C000107962

Victimisation: Theory, Research and Policy

To
Susan Doberman

Victimisation: Theory, Research and Policy

Edited by

Pamela Davies, Peter Francis and Victor Jupp

First published in hardcover 2003

First published in paperback 2004 by
PALGRAVE MACMILLAN
Houndmills, Basingstoke, Hampshire RG21 6XS and
175 Fifth Avenue, New York, N. Y. 10010
Companies and representatives throughout the world

PALGRAVE MACMILLAN is the global academic imprint of the Palgrave
Macmillan division of St. Martin's Press, LLC and of Palgrave Macmillan Ltd.
Macmillan® is a registered trademark in the United States, United Kingdom
and other countries. Palgrave is a registered trademark in the European
Union and other countries.

ISBN 978-0-333-92501-0

This book is printed on paper suitable for recycling and made from fully
managed and sustained forest sources.

A catalogue record for this book is available from the British Library.

Library of Congress Cataloging-in-Publication Data

Victimisation : theory, research, and policy / edited by Pamela Davies, Peter
Francis, and Victor Jupp.
      p. cm.
      Includes bibliographical references and index.
      1. Victims of crimes. I. Davies, Pamela, 1962- II. Francis, Peter, 1968-
III.Jupp, Victor.

HV6250.25 .V485 2002
362.88--dc21

                                                    2002068335

Contents

Contributors

Pamela Davies, Senior Lecturer, Northumbria University

Karen Evans, Senior Lecturer, University of Liverpool

Peter Francis, Senior Lecturer, Northumbria University

Penny Fraser, Research and Evaluation Officer, Nacro

Victor Jupp, Principal Lecturer, Northumbria University

Rob Mawby, Professor, University of Plymouth

Michael McCahill, Research Associate, Centre for Criminology and Criminal Justice, University of Hull

John Muncie, Senior Lecturer, Open University

Clive Norris, Professor of Sociology, University of Sheffield

Rachel Pain, Lecturer, University of Durham

Sandra Walklate, Professor, Manchester Metropolitan University

Martin Wright, Visiting Research Fellow, University of Sussex

1
Victimology, Victimisation and Public Policy

Pamela Davies, Peter Francis and Victor Jupp

Introduction

The academic study of the victim of crime can be dated to the theoretical and empirical work of von Hentig (1948) and Mendelsohn (1963). Today the study of the victim is an academic endeavour delivered by numerous scholars, and victimology is now an established perspective within the social sciences.

Developments within social research (notably around the crime survey) have informed this growth in victim studies, as have developments in social theory. A further factor has been the acknowledgement of the victim by policy–makers and practitioners (Walklate 1989; Williams 1998). Although measures allowing victim compensation (from offenders) date back to the Forfeiture Act 1870 and the Criminal Justice Administration Act 1914, it was during the latter half of the twentieth century that victim issues began formally to be addressed by the state and policy–makers (Mawby and Gill 1987). During this period compensation measures for victims of crime were formalised (Mawby and Gill 1987; Shapland et al. 1985), victim support and counselling services were implemented (Maguire and Corbett 1987) and reparation and mediation measures became commonplace (Marshall and Walpole 1985). The Crime and Disorder Act 1998 further placed the victim of crime centre stage of formal responses to community safety, crime control and punishment.

In noting that the victim of crime today is celebrated as a key player if not always a partner in discussions on crime and its control (Newburn 1995), it is important also to acknowledge that there remains important areas for concern and redress. The victimisation of certain groups remains hidden (Pain et al. 2002), while victim rights is still a contentious area of debate (Mawby and Walklate 1994). Moreover, victimisation perpetrated by the state, the criminal justice system, and big business including multi-national and global corporations remains invisible, requiring further research, problem-solving and general resolve (Davies, et al. 1999; Tombs 1999).

Teaching victimology at undergraduate and postgraduate levels and engaging in research with victims of crime provided the inspiration for this collection of essays. It has been a shared view of ours that there was a need for a book that provided a review of the theory, research, and policy relating to victims of crime. We hope that the collection provides for an accessible yet critical *understanding* of crime victimisation in relation to each of these three areas. The rest of this introductory chapter introduces the core themes covered by this volume and sets them in context. These are:

- victimological perspectives
- researching victims of crime
- victimisation and concern about crime
- risk, crime and victimisation
- victims, public policy and practice

Victimological Perspectives

Chapter 2 provides an appraisal by Sandra Walklate of the various theoretical perspectives in victimology, along with an articulation of her own framework for a critical social science analysis of crime victimisation (see also Walklate 1989; Mawby and Walklate 1994). The critical victimology pursued by Walklate is one of three main perspectives which have been articulated during the past half-century (Karmen 1990; Mawby and Walklate 1994). The three perspectives are:

- positivist victimology
- radical victimology
- critical victimology

Positivist victimology, sometimes referred to as administrative or conservative victimology can be dated back to the emergence during the mid-twentieth century of the discipline of victimology itself, and specifically the work of Mendelsohn (1963), von Hentig (1948) and Hindelang et al. (1978). Indeed, von Hentig and Mendelsohn are portrayed in much of the literature as the founders of the discipline of victimology. A number of general points can be made about this victimological perspective. First, much of the early work was speculative rather than empirically grounded. Second, that which was empirically grounded relied upon the officially recorded criminal statistics provided by central and local government departments, at least until the introduction of the victimisation survey in the late 1960s (Walklate 1989: xiii). Third, scholars working from or adopting this perspective focused attention towards victim proneness, victim precipitation and victim lifestyle. They were interested in the extent to which victims of crime contributed to their own victimisation. Thus von Hentig (1948) focused upon the role of the victim in the perpetration and thus creation of a criminal event, identifying thirteen psychological and sociological classes of victim, whilst Mendelsohn (1963) focused upon the responsibility of the victim for a criminal event occurring. As Walklate highlights, '[t]his notion of making victims responsible, to whatever extent, for their own victimisation, 'blaming the victim', has been a considerably problematic one for victimology' (1989: 2–3). The contribution of individuals to their own victimisation can be seen further in the work of Wolfgang (1958) who introduced the term victim precipitation, whilst Hindelang et al. (1978) introduced the notion of victim lifestyle which equated an individual's risk of personal victimisation to his or her own particular routine daily activities. A fourth point is that within much positivist victimological thought there has remained a clear focus upon visible victims – that is victims of interpersonal crimes of violence and street crime (Karmen 1990).

The legacy of the positivist victimological perspective is as follows. First, it has ensured the development and refinement of quantitative measures of victimisation. Second, it has clearly influenced the way the state, criminal justice agencies, and various voluntary institutions and organisations respond to victims of crime and victimisation. Positivist victimology has, however, also attracted criticism. Largely as a result of its focus upon conventional crimes, the 'private sphere' has remained until recently a neglected site for victimological research and intervention, as have victims of the state, its agencies and corporations. Moreover, a reliance upon unsophisticated data and method has meant that much positivistic research has attempted to play down the risk of victimisation and often presented a random picture of crime victimisation (Hough and Mayhew 1983). Whilst these issues have been reviewed over recent years, analysis of particular types of victimisation such as racial attack continue to remain unsophisticated. Finally, its denial of any political and/or structural analyses has meant a complacent view of the victim and more generally, an intellectual and conceptual naiveté. As Walklate details in her contribution to this volume, positivist victimology fails by offering a limited understanding of crime victimisation and of ways of tackling and responding to victims of crime.

Radical victimology does not have as lengthy an intellectual heritage as positivist victimology. Indeed, radical victimology developed in response to the partiality of the positivist perspective and as a result of the ongoing politicisation of victimology during the 1970s and 1980s. (Although it is worth noting that Mawby and Walklate (1994: 13) acknowledge the presence of a 'radical victimology' in the earlier work of Mendelsohn in that he 'argued for a victimology concerned with all victims'.) The emergence of radical victimology can be associated with on the one hand the feminist movement, new left ideals and the protest and counter cultures and on the other developments within the academy itself such as the victimisation survey and the theoretical contributions of new left thinkers. There are two variations of radical victimology. The first, associated with the work of Quinney and others mainly working in the United States of America, and a more recent variation entitled radical left realism associated collectively with the work of Jones, Lea, Matthews and Young in the United Kingdom.

In response to the positivist agenda, radical victimology has been concerned with combining analysis of the state and its actions with the lived experiences of victims of crime (Young 1986). As Young (1986: 23) argues, 'a radical victimology notes two key elements of criminal victim-isation. Firstly that crime is focused both geographically and socially on the most vulnerable sections of the community. Secondly, that the impact of victimisation is a product of risk rates and vulnerability.' A radical victimology must not 'deny the impact of crimes of the powerful or indeed the social problems created by capitalism' (Young 1986: 23). In consequence radical criminologists have engaged in locally orientated political struggles, drawn attention to state excesses, acknowledged the experiences of victims of crime in many socially deprived neighbourhoods and worked alongside the voluntary, feminist and left-wing movements as much as they have the state.

Nevertheless, as with the positivist perspective it attempted to surpass, radical victimology has also attracted criticism. First, it has in parts mirrored much of the positivist work it set out to supplant. Second, despite its focus upon state power it has provided a simplified understanding of the law and state; and third, it has offered a limited research agenda.

That said, its contribution to the development of the discipline of victimology can not be disputed. As Sandra Walklate acknowledges in Chapter 2, radical victimology's wish to contextualise victimisation within a broader socio-economic and political framework, its ability to refocus the victimological telescope towards the actions of the state and its agents and agencies, its aim to take victimisation seriously together with its engagement with local policy-makers, have contributed enormously to the victimological enterprise, not least to Walklate's own critical victimological framework.

In some texts, radical and critical are used interchangeably (for example Taylor, Walton and Young's (1973) book entitled *The New Criminology* was variously termed 'critical', 'radical' and 'new'); in others critical and radical refer to separate perspectives, and that is the case in this volume. Critical victimology is a perspective which endeavours to address the problematic aspects of both positivist and radical criminology. For Walklate, it is a perspective which 'incorporates the interests of radical victimology', and also those of feminism. As she has argued along with Rob Mawby, critical victimology 'largely emerged from a critical understanding of the achievement of radical left realism in criminology, a Bhaskarian understanding of scientific realism, and the way in which Cain (1990) has developed some of these ideas from a feminist critique of criminology' (Mawby and Walklate 1994). For Walklate critical victimology is concerned with developing understanding of what she sees as an inadequately explored question within other victimological perspectives; that is what constitutes the real? For Walklate, 'this view of victimology takes seriously the need for a development of an empirically based, rational and objective science', but in contrast to radical victimology, one which gets 'beyond the "mere appearance" of things towards understanding these mechanisms which underpin and generate their appearance'.

Researching Victims of Crime

Of central importance to the development of victimological perspectives has been research into victims of crime. This is true for the positivist work of Hindelang et al. (1978) as it is for the radicalism offered by Jones et al. (1986). While the early pioneering work of von Hentig was speculative rather than empirically grounded, others have relied upon officially recorded statistical information and victimisation surveys. Others again including Genn (1988), Walklate (1989), Bowling (1993) and Pain et al. (2002) have argued for a more qualitative methodology for researching victims of crime.

Since the early 1970s, the direct questioning of the victim of crime through crime surveys has been central to the victimological enterprise, some of the features of which are generic to social surveys whereas others are specific responses to the problems of studying victimisation. Crime surveys are carried out on a sample of the population, use methods developed during the beginning of the last century and are similar to those used for public opinion polls. In part, victim surveys developed as a result of recognised deficiencies in official crime statistics as valid measures of the extent of crime in society. For example, crimes recorded by the police rely to a great extent on members of the public reporting such crimes. There are several reasons for the public not reporting crime, including the sensitivity of the criminal act, triviality of offence or distrust of the police. The belief that officially recorded criminal statistics indicate more about the organisational processes involved in the collation and collection of data/statistics than about levels of crime and criminal activity has had an enormous impact upon engaging criminologists in alternative and competing strategies of collecting data about crime, such as the utilisation of data other than that from the police. Victim surveys collect data on the occurrence of criminal acts irrespective of whether such acts have been reported to the police and, thereby, gain some measure of the extent of the 'dark figure' of unreported crime (Bottomley and Coleman 1981; Bottomley and Pease 1986; Maguire 2002).

It was only with the growth in interest in victims of crime during the late 1970s in the United States of America and in the 1980s in England and Wales, coupled with the impact of feminist research and methodology, that new information slowly started to appear in the form of the crime survey. Since this period, crime surveys have become one of the most used research methodologies, allowing for the generation of details about the circumstances of the offence as well as the relationship between victims and their experiences of the various criminal justice agencies. These concerns have coincided with the formation of victim support schemes and the publication of victims charters (Newburn 1995).

In a variety of ways, surveys of victims of crime have been concerned with differing dimensions of victimisation. These include crime measurement and reasons for under-reporting; the correlates of victimisation; the risk of victimisation; the fear of crime and its relationship to the probability of victimisation; the experience of crime from the viewpoint of victims; and the treatment of victims in the criminal justice system. Five broad patterns in victim surveys are discernible. These are:

- local cross-sectional sample surveys
- appreciative surveys
- national trend sample surveys
- cross-national surveys
- police 'consumer' surveys

In local cross-sectional studies, a representative sample of the population of a particular area or district is selected and sample members are asked if they have been the victim of crime within a specified period of time and also whether they reported such crimes to the police. Sometimes they are asked about their experiences of, and relationships with, the police in that particular area. In the United Kingdom such surveys are exemplified by research associated with radical left realist criminology (which, in general terms, is concerned with facing up to the reality of crime from a social democratic standpoint). Left realist surveys pay attention to the experiences of vulnerable groups within a particular locality. There is the opportunity for such cross-sectional surveys to be repeated, as with the first and the second Islington Crime Surveys, thereby facilitating some comparison over time (see, for example, Jones et al. 1986; Crawford et al. 1990).

Appreciative studies are less concerned with seeking precision in estimates of victimisation in the community and more with the qualitative descriptions of the experience of crime from the victim's point of view. They may also seek to examine victims' experiences of being processed within the criminal justice system, for example by the police and by courts. Research design is typically based on purposive rather than random sampling. Appreciative victim studies are likely to be associated with victim support groups and with feminist approaches within criminology (especially in relation to women as victims of sexual crimes). In some cases such studies are closely related to social and political action to reduce victimisation of vulnerable groups and to improve the treatment of victims in the criminal justice system.

The third pattern concerns national trend studies, typified in England and Wales by the British Crime Survey (BCS) sponsored by the Home Office. The following quotation outlines the basic thinking behind its use (Hough and Mayhew 1983):

The British Crime Survey provides an index of crime in England and Wales to set beside the statistics recorded by the police. Many crimes are not reported to the police, and some that are reported go unrecorded. Recorded crime figures are thus an unreliable guide to the extent of crime. They can be misleading about trends, as readiness to report crimes to the police varies over time. The BCS avoids this problem by asking people directly about their experiences as victims.

The BCS is an example of what we earlier described as administrative criminology because of its close association with government and with official policy-making. It has been published in England and Wales in 1982, 1984, 1988, 1992, 1994, 1996, 1998, 2000 and 2001, on each occasion measuring crime and victimisation in the previous year. The BCS measures crime experienced by people living in private households. In each sweep a representative sample of over 10,000 people aged 16 and over are interviewed, although different independent samples are selected at each sweep and therefore a panel element (whereby the same people are interviewed at different points in time) is missing. (The fourth sweep of the BCS included questions for twelve- to fifteen-year-olds, while in 2000 a sample for England and Wales of 40,000 adults over 16 years of age was chosen (Kershaw et al. 2001)). To address this criticism respondents are interviewed and asked about their experience of crimes committed against them as individuals and against their household since the beginning of the previous year. The BCS facilitates an examination of trends in the extent of crime, the risk of crime and the fear of crime (Mayhew and Hough 1991). This examination is for the country as a whole or for sub-categories and also for local areas. From 2001, the BCS became an annual cycle reporting every year.

Alongside the *Criminal Statistics* (the government publication which reports crimes recorded by the police), the BCS is the main source of statistical information about crime and victimisation utilised by criminologists (Coleman and Moyniham 1996). However, as Mayhew (1996) has suggested, problems have arisen with the use of the BCS. For example, a major flaw is that it does not capture sufficiently the extent of sensitive crimes, especially sexual crimes and domestic violence. Many crimes such as fraud or shoplifting can not be covered using household surveys, while the survey does pick up some incidents which are not notifiable offences. It is acknowledged that the police and BCS data are complementary. Police figures provide a good measure of trends of well-reported crimes, are an important indicator of police workload, and can be used for local crime pattern analysis. For the crime types it covers the BCS gives a truer reflection of crime because it includes crimes which are not reported to the police. The BCS is also able to offer a better indication of trends in crime over time because it is less likely to be affected by changes in levels of reporting and recording. During the mid- to late 1980s, a Computer Assisted Personal Interviewing (CAPI) system of self-completion was introduced.

The fourth type of study is concerned with cross-national comparisons of rates of victimisation. For example, the International Crime Survey (ICS) is a large-scale survey of experiences of crime across a number of countries. A standardised interview schedule, translated into different languages, is administered to respondents by telephone using a method of random dialling of private phone numbers (Dijk et al. 1990). The survey provides a valuable source of data on victimisation among different groups and areas within countries and between countries. It does not, however, consider the experiences of victims in relation to the economic and social conditions of each country nor to the varying institutional arrangements for dealing with crime and with victims in particular. A discussion of surveying cross-national comparisons of crime victimisation is the focus of Chapter 8 in this collection by Rob Mawby.

Fifth, consultation surveys have developed as part of the increased emphasis placed in the 1990s on performance indicators and on measuring performance by levels of public satisfaction. Levels of public satisfaction are typically measured by structured questionnaires administered as part of surveys of a ward, police division, sub-division or sector. Typically, satisfaction with a wide range of services will be examined, including how victims of crime are dealt with.

Victimisation surveys have played an important role in criminology and in policy-making. They provide better estimates of the extent of crime than that provided by official statistics and they also give insights into victims' experiences of crime and of the criminal justice system. However, they do have deficiencies as acknowledged by critical victimologists including Sandra Walklate, for example in not being able to provide estimates of 'victimless' crimes, in not addressing crimes such as mass pollution affecting large populations, in being unable to explore the victimisation of 'hard to reach groups' (Pain et al. 2002) and in not providing measures of crimes, for example fraud, of which individuals are not aware (Jupp 1989; Walklate 1989). In addition, victim surveys are closely tied to the confines of the criminological and victimological enterprises. Therefore, such surveys are often viewed as inappropriate to questions raised by forms of thinking which view such enterprises as constraining and instead seek to add a critical edge by locating victimisation in wider structural issues. Sandra Walklate discusses the contributions of feminist thought to victimisation of women. Her conclusion that an analysis and understanding of victimisation should be located not within the narrow confines of criminology or victimology but within a wider consideration of the role of women in society is suggestive of research styles and strategies much wider than the victim survey.

Victimisation and Concern about Crime

In this section we map out the nature and extent of victimisation in England and Wales. In doing so we focus our attention on the 2001 BCS survey which measured crime against individuals for the year 2000 (Kershaw et al. 2001). We also set this discussion in the context of the officially recorded criminal statistics for the same year.

In 2000, there were 5.2 million notifiable offences recorded by the police. The majority of these crimes comprised offences against property and vehicles. Approximately 12 per cent of offences recorded by the police related to crimes of violence. For the same year the BCS estimated 12,899,000 crimes against adults living in private households. As in previous sweeps of the BCS, over half of all the offences involved some type of theft. Vandalism against vehicles and other household and personal property amounted to a fifth of the total number of crimes (20%), with a further fifth of crimes being of a violent nature (20%).

About three-quarters of BCS crimes measured fall into offence categories that can be compared with police recorded crime categories, and half of recorded crime can be compared with BCS crime (Kershaw et al. 2001). As already discussed, the BCS does not cover all the offences that appear in police figures (it excludes, for example, homicide, fraud and so called 'victimless crimes'). Also thefts involving households and personal thefts cannot be compared as they may fall into a miscellaneous figure of thefts within police figures. For the year 2000 BCS crimes in the sub-set totalled 9,879,000 as against 2,501,000 police recorded crimes. The BCS count is therefore approximately four times higher than that recorded by police statistics (Kershaw et al. 2001).

The BCS uncovers much more crime than recorded by the police. In 2000, for the comparable subset in total, only 25 per cent of crimes against private individuals and their households ended up in the recorded crime count. In the words of the authors, 'the remaining 75% make up the "dark figure" of crime' (Kershaw et al. 2001). This shortfall, or 'attrition rate', can be explained in the following way. First, not all incidents that are reported to the police are subsequently recorded as a crime. Second, many crimes are simply not reported to the police. It is, however, worth pointing out that reporting rates differ across crimes. For example, car thefts and burglaries are usually reported, while theft from the person and attempted motor vehicle thefts are not. The most common reason given by respondents for not reporting is lack of seriousness of the offence or that it involved a small loss. That said, not all crimes that go unreported are trivial (Kershaw et al. 2001). For violent crime the reasons for not reporting include victims often feeling the matter is private, for example domestic violence, or they are able to deal with the matter themselves. For Mayhew (1996: 35) three basic factors appear relevant to the decision-making of victims regarding whether to report. First, practical considerations governed by self-interest. Second, victims expectations and experiences of the police; and third, the relationship between the victim and the offender.

Regarding trends in crime based on BCS data, there is an irregular pattern for crime between 1981 and 2000, with crime rising between 1981 and 1995, and steadily decreasing thereafter. With regard to offence categories, all but two measures fell in the period 1997–2000, the exceptions being theft from the person (an increase of 2%) and theft of vehicles (an increase of 1%) (Kershaw et al. 2001). Moreover, the comparable subsets for police and the BCS indicate a not too 'dissimilar' picture according to Kershaw et al. (2001); between 1999 and 2000 all but one of the main offence categories measured by the BCS fell, whilst bicycle theft, vandalism and theft from vehicles fell as reported by both the police and BCS figures. Theft of vehicles increased slightly according to the BCS but fell according to police data, while attempted vehicle thefts and vandalism fell according to the BCS but increased according to police figures. Theft from the person was similar insofar as both measures showed increases, albeit to different extents (Kershaw et al. 2001).

Perceptions and beliefs of risk and victimisation, and worry and fear are also a focus of the BCS. Often, these are grouped under the banner 'concern about crime'. What emerges is a complex picture often related to particular variables such as age and gender, and residence. For example, despite the BCS indicating a reduction in crime by 12 per cent between 1999 and 2000, just over half of the public indicated they believed crime had risen during the same period, 26 per cent believing it had increased 'a lot' (Kershaw et al. 2001). The 2001 BCS indicates, however, that the public was much more positive about crime trends in 2000 than in previous sweeps of the BCS.

In terms of the likelihood of actual crimes occurring against them, in 1999 respondents reported that 'it was fairly likely that items would be stolen from their car, their car would be stolen or their home would be burgled' (Kershaw et al. 2000: 42), although on average they believed experiencing violent crime was less likely. Reasons for such perceptions are complex, although the BCS provides some evidence that perceptions are to an extent associated with actual levels of risk (Kershaw et al. 2001). For example people living in areas where victimisation risk is high are more likely to consider that they will experience victimisation; that is views are to some extent determined by or related to personal circumstance, along with the experience of crime, neighbourhood cohesion and demographic factors (Kershaw et al. 2001). Indeed race and sex are strongly related to worry about crime and feelings of safety and well being; women are more worried about burglary and far more concerned about violent crime. Black and Asian respondents are far more worried about all types of crimes than white respondents.

Risk, Crime and Victimisation

Successive sweeps of the BCS have identified that the risk of victimisation is often related to geographical area. Moreover, successive sweeps of the BCS have identified that the risk of personal victimisation is closely correlated with variables such as age, sex, race and patterns of routine activity, such as going out in the evening and alcohol consumption (see the discussion by Zedner 1997; Koffman 1996). For example, in 2000 approximately a quarter of individuals who owned a vehicle were likely to experience some form of crime against it. That said, the risk rate varied by demographic and residential characteristics, although it is worth noting that vehicle-related thefts do not always take place near to the individuals home. The risk rate is closely associated with being resident in the north of England, living in inner-city areas, flats and terraced houses and 'young better off' households (Zedner 1997: 581). The risk is highest for high-performance cars and older cars with poor security measures.

Similarly, household burglary is patterned geographically, socially and demographically across England and Wales. In 2000 there were 1,063,000 attempted and actual burglaries, a fall of 17 per cent from 1999. This follows a fall of 27 per cent between 1995 and 1999 (although this trend represents a reverse for the period from the mid- to late 1980s to the early 1990s). Particular groups are most at risk of burglary. For example, burglary is more likely to take place in inner-city areas, in flats and end-terrace houses, in rented accommodation rather than in owner-occupied households, with single adult and younger heads of households, and those without insurance (Kershaw et al. 2001). Students also experience a high risk of burglary.

The patterning of victimisation with particular variables is the same for other crimes, including violence. In 2000, 20 per cent of offences reported by the BCS were of a violent nature (wounding, common assault, robbery and snatch theft). This represented 2,618,000 crimes of violence, a slightly smaller proportion than in 1999. Risk of violent crime is highest for young men aged between 16 and 24 years, although other personal characteristics influence risk of violence, such as lifestyle, residence, gender and race. Moreover, even within local geographical areas the patterning of victimisation will be related to these factors (see for example the findings from the two Islington Crime Survey's (Crawford et al. 1990; Jones et al. 1986) and the Islington Domestic Violence Survey (Mooney 1993)).

Survey data has constantly identified that those most likely to be victimised by crime in Britain are often the most marginalised social groups living in the poorest areas (Kershaw et al. 2000; MacDonald, 1997). Vulnerability to crime and fear of crime are exacerbated by social, economic and political exclusion. The risk of personal victimisation is closely correlated with variables such as age, sex, and race. For example, since 1988 the BCS has repeatedly reported that black and minority ethnic communities have a statistically higher risk of victimisation than white people (it was not until 1988 that the BCS began to include questions relating to racist victimisation. It has also been acknowledged that the victim survey, despite advances over recent years, remains flawed in terms of its ability to measure racist violence (Bowling 1993)). According to Fitzgerald and Hale (1996) black and minority ethnic communities are significantly more likely to be victims of both household crime and personal offences; but, there are variations between and within groups as well as between different offence categories. Thus for example, risk rates for Pakistanis and Bangladeshis are higher for almost all crime types. Afro-Caribbeans are more likely to be at risk of assault and of acquisitive crimes. For the year 1999, the BCS indicated that black people had a greater risk of being the victim of burglary, car crime or violence than Asian and white people (Kershaw et al. 2000). Minority ethnic groups were also found to perceive themselves more likely to be a victim of crime than white people. In addition these populations also worry more about becoming a victim of crime and feel less safe on the streets or within their own homes at night.

Partly, the higher risk rates of black and minority ethnic households is the result of the fact that they are more likely to be over-represented in social demographic groups associated with higher risks of victimisation. As Zedner (1997) points out, members of minority ethnic communities are more likely to live in younger households of lower socio-economic status and generally to reside in socially disadvantaged communities. However, as Fitzgerald and Hale (1996) also note, this is not to suggest that 'ethnicity plays no part in their victimisation'. In their analysis of findings from the 1988 and 1992 BCS's, Fitzgerald and Hale (1996: 23–4) acknowledge that:

> for the crimes and threats which are covered by the BCS, the links between race and victimisation are strong but they are also complex. There are variations between groups both in the level of victimisation overall and in the experience of offences which they perceive to be racially motivated. And many of the links risk being overlooked, in as much as they are indirect rather than direct. Thus, although ethnic minorities are, in varying degrees, disproportionately likely to be victims, most offending against them is not racially motivated; and ethnic minorities at risk are for the most part accounted for by social, economic and demographic factors. That is, Afro Caribbeans and Pakistanis in particular are disproportionately vulnerable mainly because they are disproportionately disadvantaged. However, what should not be overlooked is the link between disadvantage and race.... The direct links between race and victimisation are more clearly to be found in the minority of incidents which are perceived as racially motivated. Yet, these links are also complex.

The Stephen Lawrence Inquiry Report 1999 defined a racist incident as being 'any incident which is perceived to be racist by the victim or any other person'. The police adopted this definition in 1999. It should be noted that this definition of an incident is wider than the normal definition of a crime as recorded in the criminal statistics and includes general threatening behaviour. The BCS 2001 estimated that the number of racist incidents, including threats, which were considered by the victim to be racially motivated fell from 382,000 in 1995 to 280,000 in 1999 (a reduction of 27%). The number of racially motivated incidents committed against ethnic minorities fell from 143,000 in 1995 to 98,000 in 1999 (a reduction of 22%). Since 1989, the numbers of racist incidents recorded by the police have increased from 4,383 to 11,878 in 1994/5, 13,878 in 1997/8, 23,049 in 1998/9 and 47,814 in 1999/2000. Variation can be found across police forces. Given the variation in the size of ethnic minority communities across England and Wales, it is no surprise to learn that in 1993/4, for example, 40 per cent of all racist incidents recorded by the police took place in the Metropolitan Police District. The sharp rise, especially when compared with the BCS, suggests that it is a consequence of reporting and recording practices rather than an increase in the number of incidents.

Nevertheless, according to the 1996 BCS, only 45 per cent of racially motivated offences were reported to the police during 1995. Ethnic minority victims were much less likely to report incidents than white victims (Percy 1998). Pakistanis are least likely to report even serious threats to the police, even though as a group it is estimated that they are the most vulnerable to this offence. The national survey of ethnic minorities conducted by the IPPR (Madood et al. 1997) in 1994, found that about half of those respondents who reported being a victim of racist harassment reported being dissatisfied with the police response. Moreover, not all racist incidents are recorded as such by the police. This may be because the victim does not refer to the racial element or the police fail to note it. The Crime and Disorder Act 1998 introduced a series of new racially aggravated offences. These were introduced on 30 September 1998. While monitoring of them is ongoing, it is possible to highlight some preliminary statistics. 21,759 offences were recorded by the police in 1999/2000 of which 49 per cent involved harassment, 12 per cent less serious wounding, 20 per cent common assault and 19 per cent criminal damage.

From this discussion it is clear that risk and vulnerability to crime and fear of crime is exacerbated by social, economic and political exclusion. However, for John Muncie, writing in Chapter 3, within this general orthodoxy, young people have not been prominent as victims of crime. Rather, the vast majority of research on youth and crime in the United Kingdom has focused upon the offending patterns and behaviours of young people, rather than on their experiences as victims. This is a point also made by Sheila Brown (1998: 116–17):

> Except in conjunction with the ideology of childhood 'innocence' – itself increasingly shaken by the demonisation of ever younger age groups – the predominant categorisations of youth do not sit easily within a 'victim' discourse . . . in popular and policy discourse such issues are often treated with cynicism, disdain or vehement denial.

That is, young people are still primarily constructed as offenders; their victimisation and fear are rarely mentioned and addressed in crime prevention policy. For example, the main emphasis of both the Crime and Disorder Act 1998 and the Youth Justice and Criminal Evidence Act 1999 was on youth offending; local policy-making does little better. The problem of crime is often reconstructed as the problem of young people, hell bent on wrecking havoc, mayhem and destruction wherever they go.

Recently, however, there has emerged a growing number of quantitative and qualitative studies exploring the complexities and dynamics of young people as victims of crime. These studies include those by Anderson et al. 1994; Aye-Maung 1995; Brown 1995; Hartless et al. 1995; Loader et al. 1998; Morgan and Zedner 1992; Muncie 1999; Pain and Gill 2001; Pain and Williams 2000, Pain et al. 2002.

What this recent explosion of research has allowed for, according to Muncie, is an understanding of the extent, nature and impact of victimisation amongst young people, of their anxieties and fears of crime, and of their experiences of institutions, organisations and individuals responsible for controlling, regulating and supporting them. Moreover, much of this research has highlighted the low levels of reporting amongst young people of their experiences and the lack of response of many criminal justice and welfare related service providers. For Pain et al. (2002):

> Within the last decade...a growing number of academic studies have identified that children and teenagers suffer a high incidence of crime and are disproportionately likely to be victims, and that fear of crime has damaging effects on their lives.... Further, there is not always a clear-cut distinction between those most likely to offend and those most likely to be victims (Walklate 1989). Offending and victimisation are unevenly distributed between young people, with certain groups experiencing higher levels of both. Some, though by no means all, of this victimisation takes place between young people. Therefore particular groups of young people, often those who have been labelled 'hard-to-reach' or 'excluded' are key to issues around crime, victimisation and youth.

For Muncie, young people are victims of crime, victims of familial violence and neglect, victims of institutional violence, are overly controlled and recipients of high levels of regulation and surveillance:

> The relative powerlessness of young people has always placed them at potential risk of adult victimisation. Such a risk is exacerbated at times when the potential of youth is subjugated to that of threat. Seeking their greater regulation ensures that they are placed in positions

of greater dependency often in those same family and institutional settings that are a key source of their victimisation. The problems facing young people are compounded when the prevailing political discourse becomes that of blaming the victim. In such contexts, the true nature and extent of youth victimisation will continue to remain stubbornly hidden from public view.

In sharp contrast to the popular image of young people as offenders, the elderly are often identified in much media and political discourse as socially and economically vulnerable to victimisation and lacking the physical or psychological strength to resist it. However, for Rachel Pain in Chapter 4, while older people often do have different risk rates of victimisation compared to younger people, the relationship between older people and crime victimisation is somewhat more complex than is often presented. Chapter 4 provides a critical review of the appropriateness of 'old age' as an explanatory category in relation to crime victimisation. This is evident in Pain's review of the research on the impact of victimisation on older people, in her review of policy approaches and also in her critical framework for understanding the victimisation of older people.

Problematising the conceptualisation of older people, and viewing older age in the context of intergenerational relations which are constructed in different ways, and which must be understood alongside other social identities, Pain argues:

> the structures of class, gender, race and ability are the key determinants of how older people experience old age. It is these which underpin where older people live, their socio-economic status and their risk of victimisation, whether from property crime, harassment in the community or abuse by carers within domestic spheres.

Certainly, the analysis of the various associations between older people and victimisation unpacks the popular stereotype that the elderly are a homogeneous, vulnerable social group especially susceptible to victimisation and least able to resist the threat of crime. The sense of multiple identities for Pain is important in understanding the relationship between old age, victimisation and crime. Moreover, she suggests that what has been constructed as a problem may not be a problem – at least not for many older people. Where the elderly are identified as the most vulnerable in our communities they are likely to be so in respect of abuse in private space and community harassment. Pain concludes that salient risks to the needs of the most vulnerable in our communities ought to determine research and policy agendas.

The chapters by Muncie and Pain illustrate the ways in which particular individuals and social groups are more at risk of crime victimisation than others. What is clear from the research literature is that the burden of crime does not fall equally on neighbourhoods and geographical areas. This theme is taken up in Chapter 5 by Karen Evans and Penny Fraser. Three areas can be identified as suffering from the highest incidence of crime. These are:

- mixed inner metropolitan or multi-racial areas with a mixture of poor, private rented housing and owner occupation
- non family areas with a mixture of affluent housing and private rented housing in multi-occupation
- the poorest local authority estates, located either in inner-city or overspill areas.

These areas, argue Evans and Fraser, have common characteristics: 'They are, in the main, low status, urban areas of low quality housing with above average concentrations of children, teenagers and young adults and with a preponderance of single-adult households.' On the basis of these commonalties, suggest Evans and Fraser, neighbourhoods themselves must be seen as victims of crime.

Charting the background to community safety in Britain, a concept imported from America in the 1980s, where the crime prevention gaze fell upon community-based action, in partnership with others, to prevent crime, Evans and Fraser explore the development of crime and victimisation prevention. Community safety has mushroomed and has taken on various guises as illustrated in the different examples given of community schemes designed to offer victimisation prevention. These include variations on the community watch or surveillance approach to working with the frightened community, a resident-led community trust approach to working with disorganised communities and finally victim-oriented community-based strategies such as removing the victim, removing/punishing the offender and involving the victim. Overall they argue for a crime reduction strategy that better understands the needs of a victimised community.

This discussion on community safety and crime prevention provides a very timely review and overview of developments in crime and victimisation reduction. It also provides an excellent link to the final set of chapters within the volume, which focus discussion upon victims of crime, the state and policy and practice.

Victims, Public Policy and Practice

A number of the contributors to this volume acknowledge the changing relationship between victimisation, victims of crime and the operation of the state, its agencies and related charitable and voluntary sector organisations. They do so in a number of ways. First, a number of them examine the victim's representation or lack of representation in criminal justice policy and practice. In Chapter 6, for example, Pamela Davies identifies how criminal justice policy and practice has traditionally neglected the victim of crime. Having outlined the reasons behind this neglect, Davies goes on to explore those policies that are victim-oriented or at least those that signify some measure of support for victims of crime. A second way in which the contributors explore the relationship between victims of crime, the state and policy and practice is through an examination of how the latter can actually result in crime victimisation. Here various contributors identify ways in which individuals experience victimisation as a result of criminal justice policy and practice and as a result of wider measures aimed at reducing crime and/or improving quality of life and well being. John Muncie, for example, examines how many young people are victims of a multitude of state practices and public policies, while Mike McCahill and Clive Norris in Chapter 7 highlight the ways in which specific crime prevention measures might also add to the nature and extent of crime victimisation. They do so through an exploration of the relationship between victimization and mechanisms of surveillance. Third, contributors to this volume consider the roles of both the state and the voluntary sector in the development and delivery of victim support, representation and compensation. Whilst several chapters acknowledge the crucial support provided by the voluntary sector, Rob Mawby's contribution in Chapter 8 examines specifically the provision of victim support and assistance drawing upon a cross-national perspective. In doing so, Mawby focuses upon service development and delivery in England and Wales, the Netherlands, the United States and Germany as well as two post-communist societies in eastern Europe. Marked variations and similarities are highlighted, particularly in relation to the organisational structure of agencies, the relationships between victim assistance programmes and partner agencies, the nature and type of service provided, and the nature of the victim population prioritised. The chapter signifies the relevance of and need for comparative analysis of support services offered to victims of crime and of criminal justice policy as it affects victims in an increasingly global world.

Finally, many of the contributors highlight recent developments, especially in the United Kingdom over the last decade, in the provision of mediation and restorative justice programmes. Martin Wright in the concluding chapter to this volume acknowledges that such programmes themselves borrow in some ways from ideas and traditions practised elsewhere in the world, most notably New Zealand. Moreover, there are indications that such philosophies appear to be penetrating the broader spectrum of criminal justice policy and practice generally.

While many of the contributors of this volume address particular aspects of victim policy and practice, it is useful to place these contributions within a broader understanding of the changing relationship between victims of crime, the state and policy and practice. Tim Newburn (1995), drawing upon the work of Van Dijk, identifies three waves in the development of victims and criminal justice policy within England and Wales:

- **1960–1975**, a period associated with the development and introduction of state compensation and probation initiatives
- **1975–1980**, a period associated with the development of rape crisis centres, shelter homes and Victim Support Schemes
- **1980s onwards**, a period associated with the institutionalisation of victim support and calls for justice for victims amongst the majority of agencies involved in crime and criminal justice.

The period 1960–75 was associated with the introduction of criminal injuries compensation, and recognition of the 'needs of victims'. The efforts of Margery Fry during the 1950s subsequently lead to a scheme being introduced under the auspices of the Criminal Injuries Compensation Board on 1 August 1964. New Zealand, Australia, Canada and some states in America also introduced state-based compensation during this decade. The European countries of Sweden, Ireland, Finland, Norway, Denmark, Netherlands, Germany and France introduced state compensation a decade later, whilst Austria, Luxembourg and Belgium did so in the 1980s (Mawby and Walklate 1994). This development, however, should not be seen as being associated with a broader victims movement and was not informed by victims' experiences. Compensation by the offender rather than the state has a longer history, although the Criminal Justice Act (1972) broadened the circumstances under which compensation could be ordered, and forms the basis of court-ordered compensation to this day.

During the period 1975–80 there was a marked increase in awareness about the role and status of victims of crime in society, including their experiences of crime and criminal justice. Almost a decade after state compensation was introduced in the UK, in 1972 Compensation Orders were introduced. The same year also saw Community Service Orders piloted, before their permanent introduction in England and Wales in 1975, introducing a notion of restoration and reparation into the arena of criminal justice policy. It was during this time that the feminist movement was also effective in influencing the ways in which public sector agencies responded to women victims as well as providing their own services for abused women. For example, there was the importation of rape crisis centres from the United States of America, and the Women's Movement was instrumental in securing their continued operation across England and Wales. These milestones in support for victims of crime and also for the feminist movement coincided with the first victim support scheme being established in Bristol. It was during this era that the National Victims Association was established. In 1972 the first UK Women's Aid refuge was set up as a result of the pioneering work of Erin Pizzey in Chiswick, London, followed by the first UK Rape Crisis centre in London, in 1976. The early years of this decade therefore saw the emergence of two strands of the voluntary sector's provisions for victims of crime. Provision and support from the voluntary sector continues to come from both the feminist movement and Victim Support.

The 1980s onwards witnessed the consolidation of a number of areas of victim provision. State compensation continued to come under the political microscope as a result of calls for cost-cutting and rationalisation across central government operations. As a result, state compensation experienced change as promoted by the Criminal Justice Acts of 1982 and 1988 where rules governing compensation were made more victim-centred. Compensation by the offender has similarly suffered modifications to its role, use and delivery.

The criminal justice system has also become more aware of victim issues and has implemented a variety of measures aimed at dealing with victims of particular crimes (such as domestic violence, child abuse, rape and racist violence). For example, 1988 saw Home Office Circular 20 issued. This, the first of a number of key Circular instructions from the Home Office on matters concerning police, police work and victims, dealt with keeping victims informed, the production of leaflets about compensation and informing the CPS of losses. Other Home Office Circulars were issued in the 1990s along with a further Circular Instruction for the Probation Service concerning contact with victims and victims' families. There has been continued development surrounding the delivery of informal measures for assisting victims. Experimental projects focusing on victim/offender mediation have been introduced. In the mid- to late- 1980s the Childline telephone advice service for children was introduced, whilst the government extended financial provision indirectly to victims through its contribution to the funding of Victim Support.

The last decade of the twentieth century witnessed several further Home Office-sponsored initiatives ostensibly in support of victims of crime. Developments included:

- 1990: The introduction and launch of the Victims' Charter.
- 1990: Home Office Circular 59/1990 instructed the police to take victims' views into account when considering the cautioning of offenders.
- 1991: Criminal Justice Act; compensation to be collected and passed on before fines; videotaped evidence in child abuse cases introduced.
- 1994: Home Office Probation Circular 77/1994; 'Contact with victims and victims' families'.
- 1995: New National Standards for pre-sentence reports on offenders included requirement to take victims' views into account.
- 1996: Victims' Charter, revised edition introduced.
- 1997: National Network of Victim/Witness Support schemes in place in Crown Courts.
- 1998: Crime and Disorder Act gave local authorities responsibility for crime prevention and introduced reparation orders requiring young offenders to make reparation to victims (where they consent).
- 1999: Victims of Crime, Home Office leaflet published.
- 2001: Release of Prisoners. Information for victims of sexual or other violent offences, Home Office leaflet published.
- 2002: Making a Victim Personal Statement, Home Office leaflet published.

There have been numerous developments involving the victim of crime in state policy and practice over the past four decades. Indeed, many have had a positive impact, especially in moving the position of and changing the status of the victim in the criminal justice system. However, the list above notes only those that emanate from the state sector in England and Wales. This list marginalises the continuing and growing provision of support and services provided by the voluntary sector, although it is evident that some sections of the voluntary sector are becoming less distinct from the state sector.

This volume clearly demonstrates that the victim-oriented policy advances achieved to date in the UK have developed within a broader global context. Rape crisis and refuge provisions were imported from the US. Innovative approaches towards the tackling of domestic violence have been published while the Duluth and Killingbeck models for tackling domestic violence are now internationally renowned. Additionally, international and European directives are effecting changes and the operationalisation of the Human Rights Act 1998 will further demand changes that affect the needs and rights of victims of crime.

That said, two points continually arise about victims, crime and criminal justice. First, there continues to be a lack of any coherent victims policy and victims of crime continue to occupy a position defined by their need rather than by a notion of rights. An examination of the ethos and practice of Victim Support, the Victims' Charters (1990, 1996) and the provisions of the Criminal Injuries Compensation Scheme suggest that victim policy in England and Wales has largely been based on a needs- rather than a rights-based model. As we move steadily into the twenty-first century victims needs are becoming ever more apparent, and an increasingly prominent global perspective on Human Rights will ensure that the question of victims' rights will be addressed. The second point that arises is that victims' 'lived experiences' of criminal justice and its agencies – namely the police, courts and prosecution process – continue to be less positive than hoped. For example, much literature details the fragile nature of police–victim relations, especially when the victim represents a marginalised and oppressed group or individual – such as ethnic minorities, women, young people and those from marginal socio-economic positions.

References

Anderson, S., Kinsey, R., Loader, I. and Smith, C. (1994) *Cautionary Tales: Young People, Crime and Policing in Edinburgh.* Aldershot: Avebury.

Aye-Maung, N. (1995) *Young People, Victimisation and the Police.* Home Office Research Study No 140. London: HMSO.

Bottomley, A. K. and Coleman, C. (1981) *Understanding Crime Rates: Police and Public Roles in the Production of Official Statistics.* Farnborough: Gower.

Bottomley, A. K. and Pease, K. (1986) *Crime and Punishment: Interpreting the Data.* Milton Keynes: Open University Press.

Bowling, B. (1993) 'Racial harassment and the process of victimisation: conceptual and methodological implications for the local crime survey'. *British Journal of Criminology,* Spring 1994.

Bowling, B. and Phillips, C. (2001) *Racism, Crime and Justice.* London: Longman.

Brown, S. (1995) 'Crime and safety in whose "community"? Age, everyday life, and problems for youth policy'. *Youth and Policy,* 48, 27–48.

Brown, S. (1998) *Understanding Youth and Crime: Listening to Youth?* Buckingham: Open University Press.

Cain, M. (1990) 'Realist Philosophy and Standpoint Epistemologies or Feminist Criminology as Successor Science'. In L. Gelsthorpe and A. Morris (eds), *Feminist Perspectives in Criminology.* Milton Keynes: Open University Press: 124–40.

Carlen, P. (1996) *Jigsaw: A Political Criminology of Youth Homelessness.* Milton Keynes: Open University Press.

Coleman, C. and Moyniham, J. (1996) *Understanding Crime Rates.* Buckingham: Open University Press.

Crawford, A., Jones, T., Woodhouse, T. and Young, J. (1990) *Second Islington Crime Survey.* London: Centre for Criminology, Middlesex Polytechnic.

Davies, P., Francis, P., Jupp, V. (1999) *Invisible Crimes: Their Victims and Their Regulation.* Basingstoke: Macmillan.

Dijk, J. J. M. van (1988) 'Ideological trends within the victims movement: an international perspective'. In M. Maguire and J. Pointing (eds), *Victims of Crime: A New Deal?* Milton Keynes: Open University Press.

Dijk, J. J. M. van, Mayhew, P. and Killias, M. (1990) *Experiences of Crime Across the World: Key Findings of the 1989 International Crime Survey.* Deventer, The Netherlands: Kluwer.

Dobash, R. and Dobash, R. (1992) *Women, Violence and Social Change.* London: Routledge.

Fitzgerald, M. and Hale, C. (1996) *Ethnic Minorities, Victimisation and Racial Harassment: Findings from the 1988 and 1992 British Crime Surveys.* Home Office Research Study 154. London: Home Office.

Genn, H. (1988) 'Multiple victimisation'. In M. Maguire and J. Pointing (eds), *Victims of Crime: A New Deal?* Milton Keynes: Open University Press.

Hartless, J. M., Ditton J., Nair G. and Phillips P. (1995) 'More sinned against than sinning: a study of young teenagers' experiences of crime'. *British Journal of Criminology,* 35, 1, 114–33.

Hentig, H. von (1948) *The Criminal and his Victim.* New Haven: Yale University Press.

Hindelang, M., Gottfredson, M. and Garofalo, J. (1978) *Victims of Personal Crime: An Empirical Foundation for a Theory of Personal Victimisation*. Cambridge: Ballinger.

Hough, M. and Mayhew, P. (1983) *The British Crime Survey*. Home Office Research Study 76. London: HMSO.

Hough, M. and Mayhew, P. (1985) *Taking Account of Crime: Key Findings from the Second British Crime Survey*. Home Office Research Study 85. London: HMSO.

Jones, T., McClean, B. and Young, J. (1986) *The Islington Crime Survey*. Aldershot: Gower.

Jupp, V. R. (1989) *Methods of Criminological Research*. London: Unwin Hyman. Reprinted 1995, Routledge.

Jupp, V. R. (1996a) 'The Contours of Criminology'. In R. Sapsford (ed.), *Researching Crime and Criminal Justice*. Milton Veyues: The Open University.

Jupp, V. R. (1996b) 'Victim Surveys'. In Burgess, R. (ed.), *Encyclopaedia of Social Research*. London: Routledge.

Karmen, A. (1990) *Crime Victims: An Introduction to Victimology*. Pacific Grove, CA: Brooks Cole.

Kershaw, C., Chivite-Matthews, N., Thomas, C. and Aust, R. (2001) *The 2001 British Crime Survey First Results England and Wales*. Home Office Statistical Bulletin 18/01. London: Home Office.

Kershaw, C., Budd, T., Kinshott, G., Mattinson, J., Mayhew, P. and Myhill, A. (2000) *The 2000 British Crime Survey England and Wales*. Home Office Statistical Bulletin 18/00. London: Home Office.

Kinsey, R., Lea, J. and Young, J. (1986) *Losing the Fight Against Crime*. Aldershot: Gower.

Koffman, L. (1996) *Crime Surveys and Victims of Crime*. Cardiff: University of Wales Press.

Loader, I., Girling, E. and Sparks, R. (1998) 'Narratives of decline: youth, dis/order and community in an English "Middletown"'. *British Journal of Criminology*, 38, 3, 388–403.

MacDonald, R. (1997) *Youth, the Underclass and Social Exclusion*. London: Routledge.

Madood, T. and Berthoud, R., with the assistance of Lakey, J. Nazroo, J., Smith, P., Virdee, S. and Beishon, S. (1997) *Ethnic Minorities in Britain: Diversity and Disadvantage*. London: Policy Studies Institute.

Maguire, M. (1997) 'Criminal Statistics'. In M. Maguire, R. Morgan and R. Reiner (eds), *The Oxford Handbook of Criminology*, 2nd edn. Oxford: Oxford University Press.

Maguire, M. (2002) 'Crime Statistics: The "data explosion" and its implications'. In M. Maguire, R. Morgan and R. Reiner (eds), *The Oxford Handbook of Criminology*, 3rd edn. Oxford: Clarendon Press: 322–68.

Maguire, M. and Corbett, C. (1987) *The Effect of Crime and the Work of Victim Support Schemes*. Aldershot: Gower.

Maguire, M. and Pointing, J. (eds) (1988) *Victims of Crime: A New Deal?* Milton Keynes: Open University Press.

Marshall, T. and Walpole, M. (1985) *Bringing People Together: Mediation and Reparation Projects in Great Britain*. Home Office Research and Planning Unit Paper 33. London: HMSO.

Mawby, R. and Gill, M. (1987) *Crime Victims: Needs, Services and the Voluntary Sector*. London: Tavistock.

Mawby, R. and Walklate, S. (1994) *Critical Victimology*. London: Sage.

Mayhew, P. (1996) 'Researching crime and victimisation'. In P. Davies, P. Francis and V. Jupp (eds), *Understanding Victimisation*, 1st Edn. Gateshead: Northumbria Social Science Press.

Mayhew, P. and Hough, M. (1991) 'The British Crime Survey: the first ten years'. In G. Kaiser et al. (eds), *Victims and Criminal Justice*. Freiburg: Max-Planck Institute For Foreign and Penal Law.

Mayhew, P., Mirrlees-Black, C. and Aye Maung, N. (1994) *Trends in Crime: Findings from the 1994 British Crime Survey*. Research Findings No. 14. Home Office Research and Statistics Department. London: HMSO.

Mendelsohn, B. (1963) *The Origin of the Doctrine of Victimology Excerpta Criminologica*, Vol. 3 (May–June): 239–44.

Mooney, J. (1993) *The North London Domestic Violence Survey*. Middlesex: University of Middlesex.

Morgan, J. and Zedner, L. (1992) *Child Victims: Crime, Impact and Criminal Justice*. Oxford: Clarendon Press.

Muncie, J. (1999) *Youth and Crime*. London: Sage.

Newburn, T. (1995) *Crime and Criminal Justice Policy*. London: Longman.

Pain, R., Francis, P., Fuller, I., O'Brien, K. and Williams, S. (2002) *'Hard-to-Reach' Young People and Community Safety: A Model for Participatory Research and Consultation*. Police Research Series Paper 152. London: Home Office.

Pain, R. and Gill, S. (2001) *Children, Crime Victimisation and Sources of Support: A Feasibility Study for Junior Victim Support*. Department of Geography, University of Durham.

Pain, R. and Williams, S. (2000) 'The exclusionary tensions of community safety: young people and fear of violence in North Tyneside'. Paper presented to the RGS/IBG annual conference, University of Sussex, January 2000.

Percy, A. (1998) *Ethnicity and Victimisation: Findings from the 1996 British Crime Survey*. Home Office Statistical Bulletin 6/98. London: Home Office.

Pointing, J. and Maguire, M. (1988) 'The Rediscovery of the Crime Victim'. In M. Maguire and J. Pointing (eds), *Victims of Crime: A New Deal?* Milton Keynes: Open University Press.

Shapland, J., Willmore, J. and Duff, P. (eds) (1985) *Victims in the Criminal Justice System*. Aldershot: Gower.

The Guardian (1996) 'Victims get a say in trials of criminal', 16 June.

Taylor, I., Walton, P. and Young, J. (1973) *The New Criminology*. London: Routledge & Kegan Paul.

Tombs, S. (1999) 'Health and safety crimes: (in)visibility and the problem of knowing'. In Davies, P. Francis, P. Jupp, V. (eds), *Invisible Crime, their Victims and their Regulation* Basingstoke: Macmillan.

Walklate, S. (1989) *Victimology: The Victim and the Criminal Justice Process*. London: Unwin Hyman.

Williams, B. (1998) *Victims and the Criminal Justice System*. London: Longman.

Wolfgang, M. E. (1958) *Patterns in Criminal Homicide*. Philadelphia, Pa.: University of Pennsylvania Press.

Young, J. (1986) 'The failure of criminology: the need for a radical realism'. In R. Matthews and J. Young (eds), *Confronting Crime*. London: Sage.

Young, J. (1991) 'Ten principles of realism'. In R. Matthews and J. Young (eds), *Rethinking Criminology: The Realist Debate*. London: Sage.

Zedner, L. (1997) 'Victims'. In M. Maguire, R. Morgan and R. Reiner (eds), *The Oxford Handbook of Criminology*, 2nd edn. Oxford: Oxford University Press.

2

Can There be a Feminist Victimology?

Sandra Walklate

Introduction

Eagle-Russett (1989: 63) states that:

> Women and savages, together with idiots, criminals and pathological
> monstrosities, were a constant sources of anxiety to male intellectuals
> in the late nineteenth century.

This anxiety was deeply embedded in what Eagle-Russett calls 'sexual
science'. This sexual science was rooted in four main principles; the law
of bio-genetics, the presumption of the greater variability of the male of
the species, the conservatism of biology, and the physiological division
of labour. Of these principles, the most powerful in the intellectual
development of criminology has been the first. The principle that 'ontol-
ogy recapitulates phylogeny' was generated by the law of bio-genetics,
and out of this the Lombrosian understanding of the notion of atavism
grew. The law of bio-genetics presumed that normally every organism
revisits the development of its own species within its own historical development; failure to do so produces abnormality, the producel of a
throwback to an earlier stage of biological development. Eagle-Russett
(1989) suggests that this law reflected a presumption that the white,
heterosexual male constituted the norm of developmental logic and as
a result by comparison women, savages and idiots were problematic indeed.

The powerful influence that these evolutionary ideas have exerted
over criminology has been well documented elsewhere. They certainly
directly informed the early work of the criminal anthropologists and
that influence was subsequently felt in the defining characteristics of
criminology. This influence has been variously identified as resulting in

a concern with differentiation, determinism, and scientism within criminology (see, for example, Taylor et al. 1973; Roshier 1989). However, what has been less well documented has been the way in which the presumptions of this evolutionary science have also had a significant influence on the later development of the (sub)discipline of victimology. It is through an appreciation of this influence that we shall consider whether or not it is possible for a feminist victimology to be constructed, and what questions such a construction might raise. However, in order to explore such issues, it will be important to consider how victimology has or has not dealt with the question of gender.

Gendering Victimology

The origins of victimology are usually located in the work of Von Hentig and Mendelsohn developed during the late 1940s. As lawyers cum criminologists, both of these writers were concerned to understand the relationship between the victim and offender. Both endeavoured to construct 'victim typologies' as one way of achieving such an understanding. Each of these writers gave a very different focus to their typologies. Von Hentig was concerned with categories of victim proneness; Mendelsohn with victim culpability. Whilst neither of these writers intended to suggest that there was such a being as a 'born victim', they were nevertheless searching for ways of differentiating the potential victim from the non-victim which could be applied in all victimising situations. Thus they focused on differentiation; a concern clearly consonant with earlier criminology.

Thinking about ways of differentiating victims from non-victims in this way reflects an underpinning worldview that there is a normal person, when measured against whom the victim somehow falls short. In Von Hentig's work this normal person, given the categories of victim proneness which he identified (women, children, the elderly, the mentally subnormal etc.), is (implicitly) the white, heterosexual male. The presumptions underpinning Mendelsohn's work are, arguably, more legalistic. They assume conceptualisations of what might be considered reasonable or rational behaviour in particular circumstances. (The question of what is considered to be reasonable and/or rational behaviour is also a gendered one; see below.) It is not until the later development of Mendelsohn's work, when victim culpability became translated into the concept of victim precipitation, that the impact of what might be considered reasonable or rational behaviour for a victim was more keenly felt. The concept of victim precipitation is particularly revealing in understanding victimology and its development, so we shall consider it a little more fully.

The notion of victim precipitation was originally formulated by Wolfgang (1957) in his work on homicide and developed later by Amir (1971) in his work on rape. Essentially this idea not only draws attention to the criminal act as involving two (or more) individuals, but also addresses the relative contribution of each party to the commission of that act. Derived as it is from a more legalistic understanding of the notion of culpability, its use has been seen to be particularly controversial when applied to rape and sexual assault.

Amir's (1971) study of rape provoked a strong reaction for a number of reasons. Not only are there empirical difficulties with his findings (for a detailed discussion of these see Morris 1987); the associated connotations of attributing blame to the victim are very difficult to deny however carefully formulated the concept might be. As an idea it clearly encourages us to consider the contribution of a victim's behaviour towards crime. Its focus on the behaviour of the victim has contributed to what Karmen (1990) has called the move from 'crime prevention' towards 'victimisation prevention'. With respect to burglary, it might be felt to be unfair, though perhaps not unreasonable, to expect people to lock their doors in order to help prevent a burglary taking place. With respect to rape or sexual assault, however, the notion that somehow the victim could have engaged in more reasonable behaviour for the incident not to have happened to them fundamentally misunderstands the nature of an incident of that kind. In other words, victim precipitation presumes equality between participants where none may exist. This presumption raises all kinds of questions as to what constitutes reasonable behaviour in situations where the individuals concerned do not possess, at a minimum, the same physical power with which to negotiate the situation. This concept cannot, therefore, be applied to situations that are a product of power relations. As a concept, it cannot see gender.

Whilst Mendelsohn's work contributed to the development of the concept of victim precipitation, Von Hentig's work can be considered to be the forerunner of a concern with victim lifestyle as a contributor to victimisation. The concept of lifestyle, in its original formulation, is largely associated with the work of Hindelang et al. (1978). Posited as a series of eight empirically measurable propositions and influenced by functionalist sociology, these propositions largely directed attention to such factors as: how much time an individual spent outside their home, what activities they were engaged in, how they moved about, etc. This way of thinking about the risk of criminal victimisation, despite the definitional difficulties associated with the concept itself (for a summary, see Walklate 1989: Ch. 1), has fed significantly into the crime survey business and has also contributed towards the reorientation of the crime prevention industry as commented on by Karmen (1990).

The concepts of victim precipitation and lifestyle form the core of much conventional victimological thinking. Fattah (1991) in reviewing the available data and explanations of differential victimisation attempts to integrate a range of victimological work generated by these concepts into a general schema. In doing so he groups forty propositions about criminal victimisation under ten key headings; available opportunities, risk factors, the presence of motivated offenders, exposure, associations, dangerous times/dangerous places, dangerous behaviours, high-risk activities, defensive/avoidance behaviours, structural/cultural proneness. This listing, whilst evidently more sophisticated than the simplistic assertion of a notion of lifestyle or victim precipitation, still reflects the central influence that these concepts have had on victimology. They all, with one exception, direct attention to the victim's behaviour and they all presume some norm of appropriate or rational behaviour which the victim fails to adhere to in some respect.

The continued dominance of work influenced by these ideas illustrates what Miers (1989: 3) has called a positivistic victimology. This he defines as:

> The identification of factors which contribute to a non-random pattern of victimisation, a focus on interpersonal crimes of violence, and a concern to identify victims who may have contributed to their own victimisation.

Whilst Miers himself does not offer a definition of what he understands by the term 'positivism', the parallels with criminology are clear; the emphasis on measurement and identification added to differentiation, determinism and pathology, combining in that same effect of 'scientism' (Taylor et al. 1973).

It is, perhaps, important to note that during the 1980s, the interests of victimology and criminology began to merge. The victim became 'politicised' (Miers 1978) and could no longer be seen as the 'forgotten party of the criminal justice system'. The interests of the victim also became equally significant to different strands of criminological work. Although feminists, for example, had long been concerned with the plight of women as 'victims' of men's violence, the criminological attention paid to crime victims arose rather more as a result of the increasing use of the criminal victimisation survey as a way of measuring the nature and the extent of the crime problem than it did from any deep commitment to the issues raised by feminist work.

There are differences in emphasis in the way in which what came to be called the 'administrative criminology' of the Home Office and that of 'radical left realism' developed their respective interests in the victim during the 1980s utilising the criminal victimisation survey. However, their use of the victim as a source of information about crime, and their implicit acceptance of the lifestyle model on which such survey methodology is based, renders a similar adherence to the principles of positivism as characterised by Miers (1989) in both strands of work. (For a development of this analysis see Walklate 1998.)

Whilst those of 'left realist' persuasion would argue that they have embraced the concerns of feminism and have challenged male presumptions of rationality especially with respect to the fear of crime, they nevertheless face methodological difficulties in removing the stains of positivism from their work (Smart 1990). So it can be seen that in many ways victimology, like criminology, has 'suffered' from the stranglehold of positivism. This stranglehold has also gendered victimology.

In one sense the process of understanding and identifying the influence of what counts as science and consequently what counts as scientific knowledge underpins the gendering of the victim in a very similar way to the way in which those same processes which have gendered the criminal in criminology. These processes do not surface in expressions directly related to evolutionism (or the law of bio-genetics) within victimology but they do surface as having been influenced by the cultural legacy emanating from those ideas. For example, if we examine Von Hentig's typology of victim proneness we find that women (children, the elderly, and people from ethnic minorities) feature as being particularly victim prone. If we examine the concept of victim precipitation, it presumes some legal notion of reasonable behaviour which, when examined carefully, frequently means reasonable, white, male, entrepreneurial behaviour (Naffine 1997).

If we examine the work of Hindelang et al. (1978) we find that their propositions are derived from a highly functionalist view of the world, a world in which the concept of lifestyle presumes that individuals adapt to their structural location; and that they do this differently and passively according to the characteristics they possess: age, race, sex, etc. Such adaptations then become reflected in an individual's routine public life, that is, their daily street activities, thereby implicitly accepting a sex role model view of gender issues and consequently accepting a very male view of what counts as a high-risk place, that is, the street.

All of these examples reflect a deeply embedded male view of the problem of victimisation; at a conceptual level in defining the scope of the discipline, and at an empirical level, in defining that which needs to be measured. At the same time these core victimological concepts have failed to take seriously or problematise some of the key findings which this work has itself generated. The lifestyle-exposure model, for example, as exemplified by criminal victimisation survey data, repeatedly reveals that young males are most at risk from violent crime and yet are least likely to express fear of it, a conundrum which has yet to be more fully explored by those who identify themselves as victimologists, but which nevertheless needs to be explained.

However, it is not only victimology that has contributed to the gendering of the victim in this way. It has to be said that much feminist work, whilst developing outside of victimology both conceptually and empirically, has also contributed to this process. Much of that feminist work, focusing as it does on the nature and extent of male violence, especially sexual violence towards women, has created the impression that only women (and female children) are victimised by such violence. This is not to downplay the political importance of all that was achieved by feminist academics and activists in drawing attention to the need to campaign against rape, 'domestic' violence, etc., nor is it intended to underestimate the importance of the feminist focus on the concept of 'survivor' rather than 'victim'. Neither, it must be said, should this be read as a denial of the overwhelming evidence that women and children suffer most at the hands of men, particularly men they know. However, despite these caveats, this work alongside mainstream victimological work leaves us with an underpinning world-view that constitutes the potential victim as being powerless and, in many instances, female. Thus women's victimisation is made visible and men's invisible. (See also Newburn and Stanko 1994.)

To summarise, much victimological work implicitly leaves us with the impression that victims are not likely to be male. Yet as more recent though limited work has suggested men can be victims and experience their victimisation as a key problem in their understandings of themselves as male (see, for example, Hobdell and Stanko 1993; Goodey 1997). Through the lens of 'hegemonic masculinity' (Connell 1987) such experiences may be differently understood; and of course, if we examine the implicit assumptions associated with this discipline we might also

want to argue that the variables of both class and ethnicity are differen-
tially addressed too. Such an observation does not change their gendered
nature. Feminists have argued that the presumptions of maleness, and
the presence of unquestioned 'hegemonic masculinity' within both criminology and victimology have their origin in the influence of positivism.
The argument has been made that positivism is in itself gender-blind.
(see, for example, Harding 1991). In order to understand and appreciate
the potential for a feminist response to both criminology and victimology,
it will be useful to review the impact that positivism, so central to the
formation of each of these disciplines, has had in perpetuating this
male view of the world.

Science Constructs the Male and the Female

Eagle Russett's (1989) study commented on earlier provides us with some
insight into the ways in which nineteenth-century science constructed
both the male and the female. She argues that it is important to locate
the emergence of these 'scientific' ideas in the broader political context
of the nineteenth century. Aspects of those politics campaigned for the
rights of blacks and the rights of women; and as those campaigns made
their presence increasingly felt, she suggests ideas about black people
and women became more rigid. Thus, it is important to appreciate the
political context in which the knowledge produced by nineteenth-century
scientists was located, offering us a glimpse of the significant links between
political processes and the production of scientific knowledge. Such
links illustrate how problematic it is to presume that any knowledge-
production process is objective. It is in relation to this issue in particular
that feminists have challenged traditional conceptions of positivism.

The belief that science could transform and control nature has its
origins in the seventeenth century. Bacon, for example, believed that the
'man of science' could 'make nature a "slave" to man's needs and desires'
(Sydie 1989: 205). In seeking this control Bacon characterised nature as
female. The association of women with nature, or being closer to nature,
as was observed with the nineteenth-century work on sex differences,
pervades philosophical thinking especially with respect to scientific
knowledge. As Kellner Fox states:

> Having divided the world into two parts the knower (mind) and the
> knowable (nature) scientific ideology goes on to prescribe a very
> specific relation between the two. It prescribes the interactions that
> can consummate this union, that is which can lead to knowledge.

Not only are mind and nature assigned gender, but in characterising scientific and objective thought as masculine, the very activity by which the knower can acquire knowledge is also genderised. (quoted in Sydie 1989: 205)

Gendering science in this way assigns women not only as the Dangerous Other (the nature to be controlled) but also confers a particular status on them as knowers in relation to men. As Smith (1987: 74) remarks:

The knower turns out after all not to be an 'abstract knower' perching on an Archimedean point but a member of a definite social category occupying definite positions in the society.

Recognising that the construction of knowledge is a product of a definite social relationship involves recognising that the rules which underpin such knowledge construction render some forms of knowledge legitimate and acceptable and other forms not.

Thus the 'scientifically validated' ideas of the nineteenth century, and their cultural legacy, need to be understood as part of a knowledge-production process that valorises positivistic conceptions of science and the scientific endeavour. Thus the surface manifestation of differentiation, determinism and pathology within criminology and victimology, are supported by a set of presumptions in relation to what it is to be 'scientific', that is, what kind of knowledge counts as scientific knowledge within positivism.

As has been suggested above, it is usual to associate positivistic 'scientific' knowledge with that knowledge which is seen to be dispassionate, disinterested, impartial and abstract. These are values which are considered to be transcendent, that is, uncontaminated by the context of time and space. These are also the characteristics associated with that kind of knowledge that is considered to be rational knowledge. (It is also important, by implication, to note the connections between transcendence and masculinity.) It is this idea of rationality (and its associated masculinity) that links a positivistic conception of science with the foundational knowledge of both criminology and victimology. So, for example, in nineteenth-century positivistic sexual science male knowledge was equated with rational knowledge, consigning women's knowledge (almost a contradiction in terms), to that of 'emotional work'. Thus the presumption, as Sydie (1989) has illustrated, of the 'natural woman' and the 'cultured man'.

Early criminology, and later victimology, reflect these deeply embedded views of positivism which also presume that the male of the species is the norm, the healthy, the searcher for knowledge, and the female of the species is closer to nature, the abnormal, the provider of nurturance. Moreover, it is within these foundational (epistemological) assumptions of victimology that we find the central tensions between conventional victimological concerns and a feminist-informed agenda.

Feminism and Victimology: A Contradiction in Terms?

The marginalisation of feminism by victimology has been commented upon on more than one occasion. Rock (1986), for example, implies that this has occurred to a certain extent in the choices made by feminists who have regarded the concept of 'victim precipitation' as 'victim blaming' not only in its everyday usage but also in the way it has been translated as 'contributory negligence' in the courts (Jeffreys and Radford 1984). Victimology has thereby been seen as a 'weapon of ideological oppression' (Rock 1986).

Some aspects of this uneasy relationship between victimology and feminism are epitomised by their respective use of the terms 'victim' and 'survivor'. Genealogically, the term 'victim' connotes the sacrificiant who was often female. Moreover, the word itself, when gendered as in French, is denoted as female. Feminists recognising the power of such linguistic usage regard the term 'victim' as emphasising passivity and powerlessness, in contrast to the active resistance to oppression that women routinely engage in to sustain their survival. But of course, whilst these terms are often presented as oppositional to one another, experientially speaking they frequently are not. It is possible to think in terms of an active or passive victim, as it is to identify an active or passive survivor. Indeed an argument can be mounted which presents these concepts as capturing different elements of the same process (Walklate 1993) and moreover, rooted in women's own experiences of their lives (Kirkwood 1993).

However, the challenge posed by feminism to victimology lies much deeper than a conceptual debate such as this one (though that is not to say that such a debate is not meaningful). It is a challenge that raises questions concerning conceptions of what counts as knowledge. In particular it is a challenge that raises the question of how we understand the nature of objectivity or the relationship between the 'academic' and the 'activist'.

The ideas associated with objectivity and value freedom that have been embraced by the social sciences have been couched, for the most part, in male terms. Terms which have been hidden by what Smith (1990) has called the 'regime of rationality'; a regime which is rooted in the idea of an 'abstract knower'. Victimology has been no exception to this. As the quote from Smith (1987: 74) cited earlier acknowledges, recognising the definite nature of the social relationship in the knowledge construction process renders some forms of knowledge more legitimate than others. The question remains, what actually constitutes rational knowledge? This is a further point of departure for feminists from positivism.

As Harding (1991: 3) states: 'From the perspective of women's lives scientific rationality frequently appears irrational.' This statement implies that what has been considered rational has all too often reflected a male, white, middle-class, heterosexual view of the legitimacy of what it is that can be known. As a consequence it is important to acknowledge that what counts as objective has an important political history embedded within it. Harding (1991) not only recognises the political significance of this, but also identifies an alternative way of understanding how the knowledge-production process might work.

Harding (1991) develops this alternative from Hegel. Women, she argues, being the 'Other', are outsiders to the social order; yet they spend their lives inhabiting and negotiating one of the major dualisms which underpins social thinking and social life: nature versus culture. Women's capacity to negotiate this dualism equips them with knowledge and experiences from both sides of it. In this sense, the knowledge that women possess is more objective. Thus the feminist concern with women as occupiers of both the public and the private domain means that women's knowledge can render visible and name processes which were once invisible and unnamed. In this way, then, the objectivity of a discipline (including victimology) is enhanced; not by detachment but by recognising that the researcher and the researched occupy the same critical plane.

For feminists the question of scientific detachment from one's work constitutes a key point of departure from positivistic thinking. This has been articulated most often by the feminist maxim that women, with women, for women should conduct empirical work. Such a statement not only argues for a different conceptualisation of the research process itself, but also challenges traditional conceptions of objectivity and value freedom. Victimology, like other social science endeavours, has been characterised as positivistic (see, for example, Miers 1989; Mawby and Walklate 1994) and has certainly been party to debate and criticism concerning the relationship between the academic and the activist (Fattah 1991). The influence of these ideas has been illustrated here through an examination of the gendered foundational ideas of victim-ology and the way in which those ideas have perpetuated not only a particular image of the victim but also a particular way of engaging in victimological research.

Thus it can be seen that the feminist challenge to victimology goes beyond a critique of the discipline as a weapon of ideological oppression. It strikes at the very heart of the discipline's understanding of what it is to be scientific, and concomitantly how the central concerns of this discipline might be defined and understood. However, the feminist response to this problematic relationship, as articulated by Harding, in some respects merely flips the coin: that is, it transposes one form of knowledge for another. It is a moot point as to how far this constitutes progress. Arguably, it is a position that keeps us trapped in the nineteenth-century dualisms of male/female, rational/irrational, and reason/emotion. Given that this may perpetuate the visibility of women and the invisi-bility of men (especially as victims) it is useful to consider if there is any way such a dualism might be transgressed; as a consequence could there be a feminist-informed victimology?

Critical Victimology: A Feminist-Informed Alternative?

In considering whether or not there can be a feminist-informed victim-ology the question is raised as to whether or not there can be a feminist-informed knowledge base beyond that which is conventionally defined as the political realm. This question is certainly raised by Carlen (1990), however, in arguing for a feminist-informed base to victimology. The position adopted here does not by definition privilege women's know-ledge over any other form of knowledge, but certainly accepts the view articulated by MacIntyre (1988) that there can be many knowledges and many rationalities. In accepting a view of knowledge and the knowledge-production process characterised in these terms, as will be seen, does not necessarily imply a loss of scientific status (nor a drift into post-modernism) but more the construction of a different under-standing of that status.

The term 'critical' has been used in a number of different ways to articulate an agenda for victimology. Miers (1990: 224) offers one version of this usage when he states: 'Many groups and individuals may claim the label, but the key questions for a critical victimology are, who has the power to apply the label and what considerations are significant in that determination?' Here Miers is drawing both implicitly and explicitly on the theoretical perspective of symbolic interactionism to inform his use of the term critical. In a similar vein Holstein and Miller (1990: 4) state that: 'Conventional victimology, it appears, presupposes that some persons or groups are objectively "victims" without explicitly considering the interpretive [and] definitional processes implicated in the assignment of victim status.'

Understanding the processes associated in acquiring the label victim is certainly a legitimate area of concern for victimology. Such an understanding highlights those assumptions that underpin what Christie (1986) has called the 'ideal victim'. Moreover, acquiring the label and/ or status of victim, especially that of a 'deserving' victim, is crucial in some circumstances if the victim is to receive appropriate agency response and support. The question remains, however, concerning the value such an emphasis on this labelling process per se constitutes a *critical* victimology.

In a different context Sumner (1990: 23) has summarised the major shortcomings associated with the symbolic interactionist stance that this usage of the term critical has so far advanced. He states that:

> it is equally problematic that 'labelling theory' (1) never specified in detail the ideological constitution of the moral and criminal categories, (2) never fully explored the links between these categories and the social structure, and (3) only dealt with the relationship between moral/legal condemnation and interest in an instrumental way.

These questions apply equally to a victimology that concerns itself with the problematic issues of the label 'victim' but not with the mechanisms underpinning the constitution of that label.

The label 'victim' is not negotiated in the vacuum of the interactive process; it is a label through which human beings (men and women) display their competence as users of the socially constructed cultural values associated with notions of the 'ideal victim' commented on above. This is why such labels have such a powerful impact, especially on those to whom they are applied. Within this kind of critical victimology there lies the potential for a detailed understanding of the interactive processes associated with victimisation, but with no real possibility of generating an alternative methodological agenda for the discipline itself.

A second delineation of a critical victimology is found in the later work of Fattah (1991). This too is defined as an interactionist stance but not in the same way as that discussed above. For Fattah (1991: 347) many of the problems of the discipline 'have to do with conceptual and measurement issues'. To overcome these problems he calls for an understanding of the dynamic relationship which exists between victims and victimisers (echoing earlier victimological concerns), and for closer links to be made between victimological and criminological concerns, hence 'interactive'. He goes on to generate a highly sophisticated conceptual framework in which he attempts to integrate criminological and victimological work (see Fattah, 1991: ch. 12).

Unfortunately, this interactive framework produces many tensions in the way in which it is developed, most aptly illustrated in the explication of gender issues. For example, Fattah (1991: 120) states, 'Males commit more crimes and are criminally victimised more frequently than females'. This statement is problematic in a number of respects, but primarily because of the empirical evidence concerning the criminal victimisation of women by men which it denies, and consequently the deeply embedded conventional view of crime, and the crime problem which it lends credence to. In other words, not only is it difficult to establish what is actually critical about this version of the victimological agenda once it has been fully explicated, but it is also a version of the usage of the term critical which fails to offer a substantially alternative methodo-logical agenda for victimology.

To summarise: two different usages of the terms critical as applied to victimology have been explored so far, neither of which has genuinely reconsidered the domain assumptions of the discipline. Each in their own terms may be more or less worthy candidates for making sense of victimological concerns, but each in their own way is still rooted in fairly traditional and conventional conceptualisations of what would count as both good and legitimate victimological knowledge. At best they are liberal in their intentions; at worst they constitute a mere token effort to address some key problems within the victimological domain. There is, however, a third version of the use of the term critical to delineate a particular way of thinking through questions of victim-ological concern. This version has been used by Walklate (1989, 1990) and developed by Mawby and Walklate (1994).

This version of critical victimology endeavours to address the prob-lematic aspects of both positivist and radical victimology by applying to this area of study a critical understanding of the achievements of radical left realism, a Bhaskarian understanding of scientific realism, and the way in which Cain (1990) has developed and applied some of these ideas from a feminist critique of criminology. This view of victimology takes seriously the need for a development of an empirically based, rational and objective science, but as the quote cited above from Keat and Urry (1975: 5) illustrated, such a science demands that we get beyond the 'mere appearance' of things towards understanding the mechanisms which underpin and generate their appearance. One of the key issues in constructing a critical victimology informed by these ideas is to develop an understanding of the question, which has been inadequately explored by the left or right realists: What constitutes the real?

Leaning on Giddens' (1984) theory of structuration, the view adopted here is that endeavours to research the real must take into account a number of processes which contribute to the construction of everyday reality: people's conscious activity; their 'unconscious' activity (that is, the routine activity which people engage in which can serve both to sustain and change the conditions under which that routine activity is constructed); the unobserved and unobservable generative mechanisms which underpin daily life; and the intended and unintended consequences of people's actions which inform both future action and knowledge.

One of the basic premises on which these theoretical propositions are constructed is a notion of duality. This kind of emphasis on the *inter-relationship* between agency and structure usefully substitutes duality for the notion of dualism on which, for example, Harding (1991) draws. As such it provides one way of understanding the dynamism between the structural location of women (one way of understanding women's powerlessness, a defining characteristic of being a victim), and women's negotiation of their structural location (one way of understanding the term 'survivor'). It is this kind of theoretical starting point, which neither treats gender as a variable nor locates it purely as a definitional category, which permits the inclusion of the critical edge of feminist work into victimology. Such a theoretical starting point also leads to the construction of a differently informed empirical agenda.

As has been noted, much empirical victimological work has been informed by the use of the criminal victimisation survey. Whilst this has not been the exclusive research instrument used, it has clearly had a significant role to play within both positivist and aspects of radical victimology. However, if we take the considerations of structuration theory seriously, and the concern to understand the complexity of human interaction through time and space, this also demands a research agenda which can take account of and document these processes. Pawson (1989) and Cain (1990) have attempted to delineate what such a research agenda, informed by realism, might look like. At a minimum their recommendations point to three defining characteristics that such research should possess; a breaking down of the barriers between quantitative and qualitative research, comparative studies, and longitudinal studies. How might such a theoretical and empirical starting point better inform the victimological agenda? In other words, what makes this a *critical* victimology?

Put rather simplistically, this kind of framework postulates the import-ance of understanding the processes that 'go on behind our backs' which contribute to the victims (and the crimes) we 'see' as opposed to those we do not 'see'. In other words, it is possible to get beyond the 'mere appearance' of things. Identifying these processes which go on 'behind people's backs' can really take us beyond those issues which people take seriously to fully understanding their 'lived realities' (Genn 1988; Crawford et al. 1990). A concern with these processes incorporates not only the interests of radical victimology but also those of feminism. For example, feminist work forces the recognition of women as occupiers of both the public and the private domain; rendering visible and naming processes and experiences that were once unspoken and hidden. Moreover, feminist work has been keen to document women's strategies of survival and resistance. Such concerns demand an understanding of human subject-ivity (conscious and 'unconscious' action) to be taken seriously. In addi-tion, this kind of theoretical framework renders problematic both the law as well as the role of the state and its contribution to the processes of victimisation, both of which are not always or consistently at the forefront of victimological work. It also allows us to deconstruct and challenge men's understandings of and relationship with their experi-ence of victimisation and their sense of themselves as men. In other words, it is possible to set an inclusionary rather than an exclusionary theoretical and empirical agenda.

Conclusion

This version of victimology is not rooted in the traditional claims of what it is to be scientific, as implied by the positivist project. The view of science proposed here places the academic and the activist in the same critical plane (Cain 1990), in which, as knowledgeable actors, both have the capacity to influence the processes of social change. This kind of victimology demands an understanding of the processes of victimisation that is socio-economically and culturally situated. Moreover, it is within that broader political and cultural context that not only might the pro-cesses of victimisation be best understood, but also an understanding of the emergence and influence of the victims' movement might best be located. Mawby and Walklate (1994) offer one way of understanding how a critical victimology, which centres the generative mechanisms of capitalism and patriarchy, offers analytical possibilities of the material conditions in which different victims' movements have or have not flourished (see especially chapters 4 and 7). They also offer a further articulation of the key concepts that might constitute such a critical perspective (see chapter 8). This version of victimology makes no special claims to privilege one form of knowledge over another. Indeed, its only special claim would lie in the requirement to formally recognise the political nature to that knowledge production process.

At a practical and empirical level it is a position which also implies that we transgress the dualism of victim and offender. This takes us beyond the recognition that not all victims are innocent and not all offenders are evil. Victims and offenders are people trying to deal with more or less difficult circumstances in their lives. They may feel and know they are responsible for those circumstances. They may feel and know that the responsibility for some of those circumstances is shared with others. They may feel and know that some things have just happened to them. How they deal with their lives will be in part dependent upon their own personal resources, the personal resources of those close to them, and the kind of support and response they receive from the various agencies with whom they have contact. Treating people with respect, that is, people who have different capabilities, is a key mechanism for ensuring that, traumatic circumstances notwithstanding, they are enabled to make use of their resources in order to understand what has happened in their lives (Walklate 2000). How they might choose to do that may, of course, be infinitely variable.

There are a number of implications that can be derived from this position, but with respect to victims it challenges the idea that victims (of crime) be given any special status. Treating victims with respect, remembering victims are people, is no more and no less than a plea to remember that victimhood is not a condition to be recommended for anyone. Challenging the dualisms inherent in academic thinking and policy and practice may be the route whereby victimology does indeed become critical. It is perhaps a moot point as to whether or not this is critical or political enough.

References

Amir, M. (1971) *Patterns of Forcible Rape*. Chicago: University of Chicago Press.
Cain, M. (1990) 'Realist philosophy and standpoint epistemologies or feminist criminology as a successor science'. In L. Gelsthorpe and A. Morris (eds), *Feminist Perspectives in Criminology*. Milton Keynes: Open University Press, pp. 124–40.
Carlen, P. (1990) 'Women, crime, feminism and realism'. In *Social Justice*, 17, 4.

Christie, N. (1986) 'The ideal victim'. In E. A. Fattah (ed.), *From Crime Policy to Victim Policy*. London: Macmillan, pp. 1–17.

Connell, R. W. (1987) *Gender and Power*. Cambridge: Polity.

Crawford, A. et al. (1990) *Second Islington Crime Survey*. Middlesex Polytechnic: Centre for Criminology.

Eagle-Russett, C. (1989) *Sexual Science: The Victorian Construction of Motherhood*. Cambridge, MA.: Harvard University Press.

Fattah, E. A. (1989) 'Victims and victimology: the facts and the rhetoric'. *International Review of Victimology*, 1, 1, 43–66.

Fattah, E. A. (1991) *Understanding Criminal Victimisation*. Scarborough, Ont.: Prentice-Hall.

Genn, H. (1988) 'Multiple victimisation'. In M. Maguire and J. Pointing (eds), *Victims of Crime: A New Deal?* Milton Keynes: Open University Press, pp. 90–100.

Goodey, J. (1997) 'Boys don't cry: masculinities, fear of crime, and fearlessness'. *British Journal of Criminology*, 48, 2, 255–66.

Giddens, A. (1984) *The Constitution of Society*. Cambridge: Polity.

Harding, S. (1991) *Whose Science? Whose Knowledge?* Milton Keynes: Open University Press.

Hentig, H. Von (1948) *The Criminal and his Victim*. New Haven, CT: Yale University Press.

Hindelang, M. J., Gottfredson, M. R. and Garofalo, J. (1978) *Victims of Personal Crime: An Empirical Foundation for a Theory of Personal Victimisation*. Cambridge, MA: Ballinger.

Hobdell, K. and Stanko, E. A. (1993) 'Assaults on men: masculinity and male victimisation'. *British Journal of Criminology*, 33, 3, 400–15.

Holstein, J. A. and Miller, G. (1990) 'Rethinking victimisation: an interactional approach to victimology'. *Symbolic Interaction*, 13, 103–22.

Jeffreys, S. and Radford, J. (1984) 'Contributory negligence or being a woman? The car rapist cast'. In P. Scraton and P. Gordon (eds), *Causes for Concern*. Harmondsworth: Penguin pp. 154–83.

Jones, T., MacLean, B. and Young, J. (1986) *The Islington Crime Survey*. Aldershot: Gower.

Karmen, A. (1990) *Crime Victims: An Introduction to Victimology*. California: Brooks Cole.

Keat, R. and Urry, J. (1975) *Social Theory as Science*, London: Routledge.

Kelly, L. (1988) *Surviving Sexual Violence*. Cambridge: Polity.

Kinsey, R. (1985) *The Merseyside Crime Surveys: Final Report*. Merseyside: Merseyside Police Authority.

Kirkwood, C. (1993) *Leaving Abusive Partners*. London: Sage.

MacIntyre, A. (1988) *Whose Justice? Which Rationality?* London: Duckworth.

Mawby, R. and Walklate, S. (1994) *Critical Victimology: The Victim in International Perspective*. London: Sage.

Miers, D. (1978) *Responses to Victimisation*. Abingdon: Professional Books.

Miers, D. (1989) 'Positivist victimology: a critique'. *International Review of Victimology*, 1, 1, 3–22.

Miers, D. (1990) 'Positivist victimology; a critique. Part 2: critical victimology'. *International Review of Victimology*, 1, 3, 219–30.

Morris, A. (1987) *Women in the Criminal Justice System*. Oxford: Basil Blackwell.

Naffine, N. (1997) *Feminism and Criminology*. London: Polity Press.

Newburn, T. and Stanko, E. A. (1994) 'When men are victims: the failure of victimology'. In T. Newburn and E. A. Stanko (eds), *Just Boys Doing Business*. London: Routledge.

Pawson, R. (1989) *A Measure for Measures: A Manifesto for Empirical Sociology*. London: Routledge.

Rock, P. (1986) *A View from the Shadows*. Oxford: Oxford University Press.

Rock, P. (1990) *Helping Victims of Crime: The Home Office and the Rise of Victim Support in England and Wales*. Oxford: Clarendon Press.

Roshier, B. (1989) *Controlling Crime*. Milton Keynes: Open University Press.

Smart, C. (1990) 'Feminist approaches to criminology: or postmodern woman meets atavistic man'. In L. Gelsthorpe and M. Morris (eds), *Feminist Perspectives in Criminology*. Milton Keynes: Open University Press, pp. 70–84.

Smith, D. (1987) *The Everyday World as Problematic*. Milton Keynes: Open University Press.

Smith, D. (1990) *Whistling Women: Reason, Rationality and Objectivity*. The Harry Hawthorn Lecture, Canadian Learned Societies 25th Conference, University of Victoria.

Sumner, C. (1990) 'Rethinking deviance: towards a sociology of censure'. In C. Summer (ed.), *Censure, Politics and Criminal Justice*. Milton Keynes: Open University Press, pp. 15–40.

Sydie, R. (1989) *Natural Women, Cultured Men*. Milton Keynes: Open University Press.

Taylor, I., Walton, P. and Young, J. (1973) *The New Criminology*. London: Routledge & Kegan Paul.

Walklate, S. (1989) *Victimology: The Victim and the Criminal Justice Process*. London: Unwin Hyman.

Walklate, S. (1990) 'Researching victims of crime: critical victimology'. *Social Justice*, 17, 3, 25–42.

Walklate, S. (1993) 'Responding to women as consumers of a police service; the UK experience 1980–1990'. In J. Vigh and G. Katona (eds), *Social Changes, Crime and Police*. Budapest: Eotvos Lorand University Press.

Walklate, S. (1998) *Understanding Criminology*. Buckingham: Open University Press.

Walklate, S. (2000) 'From the politicisation to the politics of the crime victim'. In N. H. Kemshall and J. Pritchard (eds), *Good Practice in Working with Victims of Violence*. London: Jessica Kingsley.

Wolfgang, M. (1957) *Patterns of Criminal Homicide*. Philadelphia: University of Philadephia Press.

Young, J. (1986) 'The failure of criminology: the need for a radical realism'. In R. Matthews and J. Young (eds), *Confronting Crime*. London: Sage, pp. 4–30.

3
Youth, Risk and Victimisation
John Muncie

Introduction

If victimology in general can be said to be in its infancy then a specific youth victimology is virtually non-existent. The reasons are probably not too hard to find. In political discourse young people tend to be a perennial source of anxiety and fear. Law and order enthusiasts, for example, continually warn of a delinquent syndrome in which youth delights in crudity, cruelty, violence and unruliness. The characteristic expression of this is that young people have suffered unduly from single parenting or from the permissiveness of parents and have developed into a dangerous and undisciplined mob. Government ministers have foreseen the imminent destruction of society epitomised by Margaret Thatcher's denunciation of the football hooligan in 1985 as the 'new enemy within'. In 1997 Jack Straw ominously warned that from now on there would be 'no more excuses' made for young people who broke the law. Successive British Crime Surveys from 1982 to 1998 have reported that people are more worried about being the victim of crime – particularly burglary – than they are about unemployment, ill health and road accidents. Much of this is assumed to be the work of young people. The Audit Commission (1996), for example, estimated that the under 18s make up a quarter of all known offenders, committing about 7 million offences a year. In popular and political discourse the 'problem of crime' is almost synonymous with 'youth crime'.

Young people are also routinely portrayed not so much as depraved but as deprived. However this deprivation is not viewed as one of material wealth and power (though this is usually the case), but of moral standards, parental guidance, training and self-responsibility. Young people are typically viewed as being 'vulnerable': capable of being corrupted by all manner of 'evil' influences, unless their behaviour is tightly regulated and controlled. It is a control that is often justified in terms of giving young people 'protection' (from others and themselves). Significantly though these latter concerns usually find expression in a child welfare and social work discourse, rather than that of criminology and social justice.

As a result the youth question is 'the site of a singular nexus of contradictions' (Cohen 1986: 54). At one time feared; young people are at another pitied for their vulnerability. They are simultaneously constituted as in need of control, but also protection. But a fear of youth is never far beneath the surface. Too much freedom is deemed dangerous when unsupervised and unregulated. Any behaviour that may undermine the 'natural' authority of adults is subject to regulation. Rarely are young people allowed the right to speak for themselves (Qvortrup et al. 1994: 2). Young people are 'at risk' on a number of different levels. They are vulnerable to adult victimisation but also to inordinate degrees of regulation coupled with economic insecurity and powerlessness. When adolescence is viewed as a period in which young people are *deprived* and *deficient* it is of standards of morality and discipline rather than of material independence. It is thought appropriate to 'treat' their condition through systems of continual supervision, guidance, training and support. It is a support though that is rarely designed to enable financial independence. On the other hand, when adolescence is viewed as a period in which youth is essentially *depraved* and *dangerous*, then interventions requiring a formal and punitive criminal justice response are legitimated. Many of these are epitomised by the fact that the most punitive forms of incarceration – short, sharp, shock detention centres in the 1970s and 1980s and boot camps in the 1990s – seemed to be reserved for the young. But whatever form intervention takes, it is clear that intervening in young people's lives is to be expected, essential and almost a 'natural' process. Given the dangers and potentials of 'youth', non-intervention is rendered unthinkable (Muncie 1999: 45).

This chapter explores the theme of youth victimisation by examining the degree of over-control and lack of protection afforded to young people on the streets, in the home and in institutions. It does so by reviewing current emergent shifts, not only in victimisation research, but also in contemporary social reactions to the 'youth problem'.

Victims of Crime

The vast majority of research on youth and crime in the UK has focused on young people as offenders rather than as victims of crime. The first attempt to reverse this priority was Mawby's (1979) study of 11- to 15-year-olds in two Sheffield schools. He found that 40 per cent had had something stolen from their person and that 25 per cent had suffered a physical assault. Overall 67 per cent said that they have been a crime victim. Nevertheless it was not until the 1990s that the issue was given much sustained attention. Anderson et al.'s (1990) pioneering work in Edinburgh established that criminal acts are committed against young people with 'alarming frequency'. They found that over a period of nine months half of their sample had been victims of assault, threatening behaviour or theft (Anderson et al. 1990: 39). Moreover some 52 per cent of young women and 36 per cent of young men recalled that they had suffered from adult harassment, ranging from being 'stared at', to importuning and indecent exposure. Whilst for males such offences decreased as they grew older, for females they increased to the extent that 30 per cent of 14- to 15-year-olds had experienced 'touching' or 'flashing' (Anderson et al. 1990: 59). In a follow up study in Glasgow (Hartless et al. 1995), high levels of victimisation were again found to be common with 82 per cent of a sample of 208 12- to 14-year-olds recalling they had been victimised in the previous year. 68 per cent of young women had been sexually harassed, whilst two-thirds of young men had suffered from assault *and* theft. In contrast on average only a quarter of the sample admitted that they themselves had committed an offence, leading the authors to conclude that young people are 'more sinned against than sinning'. Similarly Brown's (1998: 92) research in Teesside which compared rates of youth and adult victimisation found that 'young people endured levels of victimisation which would not be tolerated by adults'. Moreover, all three studies concluded that whatever the known rates of victimisation young people were often reluctant to report offences committed against them.

Specific questions about youth victimisation were not included in the British Crime Survey until 1992. From a sample of 1,350, in just six months a third of 12- to 15-year-olds claimed that they had been assaulted at least once, a fifth had had property stolen, a fifth had been harassed by people their own age and a fifth harassed by an adult. Again it was notable that the risks of theft and assault were substantially higher than for the adult population, but that few incidents were reported to the police (Aye Maung 1995). The 1998 British Crime Survey (Mirrlees-Black et al. 1998) confirmed that the risks of burglary or vehicle theft are greatest for those where the head of household is under 25, while the greatest risk of violence is experienced by young men aged 16 to 24.

Openly racist harassment and bullying is also reported to be endured by many black and ethnic minority children on a daily basis. Racially motivated violence (as reported to the police) increased by 250 per cent between 1989 and 1996, marking the UK as having one of the highest levels of such incidents in western Europe. All ethnic minority groups are more likely than whites to be victims of both household and person offences. Pakistanis are at most risk, being particularly vulnerable to vandalism of their houses and cars and to serious threats. Afro-Caribbeans are most at risk of assaults and acquisitive crime (Fitzgerald and Hale 1996; Percy 1998). The murder of the black teenager Stephen Lawrence in 1993 and the unrelenting campaign by his family to expose police and judicial racism catapulted racial violence and hate crime to the forefront of issues to be addressed by law enforcement and community safety agencies in the late 1990s. Six years after the murder the Macpherson report confirmed what black and Asian communities already knew or suspected about police ambivalence, racial discrimination and lack of accountability. But the report lacked an acknowledgement of the long history of violent racism in Britain. It dwelt on the failures of policing rather than on the daily experience of racist violence, threat and intimidation. Although survey research has burgeoned since the early 1980s, statistical snapshots of particular events are incapable of grasping the incessant and enduring process of such victimisation (Bowling 1999).

On reviewing this research Furlong and Cartmel (1997: 93) argue: 'In many respects, the concentration on young people as the perpetrators of crimes has left us blind to the extent to which young people are victims...while adults express concerns about "lawless" youth, many crimes are also committed against young people by adults.' Similarly Brown (1998: 96) concludes that 'young people have to *earn* their status as victims, whereas they are eagerly *ascribed* their status as offenders'.

Under-Protected: Victims of Family Violence

What is remarkable about these emergent discourses is that even they fail to note one of the more alarming facets of youth victimisation. Significantly the British Crime Survey, for example, did not ask about experience of youth victimisation and violence in the home. Children under 1 are more at risk of being murdered than any other age group with forty-four deaths per million population compared with a national average of twelve per million (Home Office 1997: fig. 4.4). The vast majority are killed by their parents or carers. In addition more than 10 per cent of the 600 homicides in Britain each year are perpetrated by parents against their under-16-year-old children. The extent of domestic child abuse remains largely unknown although research by NCH Action for Children in 1994 based on reported incidents alone estimated that at least 750,000 children were growing up in an atmosphere of fear and violence (*The Independent*, 6 December 1994). While the issue was recognised as long ago as the late nineteenth century it has generally been clouded in a discourse of cruelty and neglect or subsumed within a more general concern about juvenile delinquency. Research has been concentrated either on the degree to which parental abuse and neglect 'causes' future delinquency or on the relationship between delinquent activity and the risk of victimisation (Lauritsen et al. 1991; Esbensen and Huizinga 1991). Within criminology little has been done to expose the routine of violence – from spanking, slapping to serious assault – endured by young people in their own homes. The corporal punishment of children is widespread and often justified in the name of discipline and delinquency prevention. Ironically studies such as Straus (1994) have revealed that greater use of corporal punishment correlates not with a decrease but with *increased* rates of street violence, depression and alcohol abuse. Attempts to outlaw corporal punishment in Britain in 2000 dramatically collapsed following accusations of 'nanny state' interference.

In the child sexual abuse investigations of the 1980s in Cleveland, Orkney and Rochdale blame was passed from parents to social workers for unnecessarily removing children from their families. Notions of family sanctity and privacy have always precluded widespread use of criminal prosecutions. A psychological, medical or welfare focus obscures the fact that criminal offences have been committed. Child victims continue to be marginalised by use of the term 'abuse' rather than 'assault' (Morgan and Zedner 1992: 20). Further ambivalence is created by a prevailing political concern that the publicising of child abuse and children's rights is likely to not only undermine respect for authority and self-discipline but also threaten family life itself. Despite moments of apparent visibility the issue of child victimisation remains peripheral to mainstream law and order debates and absent from most criminological agendas (Saraga 2000). Attempts to legislate against child abuse have never approached the 'constant stream of law and order legislation for youth crime' (Brown 1998: 86). In addition, Morgan and Zedner (1992) draw attention to the fact that young people not only suffer from physical and sexual abuse and bullying but are witness to numerous and prolonged instances of parental violence in the home. Children are often 'indirect victims'. Over a third of households burgled each year include children who may be traumatised as a result, but are rarely considered to be victims themselves.

Under-Protected: Victims of Institutional Violence

Just as alarming are the growing number of revelations about the extensive abuse of children who have been in the *care* of local authorities. In the language of social work young people who are in the care of local authorities are known as 'looked-after children'. Over the past decade there have been between 7,000 and 11,000 young people in residential care at any one time in England, Scotland and Wales. Their treatment has long been a cause for concern with allegations of systematic violence by residential staff surfacing throughout the 1980s and 1990s. Significantly such victimisation, even when proved, has tended again to be clouded in terms of 'abuse' and 'mistreatment' rather than criminal violence. Any resultant inquiries have either been hidden from public view or at best restricted to identifying a small number of individuals who have taken advantage of the powerless. The main policy response has been to tighten checks on applicants for residential posts, rather than to overhaul residential care policies (Corby 1997). However the issue came to a head in 2000 with the publication of *Lost in Care* – the Waterhouse report into abuse at children's homes in North Wales. Following allegations of sexual abuse in similar homes in Leicestershire, Islington, Dumfries, Buckinghamshire, Northumbria and Cheshire, the Waterhouse tribunal of inquiry was established in 1996. It uncovered widespread and organised abuse of boys and girls in North Wales between 1974 and 1990. Although by 1996 twelve people had already been convicted, Clwyd County Council had refused to publish fourteen prior reports partly for fear of compensation claims. Waterhouse eventually heard 259 complaints, named 200 workers in more than forty homes and found evidence not only of daily physical assault but also of gross sexual exploitation and emotional abuse. It also attributed at least twelve deaths, by suicide or in suspicious circumstances, to the experience of being 'in care'.

Conditions in young offender institutions have also been a recurring cause for concern. Goldson (1997: 83) argues that not only are they 'unsuited to guaranteeing basic standards of safety and welfare, but each day is characterised by a culture of bullying, intimidation and routine self-harm'. Between 1972 and 1987, thirty-one prisoners under the age of 21 committed suicide, but there were eleven such deaths in the first eight months of 1994 alone. In 1994–5 nearly a half of young inmates reported that they had been attacked or threatened in the previous month (*The Guardian*, 3 October 1996). As Liebling (1992) established, young offenders are particularly vulnerable to the degrading and debilitating conditions of imprisonment. Young prisoner suicides tend to occur within one month or at most one year of reception into custody; often when they are on remand, awaiting sentence. A report by the Howard League (1995: 67) concluded:

> an approach which concentrates on incarcerating the most delin-
> quent and damaged adolescents, in large soulless institutions under
> the supervision of staff with no specialist training in dealing with
> difficult teenage behaviour, is nonsensical and inhumane ...

These publicised cases are arguably the tip of an iceberg of institutional violence, matched by adult complicity and indifference. They serve as a reminder of the dangers inherent in institutionalising and incarcerating young people whether in the name of care, of rehabilitation or of punitive training. Intervention at an early age – particularly in the form of secure institutions – is unlikely to prevent reoffending and may only succeed in cementing 'criminal careers'. A vicious circle ensues. The vast majority of those sent to secure units have previously been in local authority care. Half of prisoners below the age of 18 have been in care. Prior psychological or psychiatric contact is the norm. Most 10- to 17-year-olds who have committed the most serious offences have experienced abuse or loss in their earlier life (Crowley 1998; Boswell 1995). In 1998 the first of a network of secure training centres for 12- to 14-year-olds was opened. It was in direct contradiction to the United Nation's Convention on the Rights of the Child which stipulates that youth custody should be a last resort and be used for the shortest possible time. Ratified by almost all of the 190 UN member states the UK government duly signed up in 1991. But four years later UN monitoring of UK policy led it to conclude that the human rights of British children were still being consistently ignored. In particular it urged the abandonment of the then planned secure training centres and that serious consideration be given to raising the age of criminal responsibility. The UK countries have the lowest age of criminal responsibility in Europe. The Conservatives' response was unequivocal: the UN has no right to question UK policy. New Labour went further by implementing the secure training policy and removing the *doli incapax* principle which had long protected 10- to 13-year-olds from the full rigour of the criminal law. As Scraton (1997: 182–5) argues, the actions of the UK government have consistently promoted an authoritarian rather than a positive rights-based agenda.

Spurred on by a popular imagery of 'lawless youth, inadequate parents and failing teachers and social workers' youth justice in the UK, and in England and Wales in particular, has witnessed a 'sustained backlash directed against critical analysis and child centred policies and practices'.

Over-Controlled: Policing and Routine Surveillance

Public space, and particularly the street, has always provided one of the main arenas for youth leisure. Public space provides one of the few sites in which young people can 'hang out' relatively free of direct adult supervision. Yet it is on the streets where troubling aspects of their behaviour are at their most visible and where crucial elements of the relationship between young people and the police are forged. As Loader (1996: 50) put it, 'the routine use of public space is not altogether a meaningful choice. Rather it is one consequence of an age-based exclusion from both autonomous private spaces and cultural resources of various kinds.' As a result certain local places and spaces – the street corner, the city centre, the shopping mall, the precinct – take on a particular significance, arousing emotional attachments and cementing a sense of territory and identity. In popular discourse much is made of the street as a site of fear and danger, but research has revealed that youth's street activity is largely made up of 'doing nothing' or 'hanging around'. Loader's (1996: 78) interviews with police officers in Edinburgh, however, found that one of their most prominent views is that young people hanging about in groups are either directly or indirectly involved in criminal behaviour. Their objection is largely to the 'collective use of public space irrespective of whether or not others find it unsettling'. The issue here is essentially the historically recurring concern of 'who controls the streets' in which the imaginary connection between a 'dangerous' place (the street) and a 'dangerous' time (youth) is constructed and maintained. Above all police concern for youth victimisation remains peripheral and is often dismissed as trivial and self-fulfilling. Young people remain under-protected in public spaces (Loader 1996: 91–6).

Histories of police–youth relations are replete with examples of the proactive policing of young people's use of public space. In a study in Edinburgh, 44 per cent of a sample of over 1,000 11- to 15-year-olds had been 'moved on or told off', 13 per cent had been stopped and searched and 10 per cent had been arrested or detained in a police station in the previous nine months (Anderson et al. 1994: 130). Afro-Caribbean and homeless youth are especially vulnerable to police surveillance and harassment. In England and Wales in 1998–9, Afro-Caribbeans were six times more likely to be stopped and searched by police despite the fact that self-report studies suggest that they have no greater involvement in crime. Police powers have been consistently expanded. The 1994 Criminal Justice Act removed the condition of suspicion of carrying a prohibited article before a search could be made. In 1996 the police were given new powers to use 'reasonable force' to confiscate bottles and cans of alcohol from under-18 drinkers on the street. In 1995 the idea of creating 'zero tolerance' environments which discourage offending and incivility was imported into Britain as part of New Labour's campaigning agenda. In Glasgow in 1996, for instance, Operation Spotlight was specifically targeted at after-hours revellers, groups of youths on the streets and truants. As a result, charges for drinking alcohol in public places increased by 2,240 per cent, dropping litter by 320 per cent and urinating on the street by 140 per cent. New Labour has consistently backed the idea that low-level disorder, which may not necessarily be criminal, should be a priority target. The 1998 Crime and Disorder Act introduced new Anti-Social Behaviour Orders to be applied to nuisances and incivilities. To date they have been applied almost exclusively to young people. The 1998 Act also introduced curfew restrictions to children under the age of 10 and on the *presumption*, rather than actual committal, of crime. As a result all manner of myths and stereotypes about 'troublesome' people and places have come into play. Quite clearly curfews are discriminatory in that they select young people and criminalise them for doing what the rest of the population can do freely. In 1997, Strathclyde Police became the first in Britain to 'pilot' a dusk-to-dawn curfew on under-16-year-olds on the Hillhouse estate in Hamilton, east of Glasgow. They were empowered to escort children home or to the local police station if they had no 'reasonable excuse' to be on the streets – playing football, meeting friends – after dark. It was legitimised as a caring service to protect children and address public fears of harassment. Indeed local authorities throughout Britain can now authorise a local curfew on under 10s if residents demand it. Such a curfew is backed by sanctions so that parents who keep letting their kids on the street might them-selves end up in court. In such cases a parental order can be imposed requiring parents to attend training and counselling sessions on how to better look after their children. As a last resort, children are liable to be removed from home and taken into the care of the local authority. And we have already seen what can be the likely outcome of such a move.

Coupled with these legal and discretionary powers there has been a significant contraction of spaces deemed to be 'public'. Malls and shopping centres have increasingly become semi-privatised, employing security guards to deter 'undesirables' and those who do not conform to images of the ideal consumer. Lacking consumer power, the presence of young people is viewed as a threat to the normal course of commerce. Presdee (1994: 182) captures this sense of dislocation through the notion of young people being 'space invaders' of modern shopping centres:

> Young people cut off from normal consumer power invade the space of those with consumer power. The have become the 'space invaders' of the 1990s, lost in a world of dislocation and excitement; a space where they should not be. Modern consumerism demands that they look, touch, and take, or appropriate.

In these circumstances, consumption, desire, excitement, and pleasure converge with exclusion to create new conceptions of 'doing wrong'. Young people using the mall as a meeting place are, quite literally, rendered 'out of place'. The planning and design of urban space has increasingly been informed by wider concerns for population control and surveillance. The CCTV camera, along with gates, locks and alarms, has become a familiar sight in many public areas and is becoming increasingly so on housing estates and in rural villages. Pioneering research on three such schemes by Norris and Armstrong (1998) found that those targeted for surveillance were disproportionately young, male and black. Moreover they were targeted not because of their involvement in crime but for 'no obvious reason' and on the basis of 'categorical suspicion' alone.

Throughout all such attempts to regulate youth behaviour the role of the police is pivotal. Through routine surveillance, targeting and reporting practices the 'usual suspects' are identified. But such 'knowledge' is then passed on to other institutions, such as schools and social services, to 'calibrate the degrees to which the chosen few should be excluded from social life' (Ericson and Haggerty 1999: 164). In these ways new technologies of surveillance and risk management continually render particular youthful sections of the population as both 'out of time' and 'out of place'.

Governing the Young

A key element of risk management strategies is to classify people into population categories and to sort out those who pose a risk and those who are at risk. Rose (1989) uses Foucault's notion of 'governmentality' to explore how an ensemble of power emanating from institutions, procedures, calculations, tactics and reflections has come to be targeted at young people. As he argues, 'Childhood is the most intensively governed sector of personal existence' (Rose 1989: 121). Since the nineteenth century, children have been the focus of innumerable programmes designed to mould and shape their development. From birth through to the extended years of schooling and training, every aspect of their and their families lives is subject to professional scrutiny. Much of this endeavour – in the form of health visitors, teachers, social workers, doctors, psychologists, training officers and so on – is legitimated by an ideology of humanity, benevolence and protection, but has little to do with recognising youth victimisation and affording young people's rights. Rather, Rose argues, its rationale is one of extending surveillance and control over the family. This is achieved not simply by coercion, but by re-forming citizens' conceptions of themselves. In this analysis, then, the control of youth is achieved through processes of 'normalisation' as well as overt constraint. Notions of 'normality' and 'deviance' are continually relayed through professional discourses and have become progressively more internalised. In Foucault's terms, control has come to operate through the human soul in which it is not only deviance or crime that is controlled, but also every irregularity or the least departure from the norm.

> it was no longer the offence, the attack on common interest, it was the departure from the norm, the anomaly; it was this that haunted the school, the court, the asylum or the prison ... it is not on the fringes of society that criminality is born, but by means of ever more closely placed insertions, under ever more insistent surveillance, by an accumulation of disciplinary coercion ... By operating at every level of the social body and by mingling ceaselessly the art of rectifying and the right to punish, the universality of the carceral lowers the level from which it becomes natural and acceptable to be punished.
> (Foucault 1977: 299, 301, 303)

The effects of this can be found in much of contemporary social policy for the young. In 1988 – following the 1986 Social Security Act – a new era of 'repressive disciplinary welfare' (Carlen 1996: 44) was initiated with abolition of all benefits for most 16- and 17-year-olds and a gradated level of benefit introduced for those under 25. *Age* rather than *need* has become the chief determinant of benefit entitlement. In the 1970s one child in ten lived in poverty. By the end of the 1990s it was one in three. Exclusions from school have trebled in the past decade. Deprived neighbourhoods are being ghettoised. Britain has one of the worst records in the industrialised world for moving young people successfully from school to work. Despite the New Deal programme, in 1999 over 130,000 16- and 17-year-olds were in 'status zero', being neither in work nor training and not entitled to benefits. England and Wales also has one of the highest rates of imprisonment in Europe for those under the age of 21.

Reviewing shifts in housing policy, Carlen (1996: 46–7) further argues that there is now 'a much strengthened disciplining of pauperised and redundant youth *independently of the criminal justice and/or penal systems*'. When young people are 'outwith the protection of employment, family and welfare they are most likely to adopt one of the transient lifestyles which may well bring them into conflict with the law'. A ready connection between homelessness and crime – shoplifting, petty theft, begging, prostitution, drug-taking – is widely assumed such that the homeless are always vulnerable to criminalisation. Jack Straw, has maintained an exclusionary policy by calling for the streets to be cleared of the 'aggressive begging of winos, addicts and squeegee merchants' (*Guardian*, 5 September 1995). Ironically, criminalisation is known to only further increase the risk of homelessness. If apprehended, lack of a fixed address ensures that the homeless are less likely to be given bail and more likely to be remanded in custody. On release, a known criminal record makes the chances of accessing rented or hostel accommodation that much more difficult. A third of young people leaving custody are likely to be homeless or at risk of being so. Criminalising the young homeless thus only ensures that a vicious circle ensues. Carlen's (1996) interviews with 150 homeless young people in Manchester, Birmingham, Stoke-on-Trent and rural Shropshire, however, led her to argue that the real issue was not one of homelessness, but of the denial of citizenship rights to those who already face destitution. She concluded that:

- Young homeless people do not constitute an underclass with moral values different to those held by any other cross section of society – though their struggles to survive unpromising childhoods may have made them cynical about the extent to which those moral values have ever had (or ever will have) any political effects.
- Young homeless people are a threat to society not because of their minor lawbreaking activities but because the economic, ideological and political conditions of their existence are indicative of the widening gap between the moral pretensions of liberal democratic societies and the shabby life chances on offer to the children of the already poor.

- The crimes of 'outcast youth' in general should be understood in relation to 'anti-social' controls which, having deliberately excluded certain young people from citizen rights and citizen duties, in turn furnish the state with further justifications for abrogation of its own obligations.
- There is an asymmetry between the level of individual responsibility that the state exacts from young people and the level of protection it affords in return. The pursuance of youth regulation is matched by immunity from punishment for those adults who criminally victimise them. (Carlen 1996: 124)

Shifts in employment, welfare and housing policy have created a situation in which young people today have to negotiate a set of risks unknown to previous generations. The old and predictable structures of labour markets and welfare systems are being dismantled and replaced by a series of uncertainties and contingencies (Furlong and Cartmel 1997). Crises and setbacks are responded to as personal shortcomings rather than as being beyond each individual's control. Increasing numbers are excluded from the full-time secure labour market and feel the brunt of successive government campaigns, in the name of the market, against 'state dependency' (Taylor 1999). In the youth labour and housing markets adequate and effective protection and support are often notable in their absence.

Conclusion

Critical readings of 'youth regulation' have the potential to significantly broaden the traditional subject matter of victimology. By fusing the boundaries of social policy and criminological knowledges, they reveal how the control of youth, whatever form or shape it may take, does not necessarily have any rational correspondence to the intensity or nature of the deviance to which it is purportedly addressed. The object of concern has become entire youthful populations whose lives are increasingly viewed as 'at risk' and thus subjected to further escalations in disciplinary training and surveillance.

The relative powerlessness of young people has always placed them at potential risk of adult victimisation. Such a risk is exacerbated at times when the *potential* of youth is subjugated to that of 'threat'. Seeking their greater regulation ensures that they are placed in positions of greater dependency often in those same family and institutional settings that are a key source of their victimisation. The problems facing young people are compounded when the prevailing political discourse becomes that of 'blaming the victim'. In such contexts the true nature and extent of youth victimisation will continue to remain stubbornly hidden from public view.

References

Anderson, S., Grove-Smith, C., Kinsey, R. and Wood, J. (1990) *The Edinburgh Crime Survey*. Edinburgh: The Scottish Office.
Anderson, S., Kinsey, R., Loader, I. and Smith, C. (1994) *Cautionary Tales: Young People, Crime and Policing in Edinburgh*. Aldershot: Avebury.
Audit Commission (1996) *Misspent Youth*. London: Audit Commission.
Aye Maung, N. (1995) *Young People, Victimisation and the Police*. Home Office Research Study No. 140. London: Home Office.
Boswell, G. (1995) *Violent Victims*. London: Prince's Trust.
Bowling, B. (1999) *Violent Racism; Victimisation, Policing and Social Context*, rev. ed. Oxford: Oxford University Press.
Brown, S. (1998) *Understanding Youth and Crime*. Buckingham: Open University Press.
Carlen, P. (1996) *Jigsaw: A Political Criminology of Youth Homelessness*. Buckingham: Open University Press.
Cohen, P. (1986) *Rethinking the Youth Question*. Post-16 Education Centre, Working Paper No. 3. London: Institute of Education.
Corby, B. (1997) 'The mistreatment of young people'. In R. Roche and S. Tucker (eds), *Youth in Society*. London: Sage/Open University.
Crowley, A. (1998) *A Criminal Waste: A Study of Child Offenders Eligible for Secure Training Centres*. London: Children's Society.
Ericson, R. V. and Haggerty, K. D. (1999) 'Governing the young'. In R. Smandych (ed.), *Governable Places*. Aldershot: Ashgate:
Esbensen, F.-A. and Huizinga, D. (1991) 'Juvenile victimisation and delinquency'. *Youth and Society*, 23, 2, 202–28.
Fitzgerald, M. and Hale, C. (1996) *Ethnic Minorities, Victimisation and Racial Harassment*. Home Office Research Study No. 154. London: Home Office.
Foucault, M. (1977) *Discipline and Punish*. London: Allen Lane.
Furlong, A. and Cartmel, F. (1997) *Young People and Social Change*. Buckingham: Open University Press.
Goldson, B. (1997) 'Children, crime, policy and practice: neither welfare nor justice'. *Children and Society*, 11, 2, 77–88.
Hartless, J., Ditton, J., Nair, G. and Phillips, S. (1995) 'More sinned against than sinning: a study of young teenagers' experience of crime'. *British Journal of Criminology*, 35, 1, 114–33.
Home Office (1997) *Criminal Statistics for England and Wales 1996*, Cm 3764. London: HMSO.
Howard League (1995) *Banged Up, Beaten Up, Cutting Up*. London: Howard League for Penal Reform.
Lauritsen, J., Sampson, R. and Laub, J. (1991) 'The link between offending and victimisation among adolescents'. *Criminology*, 29, 2, 265–92.
Liebling, A. (1992) *Suicides in Prison*. London: Routledge.

Loader, I. (1996) *Youth, Policing and Democracy*. London: Macmillan.

Mawby, R. (1979) 'The victimisation of juveniles: a comparative study of three areas of publicly owned housing in Sheffield'. *Journal of Crime and Delinquency*, 16, 1, 98–114.

Mirrlees-Black, C., Budd, T., Partridge, S. and Mayhew, P. (1998) *The 1998 British Crime Survey: England and Wales*. Home Office Statistical Bulletin, Issue 21/98, London: HMSO.

Morgan, J. and Zedner, L. (1992) *Child Victims*. Oxford: Clarendon Press.

Muncie, J. (1999) *Youth and Crime: A Critical Introduction*. London: Sage.

Norris, C. and Armstrong, G. (1998) 'CCTV and the rise of the surveillance society'. In P. Carlen and R. Morgan (eds), *Crime Unlimited*. London: Macmillan.

Percy, A. (1998) *Ethnicity and Victimisation: Findings from the 1996 British Crime Survey*. Home Office Statistical Bulletin, Issue 6/98. London: HMSO.

Presdee, M. (1994) 'Young people, culture and the construction of crime: doing wrong versus doing crime'. In G. Barak (ed.), *Varieties of Criminology*. Westport, CT: Praeger.

Qvortrup, J., Bardy, M., Sgritta, G. and Wintersberger, H. (eds) (1994) *Childhood Matters*. Aldershot: Avebury.

Rose, N. (1989) *Governing the Soul*. London: Routledge.

Saraga, E. (2000) 'Dangerous places: the family as a site of crime'. In J. Muncie and E. McLaughlin (eds), *The Problem of Crime*, 2nd edn. London: Sage/Open University.

Scraton, P. (ed.) (1997) *'Childhood' in 'Crisis'?* London: UCL Press.

Straus, M. (1994) *Beating the Devil Out of Them: Corporal Punishment in American Families*. New York: Lexington.

Taylor, I. (1999) *Crime in Context: A Critical Criminology of Market Societies*. Cambridge: Polity.

4

Old Age and Victimisation

Rachel Pain

Introduction

> Crime is perceived to be an age war, with young offenders preying on
> innocent older victims ... Politicians have quickly, and quite unjusti-
> fiably, identified the elderly as particularly vulnerable to crime.
> (Mawby, 1988: 101)

Such images of older people and victimisation are common; they are
frequently presented as archetypal victims in media reports of crime,
crime prevention policy, government and some academic research. In
other words, they are stereotyped as a group of people who are socially
and economically vulnerable to victimisation and lack the physical or
psychological strength to resist it. While such stereotypes are increasingly
challenged by crime surveys as well as qualitative accounts of older
people's experiences, they continue to inform a range of policy initiatives
specific to older people's victimisation. Little has changed, then, since
Mawby's reflection above on the political usefulness of the association
between older people and victimisation.

A central question dealt with in this chapter is how far this association
can be justified. It will examine the evidence on victimisation and fear,
and consider why so much attention has been given to older people. It aims
to identify what is unique or special about 'old age' which makes it an
appropriate category for studying people's relationships with crime, in
the same way as issues of youth, race and gender are considered elsewhere
in this collection. One strong argument against considering older people
as a social group simply rests upon their diversity. Comprising a fifth of
the UK population and an age bracket spanning more than forty years,
older people represent a cross-section of the population divided by

gender, class, race, nationality, sexuality, ability, income, health status, and so on (Conrad 1992). It may often be inappropriate to isolate age as the primary factor in victimisation, then, and nor is it accurate to expect that all older people share the same risk of crime or make the same responses. At present in western societies older people's experiences are polarising, with a growing proportion leading affluent and active retirements, and enjoying lifestyles, cultures and identities unavailable to their parents and grandparents (Featherstone and Wernick, 1995). Others, including those dependent on state pensions, are getting poorer in real terms (Walker 1993), so that older people also make up an increasing proportion of socially excluded populations.

Questions about the meaning of old age, and its appropriateness as a category for analysis of victimisation, have received relatively little scrutiny in victimology (Midwinter 1990; Codd 1996; Pain 1997a). This chapter will consider a number of alternative ways of conceptualising old age in relation to victimisation, which are as follows:

1. Old age may be irrelevant – there may be no differences in victimisation experience by age.
2. There may be differences, but these may be explained by other socio-economic or geographical factors, or lifestyle characteristics.
3. There may be aspects of victimisation which are structured by age relations and reflect the broader social and political position of older people in Western societies.

Rather than prioritising one of these ways of thinking about age over the others, I suggest that each has relevance in different areas of victimology.

The chapter begins by presenting evidence about the victimisation of older people, examining both the incidence of crime against them and the direct and indirect impacts of victimisation. Secondly, a critical framework is developed for understanding issues around the victimisation of older people. Here the chapter will draw on theoretical developments elsewhere in the social sciences. Finally, the chapter asks whether policy approaches to older people's victimisation are justified and appropriate.

Rates of Victimisation

Both official statistics on recorded crime and crime survey data are commonly broken down by age, providing a wealth of quantitative data. In this section, some of this information is presented in order to consider whether older people are a special case when it comes to victimisation. If they are, we would expect to find evidence of significant differences in rates when compared with younger people which can not simply be explained by factors such as social class, gender or area of residence; or else evidence of victimisation from particular crimes which occur because of victims' old age.

Are older people more likely to be victimised in general?

Firstly, it is clear both from official crime statistics and survey data that older people are not at greater risk of most types of victimisation; in fact, in many cases risk is significantly lower than for younger people. Table 4.1, based on British Crime Survey (BCS) data, shows that people aged 16–24 are four times more likely to be burgled than people aged over 65, and three times more likely to be victims of vehicle-related theft. The differences in rates of violence are far greater still. Official crime statistics for the UK based on incidents recorded by the police show a similar picture; people over 60 make up just 2 per cent of victims of violence against the person, 1 per cent of victims of rape and indecent assault, and 23 per cent of female victims and 7 per cent of male victims of robbery and theft from the person (Watson 1996).

Much of the difference is due to lifestyle factors. Older people tend to go out less often, so are at less risk of burglary or street crime, and are less likely to have cars to steal. They are also less likely to frequent more dangerous places such as pubs and clubs, or engage in the risk-taking behaviours such as drinking which heighten the likelihood of victimisation for the young.

It is important to recognise that these averages do not reflect the risk faced by any one individual. Locality and socio-economic factors such

Table 4.1   Proportion of households victimised, by age of head of household

Age of head of household	Burglary	Vehicle-related theft	Violence (men)	Violence (women)[a]
	% victims once or more			
16–24	15.2	21.0	20.9	8.8
25–44	6.5	19.7	7.0	4.6
45–64	4.8	15.2	3.0	2.0
65–74	3.5	7.8	0.2	0.8
75 +	4.1	5.5	1.0	0.2

[a] Figures for violence refer to proportions of adults rather than households.

Source: British Crime Survey 1998 (table adapted from Mirrlees-Black et al. 1998).

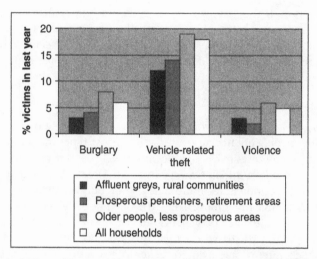

Figure 4.1   Differential rates of victimisation among older people, by ACORN area[a]

[a] ACORN ('A Classification of Residential Neighbourhoods') classifies households according to demographic, employment and housing characteristics of the surrounding neighbourhood.

Source: British Crime Survey 1998 (table adapted from Mirrlees-Black et al. 1998).

as gender, income and housing tenure also shape relative risk. Many of the indicators associated with high risk overlap, so that single young people, who are likely to rent rather than own their homes and are frequently out during the day and evening, are at greatest risk from crime (Mirrlees-Black et al. 1998). These interrelationships also mean that there are considerable differences in victimisation between older people. When the risk of these crimes is separated out into ACORN areas, the effect of locality is clear (Figure 4.1) – older people living in less prosperous urban areas run a higher risk of all victimisation types than the UK average, and twice that of affluent older people in rural areas. However, older people in inner-city areas still have risks of crime which are considerably lower than those faced by younger people in the same area, so the lower risks associated with old age can not be wholly explained by social and geographical factors.

Are there specific crimes which older people suffer because of their age?

Although crimes such as burglary and car theft affect the young more, as experiences of victimisation they are not structured by age relations. In other words, they do not usually happen *because* of this aspect of victims' identity. One example of a crime which does is child abuse, which has been related to the unequal power relationships between adults and children (Morgan 1988; Walklate 1989). Elsewhere, racist and sexual violence have been theorised in a similar way. This section considers specific forms of abuse which are targeted at older people and where old age is relevant to explanation. These incidents are much less likely to be reported to the police or crime surveys. Much of the evidence about them has emerged more recently from alternative sources.

The first is the harassment experienced by older people in public space in some local areas, especially those with high levels of crime and disorder (Garrod 1993), which Biggs (1996) has labelled 'community harassment'; 'a growing problem in which older people are scapegoated and victimised in community settings' (Biggs 1996: 78). It may include stone-throwing, name-calling, nuisance and vandalism as well as incidents more commonly conceived of and recorded as criminal, such as the mugging of older people for their pensions.

The second is elder abuse in private space, defined as the physical, sexual, psychological and financial abuse of older people taking place in a domestic or institutional context (McCreadie 1996). Rates may run as high as one in ten older people per annum. While it has been viewed predominantly as an issue for medical and social welfare services rather than one for criminal justice (Biggs 1996), elder abuse challenges certain received victimological wisdom about older people. Not only is it an age-specific crime which solely affects older people, it is likely to be a significant risk for that group, particularly when compared with the stranger-on-stranger crimes more often given attention in victimology. In addition, older people are involved as perpetrators as well as victims in a significant proportion of cases, further challenging assumptions about age and offending behaviour (see Codd 1995). Elder abuse has been theorised in terms of power relations and the vulnerable social and economic status of those at risk (Aitken and Griffin 1996). The nature of domestic spaces including the family home and care institutions, particularly the ways in which social relations are structured there, provide conditions in which older people experience a lack of power, where they may be dependent on younger carers with more social and economic capital, where intervention from outside is difficult, and where abuse largely goes unpoliced and unpunished. Difficulties with policing and resolving cases of elder abuse and, until very recently, getting the issue onto policy agendas, have been attributed to the low status of older people in Western societies (Penhale 1993).

How far these types of abuse primarily reflect age relations is not always clear-cut, however. The frailty and dependency of (a minority of) older people provide conditions in which victimisation takes place unpoliced, but old age is often not the only risk factor involved. Women are at much greater risk from both types of abuse than men (McCreadie 1996). 'Community harassment' occurring in particular localities is often aimed at others as well as older people – studies show, for example, that young women suffer much higher rates of public harassment (Crawford et al. 1990; Painter 1992). In some cases, 'elder abuse' in the home is continuing domestic violence, either within marriage or parent–child relationships which have aged (Vinton 1991; Whittaker 1996). This is not to say that age relations are not relevant, rather that it is often unwise to focus upon age as an explanatory factor alone.

The Impact of Victimisation

The idea that older people are vulnerable to particular forms of victim-isation involves more than the likelihood of victimisation alone (which, as we have seen, is lower than for other age groups for many crimes). Mawby (1988) identifies two additional dimensions of vulnerability; the effects of victimisation, and the fear of crime which non-victims as well as victims may experience. These dimensions may also be informed by survey data, but a growing number of qualitative studies are particu-larly helpful in illuminating the role of old age in responses to crime.

Vulnerability to the effects of crime

The idea that the same crime will have a greater effect on an older person than someone younger implies that older people are less able to deal with its social, psychological and/or physical consequences. This assump-tion has been widely cited in the literature, largely in an attempt to explain the finding that older people have higher fear of crime, which itself has now been dismissed as erroneous as I discuss in the next section. We should approach the notion of 'vulnerability' with some caution, then. Below, the arguments which have been put forward to explain older people's greater vulnerability to crime are evaluated. These can be grouped into physical vulnerability, socio-economic vulnerability, and cultural vulnerability. Each makes certain generalisations about older people which can be questioned.

First, the notion of vulnerability partly rests on the assumption that older people are weaker physically and psychologically than younger people, and therefore are less able to cope with and recover from victimisation. As is clear from the last section, this applies to some older people but not the majority. While illness and disability are commonly associated with all older people (Bytheway 1995), only around a third of people aged 60 and over have some form of disability, and only a small minority ever need any level of social care (McGlone 1992). Physical frailty, meanwhile, is infrequently cited as an explanation for the differential impact of victimisation on younger people, with the exception of Hough (1995) whose analysis shows that perceptions of physical vulnerability (measured in terms of physical size, health or confidence in self defence abilities) may affect the concerns of people of any age.

Second is the idea that older people are more socially and economically vulnerable than younger people. Here it has been argued that older people have less money and fewer possessions, so anything that is stolen will have more impact (and may not be insured). In addition they may be more socially isolated, lacking support networks which help speed up recovery and build confidence after a crime has been committed. Here vulnerability is explained not by the biological changes which may accompany old age, but by the enforced socially and economically constructed dependency which comes with retirement from the labour market (Walker 1993). Again, however, the factors at play are not primarily to do with old age, but concern income (older people are not the only age group over represented amongst the poor) and community structures. An increasing number of older people are experiencing greater affluence than ever, are able to choose 'safe' areas to live in on retirement, and have social and leisure lifestyles which are far from isolated or spatially restricted (Featherstone and Hepworth 1989). The growing spatial polarisation of older people – into high-crime, inner-city areas and council estates on the one hand, and more affluent rural/ suburban areas on the other – means great divergence in vulnerability to crime (see Figure 4.1).

A third and more convincing idea is cultural vulnerability. One factor which all older people have in common is that they have witnessed generational change over their lifecourses. While these changes vary between cohorts (for example those who are now in their sixties and nineties), all have witnessed rapid rises in rates of crime, and have experience of times when crime was less of a problem than today. Studies show that older people feel that they belonged to far safer and more cohesive communities in the past than they do today (Anderson 1998; Hood and Joyce 1999). Current-day reactions to crime are not solely informed by recent increases in crime and the normalisation of strategies of self-protection within daily life, but are also rooted in first-hand observation of the social, economic and cultural changes which are held to underlie these (Brown 1995; Loader et al. 1998; Pain 1995). Whether or not this means that older people are more vulnerable to the effects of crime if they are victimised is arguable. For some this may be the case, but conversely a longer lifecourse encompassing different experiences may have a more positive effect on current perceptions about crime. Towards the end of the next section, evidence is presented suggesting that older people who have grown up with lower rates of crime are more likely to see risk in perspective, less willing to allow it to restrict their lives, and therefore tend to be less fearful than younger people.

To summarise, the concept of 'vulnerability' as it has been discussed here is frequently based on ageist generalisations about older people, which apply only to some individuals in some situations. Interviews carried out by Anderson (1998) suggest that older people do not react very differently, either to the prospect of crime or to the actual experience of crime, than younger people. In both groups great diversity can be found, underpinned by different personal, social and geographical circumstances.

Fear of crime

Recent years have seen a shift in accepted wisdom concerning older people and fear of crime, from the earlier orthodoxy that they are a group who experience high fear of crime but, paradoxically, low risks of victimisation (Cutler 1980; Clarke and Lewis 1982; Hough and Mayhew 1983), to growing consensus that the issue has been misrepresented, and that older people are not necessarily more fearful than younger people (Ferraro 1995; LaGrange and Ferraro 1987; McCoy et al. 1996; Midwinter 1990; Rucker 1990). As in other areas of fear of crime research, survey methodologies are partly held to blame for these mixed conclusions (see Farrall et al. 1997); their failure to investigate the meaning of crime for older people in any depth, or the various ways in which they identify or situate themselves in relation to crime, has been highlighted (Ferraro 1995; Midwinter 1990; Pain 1995).

The British Crime Survey has shown fairly consistently that older people of both sexes worry less than younger people about most crimes (see Table 4.2). While older people have been described in the past as particularly affected by the limitations and restrictions imposed by fear (Feinburg 1981; Yin 1980), aggregate survey data do not show great differences. For example, in a new question in the 1998 BCS, 8 per cent of the total sample said that fear of crime had a great effect on their quality of life. Older people were slightly more likely to agree with this

Table 4.2 Fear of crime among different age groups

	% very worried			% feeling very unsafe
	Burglary	Physical assault	Theft from car[a]	Safety on streets
Men				
16–29	16	9	26	2
30–59	15	8	18	2
60+	14	6	12	6
Women				
16–29	24	31	21	15
30–59	23	27	15	13
60+	24	24	14	31
All	19	18	17	11

[a] Based on car owners only.

Source: British Crime Survey 1998 (table adapted from Mirrlees-Black and Allen 1998).

statement at 10 per cent, but council/housing association tenants (14%), people with disabilities (15%), and those on low incomes (16%) were all more likely to agree than older people. Also emphasising the important ways in which social identities intersect, older women living in inner-city areas were most likely of all to say they did not go out because of crime (Mirrlees-Black and Allen 1998).

Somewhat paradoxically in light of the other BCS data, Table 4.2 shows that older people are more likely to say that they feel unsafe out alone after dark (older women are twice as likely to say this as younger women, and older men three times as likely as younger men). Arguably, as older people are less likely to go out alone after dark anyway, comparisons with younger people are difficult (Mirrlees-Black and Allen 1998). However, the fact that older people also express more concern about 'being bothered by a stranger' (Mawby 1988) seems to relate to a broader range of concerns than crime itself.

In particular, qualitative research has related these fears to concerns about young people 'hanging around' and more general social and economic change within localities. These relate to the notion of cultural vulnerability introduced earlier. Fear of crime is intrinsically and intricately part of the experience of living in different localities (Girling et al. 1998), and older people are likely to have first hand experience of the changes in population, environment, reputation, economic fortunes and cultural identities which high-crime areas in particular witnessed in the second half of the twentieth century. And while few are 'prisoners of space', they may be more attached to local place and community (Rowles 1978). Brown (1995), for example, contextualises adult fears of young people's behaviour in the declining economic situation of Middlesborugh's council estates, invoking both the concept of lifecourse and distinct experience of place:

> A sixty year old East Middlesbrough resident is likely to have known an early adult life of relative economic and spatial stability, followed by a move to out of town estates and the accompanying disruption of social networks, followed immediately by the disappearance of job and income. (Brown 1995: 43)

Likewise, in the research of Loader et al. (1998), the 'youth problem' frequently cited by respondents is seen as symbolic of the concerns of older people over Macclesfield's changing economy and their own place within it, as well as the decline of the national community. Several projects using focus groups find considerable sympathy for the plight of the young amongst older people, especially the results of economic change on employment prospects (Anderson 1998; Brown 1995; Hudson et al. 1999; Loader et al. 1998). While this level of understanding challenges some stereotypes about older people's views on crime and punishment, it does not necessarily ameliorate their concerns about victimisation. It should be pointed out that similar concerns about the behaviour of the young can also be found among middle-aged people, among parents and especially among the young themselves (Hudson et al. 1999). While older people are mistakenly labelled as fearful and offered support and sympathy, young people's fears – which are much higher, and bear close relation to experiences of risk – are frequently hidden or dismissed as unworthy of attention.

The subject of fear of crime is often approached with emphasis only on the negative and oppressive ways in which people respond to it. Qualitative research has also highlighted many positive responses to crime. Some suggest that older women show more resilience than younger women in dealing with victimisation, and more resistance to the negative consequences of fear (Weinrath and Gartrell 1996; Pain 1997b). Others show how reactions to crime are contextualised in other experiences over the lifecourse. A broader and longer experience of life and its various problems, as well as cumulative experience of crime itself, can put concerns about crime into perspective. The following quotes, taken from interviews with older women and men, illustrate some of the more positive connections between old age and victimisation.

> *Moira*: I think if I had to stay in because of something like that [fear of attack] I'd be more determined to go out, you know. I can appreciate it with people if they're fearful, but I think it makes me more determined to go.
>
> *Sharon*: That's part of the reason why my handbag is so heavy. A clonk from that would knock him out for – you know. [laughs] I always put an umbrella in the bottom of my bag to make it extra heavy. Just in case I need it. (taken from Pain 1997b)

RP: *What sort of things do you worry about when it comes to crime?*

George: Well I don't worry about anything incidentally. . . . I wouldn't say I was perturbed about crime at all, I mean there's always been crime.

RP: *Does it affect you at all?*

George: Na. No, not at all. I don't think anything bothers me now, you know. . . .

RP: *What do you think it is about you that means it doesn't affect you so much?*

George: I've always been a fatalist in my life. And er I've never been afraid of anything. Not a single thing. You see I went through the war and I had three terrific accidents in the war. I was with the Northumberland Fusiliers in the war and um I had direct hits three times and it didn't perturb me. I've had two operations for cancer, and um tumours removed. It still didn't affect me. And last year – sorry, this year – we were going down the motorway, down the A1(M) and an artic lorry went into the back of us, and er we got out of that with no problems, you know, which is just I think fate, you know. I don't – burglary, it just doesn't affect me, you know. I think if they come they come, and lets face it I would be quite sorry if they did come and I was in their presence, because I wouldn't hesitate to do anything. (taken from Pain 1997a)

> *Edna*: I had a nasty experience when I was young, I mean it's not new to this age . . . I got into the taxi and then suddenly he turned off and he went along a narrow unmade road and we ended up on this bit of wasteland. I said are you going to attack me? He didn't answer you see. And I said well I'll scream at the top of my voice, that's the first thing I'll do if you touch me. And er he stood there and I said are you a married man? He said yes. And have you got

children? He said yes. I said do you know what's going to happen
if you do anything to me? I says you're going to lose your job,
you're going to lose your wife, you're going to lose your children.
And er he says I would pick you wouldn't I. He says jump in and
I'll take you back.... You see then people didn't speak about things
like that. I mean everything's more open now. But I mean it was
something that we'd feel ashamed of then and you wouldn't speak
about it.

RP: *After that, did it make you feel more wary?*

Edna: No. No, no. I've always felt that I could hold my own anyway.
It made me feel more secure, that I could deal with a situation like
that. (taken from Pain 1999)

Conceptualising Older People and Victimisation

What, then, are we to make of the categories 'older people' and 'old age'?
At the very least, we need to be critically aware of their limits. Old age
has largely been constructed in negative and static terms in victimology.
The last decade has seen a fundamental shift in theorisation elsewhere
in the social sciences (Bytheway et al. 1989; Cole et al. 1992; Harper and
Laws 1995), and old age, traditionally taken for granted as a fixed life-stage,
has come to be understood as variable and contested across different
cultures, times and spaces (Bytheway 1995). The analysis of gender in
victimology has taken a similar course; for example the deconstruction
of the category 'woman' (Walklate 1997) and recently greater recognition
of difference and multiple identities. As this chapter has shown, older
people too may be positioned in more than one way in relation to crime
and fear, yet this is less frequently acknowledged. Like women, ethnic
and sexual minorities, older people tend to be embodied, or defined by
physical characteristics (Featherstone and Wernick 1995). In Western
societies, older people are identified with physical and social decline
and dependency (Biggs 1993; Bytheway 1995; Featherstone and Wernick
1995). I have suggested that these ageist constructions underlie the
common assumption that older people are particularly vulnerable to
the negative effects of crime and fear.

On the basis that the relationship between older people and crime is
a 'tenuous link', Midwinter has suggested that old age might be abandoned as a frame of reference, if we are to avoid the dangers of 'self-
fulfilling victimology' (Midwinter 1990: 51–3). Certainly, we should
beware of making assumptions about difference, and over-analysing
categories which do not always stand up to rigorous investigation. But

if, as is proposed here and supported by other authors in recent years, a number of issues around older people and crime can be theorised in terms of power relations (Fattah and Sacco 1989; Midwinter 1990; Codd 1996), old age need not be abandoned as a relevant category of analysis. Instead, we should take explicit account of ageism and view old age in the context of intergenerational relations which are constructed in different ways, and do so alongside rather than separate from other social identities. The structures of class, gender, race and ability are the key determinants of how older people experience old age. It is these which underpin where they live, their socio-economic status and their risks of victimisation, whether from property crime, harassment in the community or abuse by carers within domestic spaces.

Policy Approaches to Reducing Older People's Victimisation and Fear

All that has been said so far suggests that policies that seek to reduce either the victimisation or the fear of older people are unnecessary, as in neither case are older people at greater risk than younger people. Meanwhile, the problem of elder abuse is largely viewed as an issue for the social work and medical professions, rather than for crime prevention, and is 'isolated from parallel debates on violence and exploitation in contemporary British society' (Biggs 1996: 67). Nonetheless, older people have been disproportionately singled out for attention in crime prevention and community safety schemes focusing on property crime and violence from strangers. Target hardening is one example, tending to focus on low-income groups who may be at higher risk – recent plans in the UK aim to widen schemes which install locks and security devices in the homes of older people.

Policy initiatives have generally been dominated by what Walklate (1989) has called 'victim-centred' approaches, especially educational measures to rectify older people's supposed misconceptions about their risk of crime. For example, the UK Home Office's *Practical Guide to Crime Prevention* continues to promulgate the idea that older people are both fearful and ignorant of the 'real' risks: 'Although you may think that elderly people are particularly at risk from crime, statistically this isn't true. Nevertheless, they can often feel very vulnerable' (Home Office 1998a: 10). The guide goes on to makes suggestions on how to reduce the risk of crime, falling back onto stereotypes of hapless, forgetful older people who are behind the times ('never keep a large amount of money in the house'; 'don't let in strangers at the door'). In Scotland,

Anderson (1998) found that older people are already highly sensitised to the full range of crime prevention measures which individuals can take to protect property and person. There is little evidence that this sort of advice reduces victimisation or fear for those who are vulnerable.

Advice is given too to relatives and neighbours in this literature to help make older people feel safer, implying that older people are unable to prevent crime themselves. In direct contrast, in many communities it is older people who take a leading role in crime prevention. In the UK, older people are well represented in Neighbourhood Watch schemes, where they are more likely to protect younger people's property during the day than vice versa, to the extent that attempts are now being made to involve young people in schemes to redress the balance (Home Office 1998b). Older and middle-aged people also predominate on residents' panels and other fora for community safety, meaning that it is frequently younger people who are excluded from consultation and involvement in subsequent initiatives (Brown 1995).

As this suggests, and as indicated earlier, one salient problem for both older and younger people in some communities is a lack of interaction and mutual suspicion. Constructions of old and young rest upon the existence of the other as victim or offender, a supposed cultural and moral clash which is employed by both politicians and academics as symbolic of crime and disorder in the UK (Mawby 1988), just as discourses centring on racial difference have been employed in the past (Lea and Young, 1984). This labelling is damaging to the social relationships between them, and concerns about young people out of control have real implications for the safety and wider social inclusion of young people as well as the old (Brown 1995; Loader et al. 1998). For both research and policy, then, an intergenerational approach is likely to be more useful than focusing on one age group alone.

There are few policy initiatives which tackle intergenerational relations which would involve small-scale, social interventions rather than the situational, environment-centred approaches which became popular in the late twentieth century. However, the recent shift of emphasis in the UK onto local issues of community safety provides a context where such interventions are more likely to be realised. One example of intergenerational work is the Lifelink project in North Tyneside, north-east England, which is currently running over a five-year period in high-crime areas of the borough. The broad aim of the project is to reduce fear of crime, but not in isolation from related issues of community integration. A range of community development methods are being employed in order to bring together different age groups who might be suspicious of or hostile towards each other. Activities have focused on the sharing of skills and experiences, including classes where schoolchildren teach computing to older people, bike clinics for children which are run by older people, and young people interviewing older people and compiling biographies of their memories.

The project has encountered the usual problems in getting people to participate, and its ultimate effects on fear of crime are difficult to evaluate as they are likely to be diffuse, long-term and partial. However, given our knowledge about old age and fear of crime – that it is only a problem in certain areas, only for some groups, and is closely linked to local social, economic and cultural change – such approaches at the local community level are more likely to have an impact than those mentioned previously. The approach has much wider benefits than reducing fear of crime alone, for example giving older and younger people in high-crime areas a role in community safety, challenging stereotypes, and reducing social isolation. Arguably, it has most benefits for children and young people, many of whom have relatively little contact with older people. The understanding of fear of crime and the values informing this type of project are appropriate for community safety planning where old age is judged to be a relevant issue.

Summary and Agenda

The evidence presented in this chapter suggests that older people do have different risks of victimisation compared to younger people. While crime may have a greater impact on some older people, rates of victimisation and rates of fear are generally lower than for other age groups. There may be reasons for this which are connected to old age, but these relate either to lifestyle differences or to positive aspects of old age rather than the negative connotations usually pointed to. On the other hand, while older people are at less risk from the crimes traditionally measured in crime surveys, in certain spaces they may be at greater risk from forms of abuse which generally receive less attention from researchers and policy-makers. In the discussion above I have highlighted the importance of issues of multiple identity; for example, it is not true to say that older people are more at risk from abuse in the home than women, who may be of any age, or those in another particular age group, young children.

There is relatively little evidence that older people are more fearful than younger people, that they have irrational perceptions of risk, or that they feel the impact of victimisation will be greater upon them. Recent research suggests that gender, race and sexuality have closer association with fear of crime than old age. However, some older people do have specific concerns about young people's behaviour in public spaces which they perceive as threatening, and this is related to wider concerns about the changing communities and localities in which they live. Age and experience also allow older people to respond in positive ways to the threat of crime: in contrast to common perceptions, with resistance and a sense of perspective.

This suggests that what has been constructed as a problem may not be a problem – at least, not for many older people. One conclusion is that recent work investigating youth, victimisation and fear is following a more fruitful road of inquiry. However, and as I argued earlier, research and policy around older people might be refocused onto the forms of victimisation where old age is relevant and which present the most salient risks – abuse in private space and community harassment. At present there needs to be much greater consultation of both old and young, and attention to the needs of the most vulnerable rather than dealing with either group en masse.

In order to achieve this it is important to develop appropriate methodologies. A range of data sources have been assessed in this chapter; all are problematic and there is a continued need for triangulation. That the literature to date has been characterised by conflicting findings reflects the related problems of varying theoretical assumptions and methodologies which are limited in the insight they can give. A central epistemological problem here is one which has been better acknowledged in research on the victimisation of children; that those representing older people's experiences tend to be young or middle aged adults. The task of assessing risk and fear for older people is not made any easier by empirical practices concerning not only what is included in crime surveys, but how it is measured. The BCS now includes a self-completion component for sexual victimisation, stalking and illegal drug use, but only asks these questions to people aged 16–59. In pilot studies, older people were found to be less capable at entering answers on the lap-top computers used, and so the opportunity to investigate how far sexual assault is an issue for older people has been lost. Yet the continuing emphasis of victimology only on public space and stranger-on-stranger crimes against older people may be as inappropriate for highlighting their victimisation as it has been for understanding women's experiences in the past (Stanko 1987). The growing number of qualitative studies in victimology, which have focused on some of the above questions with the intention of allowing older people to speak for themselves, have been central in dispelling some of the myths around old age and victimisation.

Acknowledgement

Thanks to Michelle Whitworth, coordinator of Lifelink, for providing information on the project.

References

Aitken, L. and Griffin, G. (1996) *Gender Issues in Elder Abuse*. London: Sage.
Anderson, S. (1998) *Older People, Crime and Crime Prevention*. Edinburgh: Age Concern Scotland.
Biggs, S. (1993) *Understanding Ageing: Images, Attitudes and Professional Practice*. Buckingham: Open University Press.
Biggs, S. (1996) 'A family concern: elder abuse in British social policy'. *Critical Social Policy*, 47, 16, 63–88.
Biggs, S., Phillipson, C. and Kingston, P. (1995) *Elder Abuse in Perspective*. Buckingham: Open University Press.
Brown, S. (1995) 'Crime and safety in whose "community"? Age, everyday life, and problems for youth policy'. *Youth and Policy*, 48, 27–48.
Bytheway, B. (1995) *Ageism*. Buckingham: Open University Press.
Bytheway, B., Keil, T., Allatt, P. and Bryman, A. (1989) *Becoming and Being Old: Sociological Approaches to Later Life*. London: Sage.
Clarke, A. H. and Lewis, M. J. (1982) 'Fear of crime among the elderly'. *British Journal of Criminology*, 22, 49–62.
Codd, H. (1995) 'Older offenders'. *Probation Journal*, 42, 3, 152–5.
Codd, H. (1996) 'Feminism, ageism and criminology: towards an agenda for future research'. *Feminist Legal Studies*, 4, 2, 179–94.
Cole, T., Van Tassel, D. and Kastenbaum, R. (1992) *Handbook of the Humanities and Ageing*. New York: Springer.
Conrad, C. (1992) 'Old age in the modern and postmodern world'. In T. Cole, D. van Tassel and R. Kastenbaum (eds), *Handbook of the Humanities and Ageing*. New York: Springer, pp. 62–95.
Crawford, A., Jones, T., Woodhouse, T. and Young, J. (1990) *The Second Islington Crime Survey*. Middlesex Polytechnic: Centre for Criminology.
Cutler, J. J. (1980) 'Safety in the streets: cohort changes in fear'. *International Journal of Aging and Development*, 10, 4, 373–84.
Eastman, M. (1994) *Old Age Abuse: A New Perspective*. London: Chapman & Hall.
Farrall, S., Bannister, J., Ditton, J. and Gilchrist, E. (1997) 'Questioning the measurement of the "fear of crime": findings from a major methodological study'. *British Journal of Criminology*, 37, 4, 658–79.
Fattah, E. A. and Sacco, V. F. (1989) *Crime and Victimisation of the Elderly*. New York: Springer.
Featherstone, M. and Hepworth, M. (1989) images of Aging. In J. Bond, P. Coleman and S. Peace (eds), *Aging in Society*. London: Sage.

Featherstone, M. and Wernick, A. (1995) *Images of Ageing: Cultural Representations of Later Life*. London: Routledge.

Feinburg, N. (1981) 'The emotional and behavioural consequences of violent crime on elderly victims'. *Victimology*, 6, 355–7.

Ferraro, K. (1995) *Fear of Crime*. New York: SUNY Press.

Garrod, G. (1993) 'The mistreatment of elderly people'. *Generations Review*, 3, 4, 9–12.

Girling, E., Loader, I. and Sparks, R. (1998) 'Crime and the sense of one's place: globalisation, restructuring and insecurity in an English town'. In V. Ruggerio, N. South and I. Taylor (eds), *The New European Criminology*. London: Routledge, pp. 304–22.

Harper, S. and Laws, G. (1995) 'Rethinking the geography of ageing'. *Progress in Human Geography*, 19, 2, 199–221.

Home Office (1998a) *Your Practical Guide to Crime Prevention*. London: Home Office.

Home Office (1998b) *Welcome to Neighbourhood Watch*. London: Home Office.

Hood, R. and Joyce, K. (1999) 'Three generations: oral testimonies on crime and social change in London's East End'. *British Journal of Criminology*, 39, 1, 136–60.

Hough, M. (1995) *Anxiety about Crime: Findings from the 1994 British Crime Survey*. Research Findings No. 25, Home Office Research and Statistics Department. London: Home Office.

Hough, M. and Mayhew, P. (1983) *British Crime Survey: First Report*. London: HMSO.

Hudson, B., Pain, R. and Williams, S. (1999) *Reducing Neighbourhood Fear of Crime: Final Report for North Tyneside Council*. Newcastle upon Tyne: University of Northumbria.

LaGrange, R. L. and Ferraro, K. F. (1987) 'The elderly's fear of crime: a critical examination of the research'. *Research on Ageing*, 9, 3, 372–91.

Lea, J. and Young, J. (1984) *What is to be Done about Law and Order?* Harmondsworth: Penguin.

Loader, I., Girling, E. and Sparks, R. (1998) 'Narratives of decline: youth, dis/order and community in an English "middletown"'. *British Journal of Criminology*, 38, 3, 388–403.

Mawby, R. I. (1988) 'Age, vulnerability and the impact of crime'. In M. Maguire and J. Pointing (eds), *Victims of Crime: A New Deal?* Milton Keynes: Open University Press, pp. 101–11.

McCoy, H. V., Wooldredge, J. D., Cullen, F. T., Dubeck, P. J. and Browning, S. L. (1996) Lifestyles of the old and not so fearful: life situation and older persons' fear of crime'. *Journal of Criminal Justice*, 24, 3, 191–205.

McCreadie, C. (1996) *Elder Abuse: Update on Research*. London: Age Concern Institute of Gerontology, King's College.

McGlone, F. (1992) *Disability and Dependency in Old Age: A Demographic and Social Audit*. London: Family Policy Studies Centre.

Midwinter, E. (1990) *The Old Order: Crime and Older People*. London: Centre for Policy on Ageing.

Mirrlees-Black, C. and Allen, J. (1998) *Concern about Crime: Findings from the 1998 British Crime Survey*. Research Findings No. 83, Research, Development and Statistics Directorate. London: Home Office.

Mirrlees-Black, C., Budd, T., Partridge, S. and Mayhew, P. (1998) *The 1998 British Crime Survey*. Home Office Statistical Bulletin, 21/98. Home Office, London.

Morgan, J. (1988) 'Children as Victims'. In M. Maguire and J. Pointing (eds), *Victims of Crime: A New Deal?* Milton Keynes: Open University Press, pp. 74–82.

Pain, R. H. (1995) 'Local contexts and the fear of crime: elderly people in north-east England'. *Northern Economic Review*, 24, 96–111.

Pain, R. H. (1997a) '"Old age" and ageism in urban research: the case of fear of crime'. *International Journal of Urban and Regional Research*, 21, 1, 117–28.

Pain, R. H. (1997b) 'Social geographies of women's fear of crime'. *Transactions of the Institute of British Geographers*, 22, 2, 231–44.

Pain, R. (1999) 'Women's experiences of violence over the lifecourse'. In E. Teather (ed.), *Embodied Geographies: Spaces, Bodies and Rites of Passage.* London: Routledge, pp. 126–41.

Painter, K. (1989) *Crime Prevention and Public Lighting with Special Focus on Elderly People.* Middlesex Polytechnic: Centre for Criminology.

Painter, K. (1992) 'Different worlds: the spatial, temporal and social dimensions of female victimisation'. In D. J. Evans, N. R. Fyfe and D. T. Herbert (eds), *Crime, Policing and Place.* London: Routledge, pp. 164–95.

Penhale, B. (1993) 'The abuse of elderly people: considerations for practice'. *British Journal of Social Work*, 23, 2, 95–112.

Rowles, G. (1978) *Prisoners of Space? Exploring the Geographical Experiences of Older People.* Colorado: Westview Press.

Rucker, R. E. (1990) 'Urban crime: fear of victimisation and perceptions of risk'. *Free Inquiry in Creative Sociology*, 18, 2, 151–60.

Stanko, E. A. (1987) 'Typical violence, normal precaution: men, women and interpersonal violence in England, Wales, Scotland and the USA'. In J. Hanmer and M. Maynard (eds), *Women, Violence and Social Control.* London: Macmillan, pp. 122–34.

Vinton, L. (1991) 'Abused older women: battered women or abused elders?' *Journal of Women and Aging*, 3, 3, 5–19.

Walker, A. (1987) 'The social construction of dependency in old age'. In Loney, M. (ed.), *The State or the Market?* London: Sage, pp. 41–57.

Walker, A. (1993) 'Poverty and inequality in old age'. In J. Bond, P. Coleman and S. Peace (eds), *Ageing in Society: An Introduction to Social Gerontology.* London: Sage, pp. 280–303.

Walklate, S. (1989) *Victimology.* London: Unwin Hyman.

Walklate, S. (1997) 'Risk and criminal victimisation: a modernist dilemma?' *British Journal of Criminology*, 37, 1, 35–45.

Watson, L. (1996) *Victims of Violent Crime Recorded by the Police, England and Wales, 1990–1994.* Home Office Statistical Findings 1/96. London: Home Office.

Weinrath, M. and Gartrell, J. (1996) 'Victimisation and fear of crime'. *Violence and Victims*, 11, 3, 187–97.

Whittaker, T. (1996) 'Violence, gender and elder abuse'. In B. Fawcett, B. Featherstone, J. Hearn and C. Toft (eds), *Violence and Gender Relations: Theories and Interventions.* London: Sage, pp. 147–60.

Yin, P. P. (1980) 'Fear of crime amongst the elderly: some issues and suggestions'. *Social Problems*, 27, 492–504.

5

Communities and Victimisation

Karen Evans and Penny Fraser

Introduction

In Britain and in America numbers of recorded crimes rose to unprecedented levels in the last two decades of the twentieth century. Criminal statistics show, for example, that recorded crime in England and Wales rose by 91 per cent between 1981 and 1995. Over the same period figures derived from the British Crime Survey (BCS) showed an increase of 83 per cent.[1] Crime, risk and fear of victimisation was no longer a problem that people could keep at a distance. They affected the 'daily considerations of anyone who owned a car, used the subway, left their house unguarded during the day, or walked the city streets at night' (Garland 2000: 359). One particularly significant feature of the impact of crime on society cannot be overlooked. Looking at crime statistics for the country as a whole obscures the fact that the burden of crime does not fall equally on all areas. The distribution of crime is in fact decidedly unequal with some areas suffering disproportionately. Just as some groups in society are more vulnerable to victimisation, it seems that this could also be said to be true of different neighbourhoods.

In this chapter, we examine the relationship between victimisation, crime and neighbourhood, and consider the appeals to community that characterise attempts to understand this relationship. The term 'community' possesses a range of complex meanings, not least in relation to crime. Degeneration of community, as Crawford explains, 'is viewed as both the cause and effect of crime and the fear of crime', so that, 'rebuilding community, it is supposed, will lead to less crime' (Crawford 1997: 151). But precisely what is it about 'community' that can bring about such consequences? As a vehicle for interventions to prevent crime, community, as Currie points out, can be conceptualised in two main ways. Firstly as a set of attitudes, which community crime prevention would seek to alter, promoting more 'social' behaviour, through an enhanced sense of community. Secondly, and in Currie's view more significantly, by emphasising the basic institutions of family, work, school or religion which are fundamental to thriving communities and which help 'real communities' to withstand crime through effective 'informal social control' mechanisms and community mobilisation (Currie 1988 in Crawford 1997: 156). Discussion of community in crime prevention, however, often merely refers to a shared geographical location, although recent developments in crime prevention have considered 'virtual' communities of victims, to refer to groups of people who by virtue of their victimisation risk may be envisaged as 'communities' even though they may not share a common geographical space.

The Spatial Patterning of Crime

Since Shaw and McKay first presented their mapping of 'delinquent areas' in Chicago in the 1930s and 1940s, there has been a recognition that crime and place can be closely related. Shaw and McKay's maps plotted the place of residence of known offenders, and demonstrated that they were concentrated in particular neighbourhoods. These were residential areas, close to the central business district of Chicago and featured a largely impoverished and transient population, new to the city, and to America itself, and so without roots and social contacts (Shaw and McKay 1942). The Chicago school of sociologists set out to discover why offenders might be concentrated within these areas and looked for factors present in such neighbourhoods which might contribute to their residents' offending behaviour. These academics famously turned to a discussion of 'social disorganisation' as the major factor affecting the 'criminality' of such areas. Their work was built upon by a number of writers who were equally concerned to explore the ways in which the social relationships within a neighbourhood, or the lack of such relationships, might contribute to the total numbers of residents in that area who became involved in offending (for further elaboration see the discussion in Croall 1998).

It was not until the early 1970s that rates of *victimisation* within different neighbourhoods began to be explored. The incidence of crime was mapped across cities and the mapping of offence location, rather than offender location, demonstrated that victimisation was also spatially patterned (see for example Baldwin and Bottoms 1976). In America, Oscar Newman (1972) uncovered a relationship between numbers of offences and characteristics of the built environment. This work was taken up in Britain by the Home Office (Mayhew et al. 1976 for example) and by the work of Alice Coleman (1985). High-crime areas were studied and particular features of the architecture and physical environment of these places were seen as key to understanding their high crime rates. Whole estates were redesigned to remove these features, and plans for new buildings avoided their use altogether. This environmental control of crime proved to be a popular crime prevention technique, but it was acknowledged that there were other aspects to the spatial patterning of crime which had yet to be explored and researchers looked for explanations in the operation of housing markets (Bottoms and Wiles 1986), the impact of poverty (Kinsey 1985; Young 1992) and different patterns of socialisation (Bronfenbrenner 1979).

During the 1980s further interest was generated in the study of the link between victimisation rates and neighbourhood. Large-scale victimisation studies, which had been developed in the United States in the 1960s, were conducted across Europe and in Britain from 1982. Data generated by these surveys gave a more accurate image of victimisation than relying on numbers of recorded crimes alone (Mawby and Walklate 1994: 24–32). The first British Crime Surveys were analysed in such a way that the distribution of criminal victimisation within different residential areas across the country could be illustrated. This analysis showed crime to be concentrated in the poorer neighbourhoods within British cities where rates of burglary and crime against the person were particularly high (see Hope and Hough 1988). Further analysis has shown victimisation to be even more concentrated than previously thought. Using 1982 BCS data, a sample of representative communities across England and Wales were ranked according to incidence of crime into ten groupings or deciles, which were ranked from the lowest to the highest crime areas. A remarkable distribution of crime was uncovered by resulting graphs which showed there to be a gradual increase in crime across the majority of areas, as well as a massive increase in incidents of crime for a minority of high crime areas (see Trickett et al. 1992). Further, for property crime there was an incidence rate in the highest decile twenty-five times higher than that of the second highest decile. The increase was even more marked for personal crime. The incidence rate for the highest decile was shown to be seventy-six times higher than that of the third highest. So crime was shown to be very heavily concentrated in a small minority of areas. In addition, however, the rate of victimisation per household was also shown to increase in these areas, demonstrating that those households and individuals which had been victims of crime were likely to have been victimised on more than one occasion. This phenomenon has been labelled 'repeat victimisation', and means that once victimised in such an area the chances of being victimised again are far higher (Farrell and Pease 1993). This phenomenon has been recognised as having significant implications for crime prevention work as it further outlines the extent of the social and spatial concentration of crime (Crawford 1998).

So which areas suffer from the highest incidence of crime? Three types of area have been associated with a heightened risk of property and personal crime and they have been classified as follows:

- mixed inner metropolitan, or multi-racial areas with a mixture of poor, private rented housing and owner occupation
- non-family areas with a mix of affluent housing and private rented housing in multi-occupation
- the poorest local authority estates, located either in inner city or overspill areas.

These three types of areas have certain characteristics in common. They are, in the main, low-status, urban areas of poor-quality housing with above-average concentrations of children, teenagers and young adults and with a preponderance of single-adult households.

The Relationship between Crime and Locality

How can this unequal distribution of crime be explained? This is a crucial question, as consideration of the major causes of offending and victim- isation will influence the choice of crime-prevention tools. Different analyses of community crime rates each seek to explain whether and how: 'community crime rates may be the result of something more than the mere aggregation of individual propensities for criminality or victimisation' (Hope 1995: 23). Wilson and Kelling, in their influential 'broken windows' article (1982), demonstrated that a snowball effect occurs when the level of disorder or incivility reaches a certain point. Farrell (1995) has identified particular thresholds or 'tipping points' where a qualitative shift in the extent of crime occurs. Where a neigh- bourhood acquires a reputation for being a high-crime area it can be difficult to attract new residents into the area and the more capable and community-orientated residents may leave. This can leave a neighbour- hood in a state of decline, where fear of crime is high and people do not feel able to intervene when they witness crime and disorder incidents.

In these circumstances people may lose confidence in their area and in their capacity to act to change things for the better. Within such areas residents are less likely to look out for one another, to intervene to prevent crime or to confront young people who are causing a nuisance. There are likely to be more opportunities in these areas for criminal incidents to take place and for the offender to be successful in the crime and remain undetected (see Sampson 1987; Skogan 1988). Under these circumstances, it could be argued that neighbourhoods themselves can be seen as victims of crime. Individual residents can do little to combat the spiral of decline in their area and many do not have the resources to enable them to move out. Furthermore, if a neighbourhood gains a reputation for crime, fear and lawlessness then the area's residents may face related difficulties in obtaining finance, employment and insurance for their property. Yet, increasingly, residents belonging to such areas are being co-opted into the 'fight against crime'.

Cohen and Felson (1979) have argued that a combination of factors need to be present in order for a crime to be committed. These are:

- motivated offenders
- vulnerable victims
- the opportunity to commit crime

This work has had a significant influence on policy, suggesting a number of crime prevention approaches which could centre on demotivating offenders, strengthening the capacity of the victim to evade crime, or eliminating opportunities for crime to take place. The relevance of each of these factors to understanding the dynamics of highly victimised neighbourhoods is discussed below.

Motivated offenders

The 'social disorganisation model' argues that anti-social and offending behaviours are 'normalised' in certain areas. The 'normalisation' of offending behaviour is seen as more likely to occur where people have weak social ties to sources of conformity such as school, job opportunities and community and stronger ties to sources of non-conforming behaviour such as gang cultures, unemployment and criminal opportunities. Crime prevention policies which follow this model centre on the offender, seeking to deter offending by various means. They concentrate on the individual, presenting alternatives to offending, 'diversionary activities', or employ more punitive deterrents which act in a more general way on offender motivation, using the threat of punishment, for example, to persuade people that crime is not worth the risk. Imprisonment can be used simply as a threat, or as a mechanism by which offenders are removed from a neighbourhood altogether. The use of the threat of imprisonment as a crime prevention tool certainly grew in favour during the latter part of the twentieth century.

Vulnerable victims

One of the conclusions of Trickett et al.'s work on the spatial patterning of victimisation is that there may be concentrations of particular groups within high-crime areas who may be more likely to become victims of crime. One of the features of the three types of area most subject to criminal victimisation is that they are more likely to have a youthful population. Data from the BCS has illustrated that young people are more likely to become victims of personal crime, partly because they share similar characteristics to offenders. Single-adult households are also more likely to be victims of property crime, partly perhaps because their properties are more often left unguarded. Hence, victimisation is less likely to be a product of individual characteristics of victims than of the social and economic make-up of the neighbourhood in which victims of crime reside. However, crime-prevention models which aim to reduce the vulnerability of victims have, to a great degree focused on individual crime-avoidance strategies. Crime prevention literature therefore often advises the individual as potential victim to take precautions to prevent crime – this can mean purchasing alarms to protect buildings and cars, or perhaps avoiding being out on the streets at certain times. Although this advice can seem like common sense, it can also be seen as an approach which puts a great deal of responsibility on the individual or organisation to take steps to avoid becoming a victim of crime, rather than being concerned with affecting wider social and economic processes which can contribute to crime. Advice to women in particular focuses on individual victimisation-avoidance strategies. Feminist writers, especially, have criticised much of the crime-prevention advice issued to women as encouraging a point of view which sees the cause of crime as resting with the victim, rather than with the perpetrator (Stanko 1990). This approach can lead to 'victim blaming' (see Mawby and Walklate 1994: 9–10), where the victims of crime are seen as in some way responsible for their own victimisation.

The opportunity to commit crime

The changing nature of urban lifestyles in the second half of the twentieth century opened up a wide range of criminal opportunities. Greater numbers of homes became unoccupied during the day (with both male and females members of the household out at work and more single-occupier homes); also increases in car ownership (fewer people walking the streets of their neighbourhoods providing a measure of informal social control as well as greater opportunities for theft and break-ins to private vehicles) and a rise in the quantity and range of consumer goods have arguably produced more opportunities for crime to be committed. Changing technologies produce a different 'breed' of professional criminal.

A whole new industry has grown up around the provision of 'situational crime prevention', a practice which has sought to minimise opportunities for criminal victimisation by manipulating the built environment, securing and 'target-hardening' properties and 'designing out crime' through the work of architects and planners. Designing out crime has included the application of security features such as immobilisers and alarms in cars, constructing buildings with built-in security measures such as strong doors and windows or by designing environments which encourage natural surveillance of surrounding properties. Many local authority housing estates throughout Britain have been redesigned using these principles, concrete walkways have been removed between blocks of flats, open space between housing has been incorporated into private gardens and housing has been 'turned around' so that the fronts of houses face one another. It is thought that these structural changes can improve guardianship of property, encouraging a sense of neighbourliness and surveillance of shared and semi-private spaces. Although popular, this strategy has been criticised as crude 'architectural determinism' which does not take into account the complexity of the relationship between crime and community (Merry 1981).

Crime and Community

Since the Chicago sociologists first discussed social disorganisation in the city there has developed an interest in the social relationships which could be said to constitute the study of community. For the Chicago school it was lack of social ties which contributed to criminality and this argument has continued to be persuasive throughout academia. In the 1980s Skogan typified the high crime community as one in which residents are:

> deeply suspicious of one another, report only a weak sense of community, have low levels of influence on neighbourhood events...

and feel that it is their neighbours whom they must watch carefully.
(Skogan 1988: 45)

In 1988 Hope and Shaw pointed out that little of what had constituted
community crime prevention up to that time had actually sought to
strengthen or alter such ties or to build the social relationships which
might be said to constitute the building of community. Instead, they
argue, community crime prevention has focused on changing the behaviour of certain individuals and families, or targeting measures on particular
high-crime neighbourhoods. The term 'community', they further argue,
has been deliberately utilised in order to invoke practical and emotional
support for various crime prevention measures from the residents of
such localities. The appeal to 'community' could therefore be seen as a
disguise for an approach which actually considers that a minority of
people whose values and beliefs somehow conflict with those of the
majority in society constitute the major problem in terms of increasing
levels of crime. Indeed such sentiments have fuelled the theories of the
underclass which were current in the late 1980s and early 1990s (see
Murray 1990). These ideas have not gone unchallenged (Campbell 1993;
Walklate and Evans 1999) but still hold a great deal of currency in the
popular imagination. It is assumed that there has been a wholesale 'loss
of community' in high-crime areas and that crime prevention must look
to a rebuilding of community if crime rates are to be reduced.

There is another sense in which the crime-prevention gaze has fallen
upon the community. Until the early 1980s it was generally felt that crime
prevention was the responsibility of the police alone, although individuals
were supposed to help by taking steps to reduce their chances of victimisation, by taking care of their own personal safety and also securing
their own property against theft. A much broader concept of crime
prevention was introduced from the late 1960s in the United States,
reaching Britain in the 1980s. This approach emphasised the responsibility of the community to act, in partnership with others, to prevent
crime. The term 'community safety' was adopted to characterise this
broader approach. A Home Office circular on crime prevention, published
in 1984, explained the idea behind community safety. It argued: 'Just as
the incidence of crime can affect the whole community, so too its prevention is a task for the whole community' (Home Office Circular 8/84).
The circular went on to stress that the term 'community' referred to
a range of agencies working in a particular area, both in the public and
private sectors, and not only individuals resident locally. The embracing
of the notion of community safety was also influenced by the Scarman

Report published after the inner-city riots of 1981, which recommended a number of ways in which police and community relations could be improved. By 1997, the Local Government Association (LGA) report *Crime: The Local Solution. Current Practice* identified most local authorities in Britain as being engaged in community safety work. The narrow, police-driven, perspective which crime prevention had formerly denoted was beginning to be broken down. In 1996 the Local Authority Association's Community Safety Working Party came up with an extended working definition of the term. They stated:

> Community safety is the concept of community-based action to inhibit and remedy the causes and consequences of criminal, intimidatory and other related antisocial behaviour. Its purpose is to secure sustainable reductions in crime and the fear of crime in local communities. Its approach is based on the formation of multi-agency partnerships between the public, private and voluntary sectors to formulate and introduce community-based measures against crime.

In passing the Crime and Disorder Act in 1998 the new Labour government sought to enshrine in legislation a notion of community safety. The Crime and Disorder Act typifies the move to community responsibility inherent in 'community safety' and introduces a new range of crime controls which place more responsibility on individuals and community members to play a part in reducing crime.

Tackling Victimisation: Exercises in 'Community Crime Prevention'

The term 'community crime prevention' is generally taken to refer to efforts to tackle crime that in some way or another involve members of the community. In their round-up of crime prevention in Europe and North America, Graham and Bennett found no clear agreement or precise definition of community crime prevention. They offer a working definition, where:

> Community crime prevention is defined as encapsulating both situational measures and measures to prevent criminality within a community-based framework of action . . . including measures which emphasise the need to change the social, economic and demographic conditions which are believed to sustain crime in communities including the development and strengthening of communities as

well as measures which emphasise the need to involve members of communities in reducing opportunities for committing offences. (Graham and Bennett 1995: 71)

A key driver of efforts to realise community crime prevention is the existence in areas with low crime rates of high levels of social control and community cohesion. It is believed that replicating the conditions of low-crime areas is likely to be an effective way to reduce victimisation rates in high-crime areas. A particular emphasis is placed on informal social control mechanisms – those ties that link people together in relations with each other and with community-based institutions (e.g., schools, family and work) (Sampson and Laub 1993: 18). Also emphasised is the goal of capacity-building communities to increase levels of 'social capital' – resources and skills that individuals can draw upon throughout their lifecourse and that derive from positive and 'interdependent' relationships with local social institutions such as school, family and workplace (Sampson and Laub 1993: 19).

But this oversimplifies the factors that generate or inhibit crime in poorer neighbourhoods. An important distinction between the types of social relations in neighbourhoods has been made in relation to the chances of successful community crime prevention (Hope 1995). The first type of social relatism is the 'horizontal' relationships that exist, for example between people sharing a geographical space which are characterised by loyalty, affection or reciprocity or the absence of these attributes. The second dimension – the vertical dimension – denotes the relationships that connect residents and local institutions to resources and influence in the wider public sphere. As Hope states:

the paradox of community crime prevention ... stems from the problem of trying to build community institutions that control crime in the face of their powerlessness to withstand the pressures towards crime in the community, whose source, or the forces that sustain them, derive from the wider structure. (Hope 1995: 24)

Hope further identifies/describes several community crime-prevention models. The first model, following Shaw and McKay, characterises communities as disorganised and posits solutions which foreground community development, tenant involvement, mobilising the resources found within active communities which can help to combat crime and empower communities to access further resources (Hope 1995: 35). The second model is associated with frightened communities and promotes self-policing or defence, organised community surveillance and environmental modifications. The third model reacts to a perceived disintegration of social ties, seeking to preserve order (concentrating on controlling incivilities or 'nuisance') and protect the vulnerable (targeting crime prevention at those most at risk of victimisation rather than across the community).

In the following we consider recent examples of community crime prevention that illustrate some of the ways in which criminal victimisation is tackled through community-based institutions or sets of relationships.

1. Strengthening community ties through community surveillance: working with the frightened community

Various 'watch' schemes are often regarded as the embodiment of community crime prevention – business owners, shopkeepers, publicans or householders work together to respond to the risk of crime in their locality. Physical proximity and neighbourhood ties are mobilised to promote a shared vision for a safe community where notions of guardianship, surveillance and self-organisation come together to ensure the effectiveness of each scheme. Schemes like Neighbourhood Watch have claimed support from many areas: not only can they increase positive contact between neighbours but they also require active attention from the local police who, as a result, can become better acquainted with the worries and fears of local people. Indeed, Neighbourhood Watch is frequently regarded as a key plank in community policing strategies.

However, research on Neighbourhood Watch schemes in England and Wales has shown that they are easier to establish and sustain in 'homogeneous, stable neighbourhoods' where participation rates in voluntary and community organisations is common and where residents tend to own their own dwellings (Graham and Bennett 1995; see also Hope 1988). Conversely, in areas where communities are more heterogeneous, where resident turnover is higher and where there are high proportions of residents from low socio-economic backgrounds, Neighbourhood Watch schemes are less successful (Laycock and Tilley 1995). Trust between neighbours is fundamental to the efficacy of such schemes and this trust may be easier to sustain in homogeneous and stable communities and difficult to generate and maintain where there is higher resident turnover, or where fear of victimisation is high – especially if people fear that known Watch members may be especially targeted. For these reasons, efforts have sometimes been made where Neighbourhood Watch has been unsuccessful, to establish community – police partnerships which use some of the key techniques of watch schemes, but do not use their name. The CAPE (Community and Police Enforcement) scheme in Newcastle upon Tyne's West End is an example of one such alternative.

Community and Police Enforcement in Newcastle's West End

Background

Some of the usual ways in which the police work in partnership to prevent crime and improve reporting of crime and anti-social behaviour had been eroded during the early 1990s in part of Newcastle's West End. High levels of fear, not just of crime but of secondary harassment or intimidation of people prepared to report and speak out about crime, prevented people from coming forward to the police. Neighbourhood Watch, which had been in operation before 1991, had become negligible by 1996. Northumbria Police required 60 per cent of eligible residents in a designated Watch area to become members before they could service any Neighbourhood Watch scheme. This was an impossible target for the area. Trust in the police had dwindled, and the high turnover of uniformed officers servicing the schemes meant that relationships of trust between residents and designated officers was difficult to establish.

Taking Action

A decision was taken to hand the post of Neighbourhood Watch co-ordinator at the West End Police divisional headquarters over to a civilian officer. The post was initially co-funded for three years by Newcastle City Council's Urban Crime Fund and subsequently solely by Northumbria Police. An alternative to the orthodox Neighbourhood Watch style of working was developed. The scheme that emerged aimed to: increase reporting of crime; improve the relationship between police and local residents; and ensure that residents were given the necessary support to enable them to report incidents, to give witness or victim statements and to attend court appearances without fear of reprisal from within their community.

Community and Police Enforcement in Newcastle's
West End (*Continued*)

The CAPE (Community and Police Enforcement) Scheme

The scheme encourages wider police–community contact, mainly through the use of community beat officers. These officers carry a pager allowing CAPE members to leave information and intelligence reports at any time of the day. A leaflet explaining the role and procedures involved in CAPE is produced for new or potential members. Regular meetings are held to update CAPE resident-members on progress made and to raise general issues of concern relating to the policing of the area. A newsletter also keeps members in touch. There are no window stickers or other overt identification of membership in the scheme. A particular feature of the scheme is the support given to members who experience or witness crime; this support could include keeping in touch with – and keeping a lookout for – the witness, or attending court with them. In March 1998, when the Home Office carried out research on the CAPE scheme in one neighbourhood, 10 per cent of households were represented as members of the scheme.

According to Home Office research, membership of the CAPE scheme has reduced fear among members and increased confidence about what would happen if they reported a crime – as a consequence members told the researchers that they were less likely to drop charges and members were repeatedly less frightened of victimisation resulting from their involvement in the scheme.

Sources: Nacro (1999); Home Office (2000).

2. Promoting social order in communities: working with disorganised communities

Community crime-prevention initiatives have sought to introduce higher levels of social order into what are considered to be socially disorganised areas. Crime prevention or 'community safety' schemes have been set up in neighbourhoods, focusing as much on a range of general social projects as on specifically crime-focused ones. This approach recognises that crime risks are both accompanied by, and associated with, a range of other risks (for example, poor housing, deprivation, unemployment, poor educational achievement and poor health – see

Wiles and Pease 2000: 36). Community safety work has therefore been increasingly closely allied with other services such as youth and family work, health promotion, improved housing, increased employment opportunities and nursery provision. The precise nature of the relationship between these different elements of provision is far from unequivocal and any causal links can be very difficult to disentangle. However, as Wiles and Pease point out, recognising the interrelationships between sets of risk factors enables politicians, policy-makers and practitioners to at least start to address social problems more holistically and systematically. The Crime and Disorder Act of 1998 enshrined this principle further, placing a statutory requirement upon each local authority in England and Wales to consider the crime and disorder implications of activities undertaken by the authority in the discharge of its duties. Under Section 17 of the Crime and Disorder Act, major decisions taken by a local authority can now be subject to review and their likely impact on crime and disorder assessed, so that any negative consequences can be avoided. However, as Wiles and Pease have also noted, Section 17 is also open to criticism for focusing too narrowly on the consequences of local authority policies on levels of crime and disorder while ignoring other risk factors such as increasing inequalities, poor health or accidents which may also be shared by high-crime communities (Wiles and Pease 2000: 28).

The Crime and Disorder Act further seeks to maintain social control in communities by the use of measures such as anti-social behaviour orders, child safety orders, parenting orders and child curfews. These measures are designed to control antisocial or disorderly behaviour within communities. Some of the most effective crime and disorder prevention, however, is designed and delivered by residents and addresses deficits in local social provision for young people. The effectiveness often derives from local knowledge of the area's young people and being able to command the respect and trust of a diverse range of residents and interest groups in the community. The resident-led Community Trust set up on the Kingsmead Estate in Hackney is illustrative of this approach.

Kingsmead Community Trust

Background

In 1993 hardly anyone wanted to live on the Kingsmead Estate in Hackney. Crime, vandalism and anti-social behaviour appeared to be out of control. 27 per cent of flats were unoccupied and the

Kingsmead Community Trust (*Continued*)

communal facilities were regularly vandalised. A climate of fear
had taken hold and the estate had become so notorious that 75
per cent of council housing applicants refused offers of housing
on the estate. Burglaries on the estate in 1993 accounted for
one-tenth of the burglaries for the whole of Hackney.

First Steps

1993 was a turning point for Kingsmead. By establishing a unique
partnership arrangement with the police, the council won court
orders against four young people on the estate. These injunctions
banned them from entering any other property on the estate or
threatening other tenants or staff. They were obtained using
signed affidavits by other tenants against the accused. Criminal
charges by the police followed on from this action.

Kingsmead Community Trust

At the same time as the injunctions procedure was being developed,
a group of residents, concerned about the neglect of Kingsmead's
economic and social life, and above all anxious that provision
should be made for the estate's young people, started to negotiate
with the council around the setting up of a community trust on the
estate. The Kingsmead Community Trust aimed to 'help realise the
potential of Kingsmead through encouragement and the development
of a successful community spirit, enterprise, training initiatives
and recreational leisure-time occupation for the youth, single parents
and women returners, the elderly citizens and persons with disability
on the estate'. A range of sponsorship and grants was obtained,
enabling the Trust to run activities including youth provision for
young people barred from an existing youth club on the estate. The
Trust served as a focal point for the community, including its relations with the local police, who worked with the Trust and residents
to develop a sensitive community policing strategy for the estate.

   By early 1995, the proportion of empty properties was down to
7 per cent, the burglary rate had nearly halved and residents were
describing Kingsmead as one of the better estates in the area.

Source: Nacro (1996).

3. Relieving the pressure on victims: working with disintegrating communities

Victims, residents and others are frequently exhorted to become focused on crime prevention in the course of their daily routines, habits and lifestyles. Garland expresses it thus: 'where the State once targeted the deviant for transformative action, it now aims to bring about marginal but effective changes in the norms, routines and consciousness of everyone' (Garland 1996: 454, quoted in Hughes 1998: 128). What victim-oriented, community-based strategies can help relieve the pressure on victims to take responsibility for their own safety? Three main approaches are:

- removing the victim
- removing/punishing the offender
- involving the victim

Removing the victim. This strategy is sometimes adopted where fear of retribution against the victim and isolation within the community are anticipated following a report being made to the police. It is a strategy that has been employed where persistent or potentially life-threatening victimisation is taking place and can accompany a criminal prosecution or can be employed where there is insufficient evidence to effect a prosecution. It can be deemed appropriate where there is evidence, for example, of racial abuse of residents by neighbours, but where evidence is difficult to gather. If the victim is housed in social housing then one short-term solution may be to rehouse them away from the perpetrators for their own safety. The rationale for this is similar to that in respect of domestic violence, where the threat usually comes from within the home. But what does this approach actually achieve?

In some situations, the opportunity to leave a place of residence and start afresh somewhere new may be welcomed by the victim. In other cases, however, but for the victimisation there may have been a significant attachment to the community (for example through children's attendance at local schools, employment, social and family ties, and the availability of nearby facilities). Removal of the victim from what was otherwise an embedded relationship with their place of residence may be very much against the victim's and their family's longer-term interests and has perhaps been used as an easy option when an evidence-gathering operation to enable the prosecution of offenders has been discounted. With the introduction in the Crime and Disorder Act (1998) of a raft of measures such as Anti-Social Behaviour Orders and Child Safety

Orders for which the burden of proof is lower than for other forms of criminal prosecution, the government may claim that it is now easier for victims of such crimes to stay put while sanctions are placed on the perpetrators.

Removing/punishing the offender.   Where a criminal prosecution is successful, an offender can be removed – into custody or care – or given a court disposal designed to inhibit them from committing the offence(s) again. With the protection of communities and witnesses in mind, the Anti-Social Behaviour Order can include a requirement for the offender to keep away from the victim for a period specified by the court (the Anti-Social Behaviour Order must be of a minimum of two years' duration). Such an Order can be given where there is evidence of behaviour that has either caused or which is likely to cause alarm, harm or distress to another. Failure to abide by the condition of the Order means that an offender can be returned to court, one outcome of which could be a custodial sentence (up to five years maximum) or an additional fine. Removing or restraining the offender in this way can be seen as giving respite, not only to the individual victim of crime but also to a highly victimised community.

Citizen action can sometimes be a powerful force at the local level, when mobilised to take action against actual or suspected perpetrators of crime. Citizen action can include acts of vigilantism, seeking to exact punishment against actual or suspected perpetrators, resisting action or perceived action taken by the state which it is believed would harm the community, or lobbying for extra resources to improve home security (see Johnston 1996 for a description and analysis of vigilantism). We have witnessed recently in the UK, in response to the decision to house convicted sex-offenders on a housing estate in Portsmouth, actions taken by a community that perceived itself to have been victimised or at risk of victimisation in a general sense. This action may have made its participants and their community feel engaged and empowered, but may also have increased feelings of fear and vulnerability.

Involving the victim.   Criminal justice in the late twentieth century has been characterised by an enhanced set of roles and responsibilities for and responsibility towards victims, and more generally the voice of the victimised (see Garland 2000). For agencies like Victim Support working directly with victims of crime, attention to the 'forgotten party' in the criminal justice process was long overdue. One of the ways in which victims are being accorded a voice is through the statutory responsibility for the probation service to undertake victim-contact work in the cases of victims of serious violent or sexual offences. Probation Circular 61/1995 requires probation services to 'provide victims with information about the custodial process and post-release supervision and obliges probation services to seek victims' views about release conditions' (Crawford and Enterkin 2000: 30). This move recognises that offenders and victims frequently occupy the same geographical space. Research conducted by Crawford and Enterkin showed that victims found high-quality and well-delivered victim-contact work of benefit. In respect of public protection issues, however, there were potentially both positive and negative factors at play. Probation services found the contact work with victims helpful in planning post-release supervision and risk assessments. Concerns centred around the victim-contact work actually enhancing risk to victims (for example, if an offender perceived his/her victim to have had an undue influence over his/her post-release conditions) (Crawford and Enterkin 2000: 31), acknowledging that victims and offenders are not disembodied actors in the criminal justice process, but members of dynamic and interrelated communities.

Victims can now be directly involved in the implementation of sanctions against offenders in certain circumstances, should they wish. As Nellis points out, the notion of justice itself is 'a process of reconciling interests' (Nellis 2000: 76). For liberal Western democracies, justice as embodied in the legal system concentrates on the protection of individual rights. An alternative interpretation, one promoted by a variant of communitarianism, emphasises the 'over-riding importance of healing rifts in community' (Nellis 2000: 77), with a primary (but not exclusive) focus on reconciliation (Nellis 2000: 77). This quality of justice is 'finding some practical expression in family group conferencing initiatives' (Nellis 2000: 78) and in notions of victim–offender mediation/restorative justice.

Conclusion

This chapter has looked in detail at a number of perspectives which have informed the understanding of the link between communities and victimisation. It has emphasised the contexts in which crime and community have been linked and has considered some of the responses in practice to this emerging imperative to involve communities in crime reduction. Different models of community crime prevention have been considered, along with some of the difficulties involved in developing and mobilising communities in the prevention of crime and victimisation. Of course much of this thinking and practice is new and, as we explain, community crime prevention has been criticised for not engaging with the reality of social relationships in high-crime areas. To fully engage with this reality involves a balancing act between the needs of a victimised community and the needs of the offender who may be embedded within that community (Hope 1998). This is a difficult act to success-fully carry out. To a great extent then community crime prevention has focused on the physical rather than the social fabric in which commu-nities are found and has offered little more than the same old solutions with the added rhetoric of community to engender higher levels of support and participation.

However, there is a new agenda, typified in the approach of the government's New Deal for Communities and the National Strategy for Neighbourhood Renewal which links the needs of the community to more than just its physical regeneration. This approach could see the notion of communities and victimisation becoming more central to crime reduction and may signal a move away from the previous emphasis on area-based and/or individual-based strategies to tackle crime in order to fully incorporate the building and sustaining of communities on many different levels.

Note

1. The 1996 British Crime Survey England and Wales, Home Office Statistical Bulletin 19/96.

References

Baldwin, J. and Bottoms, A. E. (1976) *The Urban Criminal*. London:Tavistock.

Bottoms, A. E. (1990) 'Crime Prevention Facing the 1990s'. *Policing and Society*, 1, 1, 3–22.

Bottoms, A. E. and Wiles, P. (1986) 'Housing tenure and residential community crime careers in Britain'. In A. J. Reiss and M. Tonry (eds), *Communities and Crime*. Chicago: University of Chicago Press.

Bronfenbrenner, U. (1979) *The Ecology of Human Development*. Cambridge, MA: Harvard University Press.

Campbell, B. (1993) *Goliath: Britain's Dangerous Places*. London: Methuen.

Cloward, R. A. and Ohlin, L. E. (1960) *Delinquency and Opportunity*. Glencoe: Free Press.

Cohen, L. and Felson, M. (1979) 'Social change and crime rate trends: a routine activities approach'. *American Sociological Review*, 44, 558–608.

Coleman, A. (1985) *Utopia on Trial: Vision and Reality in Planned Housing*. London: Hilary Shipman.

Crawford, A. (1997) *The Local Governance of Crime: Appeals to Community and Partnerships*. Oxford: Clarendon Press.

Crawford, A. (1998) *Crime Prevention and Community Safety: Politics, Policies and Practices*. London: Longman.

Crawford, A. and Enterkin, J. (2000) 'The probation service, victims of crime and the release of prisoners'. *Criminal Justice Matters*, 39, 30–2.

Croall, H. (1998) *Crime and Society*. London: Longman.

Currie, E. (1988) 'Two visions of Community Crime Prevention'. In T. J. Hope and M. Shaw (eds), *Communities and Crime Reduction*. London: HMSO.

Farrell, G. (1995) 'Preventing repeat victimisation'. In M. Tonry and D. Farrington (eds), *Building a Safer Society: Crime and Justice, a Review of Research*, vol. 19. Chicago: University of Chicago Press.

Farrell, G. and Pease, K. (1993) *Once Bitten, Twice Bitten: Repeat Victimisation and its Implications for Crime Prevention*, CPU paper 46, London: Home Office.

Gardner, J. von Hirsch, A., Smith, A. T. H., Morgan, R., Ashworth, A. and Wasik, M. (1998) 'Clause I: the hybrid law from hell'. *Criminal Justice Matters*, 31, 25–6.

Garland, D. (1996) 'The limits of the sovereign state: strategies of crime control in contemporary society'. *British Journal of Criminology*, 36, 4, 445–71.

Garland, D. (2000) 'The culture of high crime societies: some preconditions of recent "Law and Order" Policies'. *British Journal of Criminology*, 40, 3, 347–75.

Gelsthorpe, L. and Morris, A. (eds) (1990) *Feminist Perspectives in Criminology*. Milton Keynes: Open University Press.

Gottfredson, M. R. and Hirschi, T. (eds) (1987) *Positive Criminology*. Newbury Park, CA: Sage.

Graham, J. and Bennett, T. J. (1995) *Crime Prevention Strategies in Europe and North America*. Finland: HEUNI.

Home Office (1990) *Safer Communities: The Local Delivery of Crime Prevention through the Partnership Approach*. Home Office Standing Conference on Crime Prevention. London: Home Office.

Home Office (2000) 'Community and police enforcement in Newcastle'. Home Office Briefing Note 2/00. London: Home Office.

Hope, T. J. (1988) 'Support for Neighbourhood Watch: a British Crime Survey analysis'. In T.J. Hope and M. Shaw (eds), *Communities and Crime Reduction*. London: HMSO.

Hope, T. J. (1995) 'Community crime prevention'. In M. Tonry and D. P. Farrington (eds), *Building a Safer Society: Strategic Approaches to Crime Prevention*. Crime and Justice: vol. 19. Chicago: University of Chicago Press.

Hope, T. J. (1998) 'Communities and crime'. In D. Goldblatt and C. Lewis (eds), *Reducing Offending: An Assessment of Research Evidence on Ways of Dealing with Offending Behaviour*. Home Office Research Study No. 187. London: Home Office.

Hope, T. and Hough, M. (1988) 'Area, crime and incivility: a profile from the British Crime Survey'. In T. Hope and M. Shaw (eds), *Communities and Crime Reduction*. London: HMSO.

Hope, T. and Shaw M. (1988) *Communities and Crime Reduction*. London: HMSO.

Hughes, G. (1998) *Understanding Crime Prevention: Social Control, Risk and Late Modernity*. Buckingham: Open University Press.

Johnston, L. (1996) 'What is vigilantism?' *British Journal of Criminology*, 36, 2, 220–36.

Kinsey, R. (1985) *Merseyside Crime Survey: First Report.* Liverpool: Merseyside County Council.

Kinsey, R., Lea, J. and Young, J. (1986) *Losing the Fight against Crime.* Oxford: Blackwell.

Laycock, G. and Tilley, N. (1995) 'Implementing crime prevention'. *Crime and Justice: A Review of Research,* 19, 535–84.

Mawby, R. I. and Walklate, S. (1994) *Critical Victimology: International Perspectives.* London: Sage.

Mayhew, P., Clarke, R. V., Sturman, A. and Hough, M. (1976) *Crime as Opportunity.* London: HMSO.

Merry, S. (1981) 'Defensible space undefended'. *Urban Affairs Quarterly,* 16, 397–422.

Murray, C. (1990) *The Emerging British Underclass.* London: Institute for Economic Affairs.

Nacro (1996) *Crime, Community and Change: Taking Action on the Kingsmead Estate in Hackney.* London: Nacro.

Nacro (1999) *Community Safety Community Solutions: Tackling Crime in Inner City Neighbourhoods.* London: Nacro.

Nellis, M. (2000) 'Creating community justice'. In S. Ballintyne, K. Pease and V. McLaren (eds), *Secure Foundations: Key Issues in Crime Reduction and Community Safety.* London: IPPR.

Newman, O. (1972) *Defensible Space: Crime Prevention through Environmental Design.* London: Architectural Press.

Reiss, A. J. and Tonry, M. (eds) (1986) *Communities and Crime.* Chicago: University of Chicago Press.

Sampson, R. J. (1987) 'Communities and crime'. In M. R. Gottfredson, and T. Hirschi (eds), *Positive Criminology.* Newbury Park, CA: Sage.

Sampson, R. J. and Laub, J. H. (1993) *Crime in the Making: Pathways and Turning Points through Life.* London: Harvard University Press.

Shaw, C. R. and McKay, H. D. (1942) *Juvenile Delinquency and Urban Areas.* Chicago: University of Chicago Press.

Skogan W. G. (1988) 'Disorder, crime and community decline'. In T. Hope and M. Shaw (eds), *Communities and Crime Reduction.* London: HMSO.

Stanko, E. A. (1990) 'When precaution is normal: a feminist critique of crime prevention'. In L. Gelsthorpe and A. Morris (eds), *Feminist Perspectives in Criminology.* Milton Keynes: Open University Press.

Tonry, M. and Farrington, D. P. (eds) (1995) *Building a Safer Society: Strategic Approaches to Crime Prevention.* Crime and Justice; vol. 19. Chicago: University of Chicago Press.

Trickett, A., Osborn, D. R., Seymour, J. and Pease, K. (1992) 'What is different about high crime areas?' *British Journal of Criminology,* 32, 81–9.

Walklate, S. and Evans, K. (1999) *Zero Tolerance or Community Tolerance: Managing Crime in High Crime Areas.* Aldershot: Avebury.

Wiles, P. and Pease, K. (2000) 'Crime prevention and community safety: Tweedledum and Tweedledee?' In S. Ballintyne, K. Pease and V. McLaren (eds), *Secure Foundations: Key Issues in Crime Reduction and Community Safety.* London: IPPR.

Wilson, J. Q. and Kelling, G. (1982) 'Broken windows: the police and neighbourhood safety'. *The Atlantic Monthly,* March, 29–37.

Young, J. (1992) 'Ten points of realism'. In J. Young and R. Matthews (eds), *Rethinking Criminology: The Realist Debate.* London: Sage.

6
Crime Victims and Public Policy

Pamela Davies

Introduction

This chapter outlines the agencies and processes that the victim of crime comes into contact with when entering the formal parts of the criminal justice system. In addition, the chapter briefly assesses criminal injuries compensation and restorative justice developments as well as the new responsibilities that the National Probation Service has to victims of crime. The chapter draws upon two perspectives in detailing this journey. One is an account as identified by official policies adopted and prescribed by the Home Office, the police, the CPS, the courts and the Probation Service. This can be seen as the 'official' or 'top-down' view of policies and practices. The second perspective will consider these processes and provision from a bottom-up approach, from the standpoint of the victim – a victim's perspective.

Structuring the chapter according to the above criteria, it is possible to view the criminal justice system and its interaction with victims of crime in an uncritical way and also subsequently to view this inter-action as problematic. The twofold account therefore allows us to raise a number of important issues and debates for those concerned about the victim in the criminal justice system. These include for example, the important debates concerning victims' rights/needs, the state and its provisions/obligations, the relationship between police, courts, the law and other agencies including the voluntary sector.

The chapter will emphasise the state or 'official' dealings with victims. It is recognised that outside the scope of this discussion a number of voluntary organisations and feminist-inspired groups play a vital role in providing help and support to different types of victims. Some of these bodies have succeeded in influencing victim policy and have inspired changes which have been incorporated in 'official' criminal justice policies. It is acknowledged that this will inevitably provide only a partial picture of victimisation, even a stereotypical view of the crime victim and a traditional representation of the criminal justice system where 'police' and 'victims' are on the whole referred to in ideal-typical terms.

Victims and the Police

Although they represent a very small minority of the total number of victims of crime, those victims that come into contact with the police are at the gates of the formal institution of the criminal justice system. Some of these victims will have limited initial contact and then no further contact with the police. Others will continue to come into contact with the police and some fewer still will continue to be processed through the gates of the criminal justice system (by the police) into the hands of more representatives and professionals belonging to the court process. The police therefore, represent an important benchmark in any review of the way in which victims in the criminal justice system are treated. This is acknowledged by a number of writers (see, for example, Mawby and Walklate 1994; Shapland et al. 1985; Southgate et al. 1984). Three points of police/victim contact are examined below. These are how a victim comes into contact with the police, what happens when a victim reports a crime to the police and follow up contact between the victim and the police.

How does a victim come into contact with the police?

Whichever way a victim comes into initial contact with the police, be it via the telephone or in person. The way in which the police respond is vitally important to the victim and to the image of the police service. From the police point of view the initial communication with a victim needs to elicit as much information as quickly as possible so that a decision can be made about the incident's priority in terms of a police response. For the victim the chances are that this communication will not be such a routine activity as that of the police representative responding to it and the victim's decision to contact the police may have taken a great deal of courage.

From the first point of contact impressions are formed about the police by victims and the public alike and vital information is gained about a crime, perhaps for the first time, by the police. The fact that police rely almost entirely upon the public for information about crime is well known (Kinsey et al. 1986; Mawby and Walklate 1994). Crimes that come to the attention of the police where a victim is readily and easily identifiable tend to be the more traditional types of crime, both serious and less so. Crimes of the powerful and their often more generalised victims are not the focus of so much attention as personal and property crimes that are the everyday business of our local police services (Croall 1998). It is therefore the victims of these latter types of crime that form the basis of the police's idea of what a victim looks like, and this in itself can be problematic for crime victim policy. For some victims this initial contact may result in their being processed no further even if the crime is of a violent nature. Although policy has now changed, until recently victims of domestic violence could be referenced off as 'advice given' and the incident would effectively be brought to a close for policing purposes. Whether or not recent policy changes have been effective in respect of the police's response to this type of inter-personal, non-stranger violence is still a matter of debate.

The relationship between the victim and the police, from the very earliest moment of contact, is structured in terms of unequal power relations. Undoubtedly the victim would prefer not to be a victim in the first place and would also prefer not to be in contact with the police. On the other hand one of the main functions of the police rests entirely upon the existence of crime victims. That apart, both parties require the co-operation of each other. The victim may believe the police can do something about their being victimised, whether that be to catch the offender and bring them to justice, stop crimes happening again, or simply to provide a crime number for the purposes of insurance. The police need victims to come forward to tell them about the volume, nature and extent of crime, the information surrounding the commission of crimes and the 'clues' as to who the perpetrators might be in order for offenders to be caught. Further into the criminal justice process the reliance of the police on the victim remains paramount in the pre-trial, trial and court stage, often as witnesses to provide evidence.

Realistically, however, the police and criminal justice system have nothing tangible to offer the victim. There are no guarantees that property will be returned, that the offender/s will be caught or that justice will be done. Worse still, according to some commentators, the victim is at risk of becoming re-victimised by the police and the courts. This experience of the criminal justice system is where secondary victimisation can take place (Victim Support 1995). Perhaps the question that is often asked about why victims fail to report crimes to the police should be turned on its head. From a more victim-oriented perspective the question ought to be: Why *should* a victim report a crime and thereby enter into contact with the police?

The above demonstrates clearly how the relationship between the victim and the police is unusual and unequal. It may seem that the victim ought to be in a powerful and prime position, as holder of vital and key evidence. In reality this is not the lived experience of many victims. The police have increasing power over the victim as the case progresses. This power comes in the form of greater information and knowledge about police, CPS and court processes and what happens after this initial contact in many respects is already informed and structured by this first encounter.

What happens when a victim reports a crime to the police?

Most victims will be unaware of how their crime is considered alongside the many hundreds of others that are reported to the police every day. The police will be asking whether the report requires an immediate response and decisions will be made about the priority of the incident. The victim having reported the crime is likely to want to know what will happen next and when. It is clear that the victim's and the police's concerns about what happens next are not in harmony.

At this point it is worth mentioning some of the ways in which police prioritise crimes because depending on what the nature of the crime and victimisation is, the police may respond quite differently. Practices such as 'crime-screening' can make individual experiences of the police response vary widely. Some of the procedures that ensue are standard practice in the police service and are guided by national directives in the form of Home Office circulars, one such being Home Office Circular 20 (1988) entitled *Victims of Crime*. Other decisions and priorities depend on local policy decisions and current initiatives that the police may be supporting, for example there may be a crackdown on house burglaries or a 'zero-tolerance' campaign might be in place. Some policies will remain fairly stable over time and others will change according to the local tolerance of crime and police management decisions and community safety priorities. Some crimes on the other hand simply lend themselves to being detected and police are likely to be able to achieve an impressive clear-up rate if enough time, energy and resources are allocated. Other crimes have not been taken seriously enough, for example domestic abuse (Edwards 1984, 1989) and have not traditionally attracted a high policing priority. So-called 'domestics' have often been seen as 'rubbish' police work (Reiner 1992). White-collar crimes and 'crimes of the powerful' have never been as zealously policed as the more visible crimes on the streets, leaving victims of such forms of victimisation hidden and/or neglected entirely by the police and the criminal justice system (Davies et al. 1999). All of the above can affect victims' experience and contact with the various agents of the criminal justice system.

According to the *Victim's Charter* (Home Office 1996) at this stage victims can *expect* the police to do several things. These include providing a quick response and various verbal and leafleted information. In addition, victims can expect the police to ask them about their victimisation experience so that this can be included in files for the CPS. Following a crime report it is possible that the police will pass on the victim's details to the local Victim Support team. The British model of victim support can briefly be described as a community response to victims in which members of the community voluntarily offer the victim emotional or practical support. Its origins can be traced back to a scheme in Bristol in 1974. Originally Victim Support largely addressed the *needs* of crime victims. The current model of Victim Support has moved towards a model of uniform standards and a model that also encompasses concern for victims' *rights* (Wright 1996). Since the mid-1980s Victim Support has enjoyed government funding but has continued to rely on voluntary workers thereby maintaining a semi-independent and rather unique status.

In England and Wales the referral of victims to Victim Support comes primarily from the police via a direct referral system. In principle Victim Support offer their services to victims of any kind of crime, although in the past they have been criticised for focusing, like the police, on the more common types of crime such as burglaries. Volunteers are now trained to support a wider variety of crime victims, and caseloads now include more serious cases including relatives of murder victims and also rape victims. Victim Support may then contact a victim to inquire whether they would like further contact from the service, often they will offer to send a volunteer round to talk to the victim and their family irrespective of what any further developments in the 'official' case might be. The police's relationship with other agencies such as Victim Support is an important factor in responding to the needs of crime victims. The police's relationship with Victim Support varies from scheme to scheme and even from police officer to police officer (Newburn and Merry 1990) but it is generally a good one. This cannot be said of the police's relationship with all voluntary and in particular feminist support groups, many of which tend to have an antagonistic relationship with the police as part of their oppositional stance to the criminal justice system.

If it was not already clear that some crimes are policed more than others, the variability in the way in which crimes are policed and therefore victims are viewed is further complicated by cultural aspects of policing and media reporting of crime and its control. As already mentioned women victims of domestic violence have had their crime down-crimed (Edwards 1984, 1989). The police stereotype of a victim also includes unconscious notions about victim-blaming (Brake and Hale 1992), deserving and non-deserving victims, the innocent victim and the negligent or provocative victim (Shapland et al. 1985: 67). The media have also contributed to these unfair and inappropriate presentations of some crime victims whilst such stereotypes have been reinforced by the courts, as have notions surrounding contributory negligence (Jeffreys and Radford 1984; Jones et al. 1994) and victim precipitation. Victims such as prostitute women, gay men, lesbians and ethnic minority populations may be afraid of a possible unsympathetic reaction by the police. Crime victims may also fear, or be at risk of, being treated as second class citizens or illegal immigrants (Lopez-Jones 1999; Wright 1996). Recent criticism of the police response to crime victims has come from rural environments where many feel that their homes are largely unprotected by the police or that crimes committed in more remote locations are not adequately policed (*The Daily Telegraph*, 25 April 2000: 1–2). Such issues affect the reporting of crime to the police by crime victims, as well as the recording of 'official' crime by the police.

Returning to the *Victim's Charter*, according to the original version (Home Office 1990), the police *should* ensure and aim for a number of things to happen during this stage of the police and victim contact. The 1990 *Charter* has been criticised as an optimistic and naively hopeful publication on behalf of the Home Office. Nowhere was there any timetable to suggest when these things *should* be happening. Nowhere was there any mention of resources to ensure any of these things could be made to happen and there were no enforcement mechanisms or apparent penalties or remedies should the victim not receive any of these pieces of information and communication during their contact with the police. Clearly a critical assessment might condemn the *Victim's Charter* as a political gesture, empty of any real concern for the victim (Mawby and Walklate 1994). The 1996 *Victim's Charter* (Home Office

1996) is a much shorter document than the original whose semantics have changed significantly from a document that claimed to be rights-based to one that is no more than a service standard. We are no longer told what the police *should* do but what we can *expect* to happen. Most of the criticisms noted above remain pertinent in respect of the more recent version of the charter also.

Follow-up contact between the victim and the police

If no offender is apprehended the majority of victims are unlikely to hear any more from the police and contact with the criminal justice system ends here. If an offender is caught by the police and admits to the offence, a caution may be an appropriate consideration for the offender. However, if the case does not go to court, as in the latter example, the victim will not be eligible for compensation direct from the offender, and compensation by a civil court action would be the remaining option. Research conducted in the 1980s suggested that the majority of burglary victims heard nothing from the police in terms of outcome (Maguire 1982) and the victims in Shapland et al.'s study (1985) were dissatisfied with the information from police sources. The necessity for a follow-up visit was generally seen to be determined by the police's need for information rather than victim's needs, according to research on police–victim communication by Newburn and Merry (1990: 9). Despite service standards on police–victim contact as outlined in the *Victim's Charter* (1996) many victims still rely heavily on Victim Support for follow-up information. Various aspects of the police's lack of response to the murder of Stephen Lawrence in 1993 have recently been widely reported. This murder investigation and the subsequent public inquiry revealed a culture of racism in the police service (Cathcart 2000) and a sequence of events where the police failed both Stephen Lawrence and his family who became victims of this violent murder as well as victims of institutional racism.

Victim–police, police–victim tensions

The police continue to be an important point of contact for many victims of crime. Any review of the performance and effectiveness of the police can be expected to monitor various aspects of the police–victim encounter. For those concerned about improving the different forms of support that victims might receive at, or shortly after, the offence, the police are certain to feature in the analysis. There are clearly several tensions between victims and police. Some of these tensions arise from the inherent nature of police work which is historically and primarily preoccupied with preventing/managing crime but which inevitably brings them into close contact with victims. This leaves the victim in a clear second or even third place from the police perspective, after the crime and the offender, who take precedence. Although practices are visibly changing – in most instances for the better – in respect of how the police respond to and support crime victims, it is difficult to see how victims can ever become more fundamentally central to the core function of policing in this country. Further tensions between victims and the police become visible when a less ideal-typical view, and more realistic but complex view of victims and offenders is adopted. Police can themselves be victimised in a variety of ways both as civilians and in their capacity as employees of the police service. Police can also be victimisers and some of the ways in which this occurs in the contexts of youth for example, is explored in this volume by John Muncie.

Victims, the Crown Prosecution Service and the Courts

If the victim was also a witness to the crime they may also take on the status of victim-witness and be drawn into a further set of contact points with the police to help them compile evidence for the CPS and the courts. The CPS receive all the files containing the charge, facts and evidence in support of the case from the police. The main job of the CPS is to decide whether or not there is a case to answer and, if so, whether to prosecute. This decision is made according to whether it is in the public interest or not, and whether there is sufficient evidence and a realistic prospect of conviction. The CPS will check that cases referred by the police include a statement of any injury or loss by the victim. If the victim suffered personal violence, the victim should be told if the accused is released on bail. The *Victim's Charter* suggests the police will normally do this.

If the CPS decide there is a case to answer the victim may then be called upon to give evidence in court. In some cases this could be days later, in other cases it could be weeks, months or even years later. Not all victim-witnesses will end up in the witness box. Mawby and Walklate (1994) suggest that out of a hypothetical population of 100, a quarter, or twenty-five people, may become victims, possibly one out of those twenty-five will experience being called as a witness in court. This stage involves communication and liaison between several agencies and actors in the criminal justice system, for example, the police, the CPS the victim, Victim Support and the courts.

From a victim-oriented perspective, the role of the CPS in respect of the victim is negligible. Improving communication work with victims has largely been left to the police to handle. If the CPS decide not to prosecute, the victim is often left to assume that no further action is being taken by the criminal justice system. Clear research evidence has identified the lack of information about bail, charges and other pre-trial decisions as being a source of dissatisfaction for their victims (Shapland et al. 1985). One official publicity document, the Court Service's publication *Charter for Court Users* (Court Service 1995), makes no substantive mention of victims at all.

The victim at court

The CPS has a responsibility to ensure that witnesses attend court and are aware of the proceedings. There remains a potentially significant level of police contact with the victim-witness via the officer in charge of the case. Further victim contact takes place with the Crown Court Liaison Department and in many instances the police, or the victim her/himself may co-opt the help and support of Victim Support services in a court-based setting. In some parts of the country the police contact includes police members from Child Protection and Domestic Violence Units.

The mechanisms of communication with the victim are generally as follows: a warning notice or 'witness order' is issued from the court stating their required attendance at court; they should also receive a Home Office leaflet (Home Office 1989) explaining the role of the witness in court. At this stage no date is appointed for the court hearing. Victim Support will often be the body informing the victim of their court date, although the CPS also have a responsibility to the victim-witness concerning notification of the court date. It is likely however, to be either the police or a Victim Support volunteer who provides any further significant level of contact with a victim. Even with regard to the provision of support from this service the availability of such support does vary depending upon the area in which a victim lives (Mawby and Walklate 1994: 188).

Once called to court a victim must ensure that they arrive on time. Victims at court may find themselves queuing for a place in the public gallery, along with any other onlookers, to watch and hear the progress on their case (Zedner 1997, 2002). At this stage the 1990 *Victim's Charter* provides perhaps one of the most telling portrayals of what the victim might then face. Victims should *not* expect there to be separate waiting areas for victim-witnesses, people facing charges, and their families. The 1996 version tones down this statement in the small print; 'In some courts a lack of space may mean that you cannot reserve a seat or wait in a separate area' (Home Office 1996: 4). Refreshment facilities and private payphone areas are rarely on offer. Victims can expect to wait around until they are called into give evidence. Often the only place for victims in court is as 'evidence' (Zedner 1997, 2002). In such cases victims will be required to learn about how to become a witness in court in addition to the burden of being a victim.

Once at court the victim-witness may be offered support from a Crown Court-based victim service. The Home Office initially funded seven Crown Court centres. These projects were launched on 22 February 1990 on European Victims Day to coincide with the government's publication of the *Victim's Charter* (Home Office 1990). All Crown Court centres now have a witness service run by Victim Support to provide practical and emotional support to victims and witnesses in court. Their service spans from the time it is known that a victim-witness will be required to attend court through to the actual court appearance, and the service liaises with a number of criminal justice personnel in that period in the interests of the victim. The service is free and confidential: they cannot discuss evidence but aim to ease worries about appearing in court by explaining and demonstrating what might be expected to happen on the day in advance of the court date and also offering reassurance and/or assistance on the day.

Research conducted by Shapland et al. (1985) suggested there were some serious problems concerning the witness warning system at the Crown Courts. Victims were dissatisfied, aggravated and inconvenienced by the system. The quality of a victim's experience is very much contingent upon this complex system of notification – with its multiplicity of officials – being implemented properly and with due regard to victims' needs. In reality the pre-trial preparation stage suggests a likelihood that the victim's needs (for example, for information, advice and assistance from the various criminal justice and court-based personnel) are relegated to the needs of the court and the demands made by the bureaucracy of the criminal justice process. This process is demanding of victim-witnesses yet rarely supportive to them. Critics of the victim in court's experience have named this experience 'secondary victimisation'. Victim Support for example (1988) have pointed out that victims regularly experience not only discomfort and inconvenience at court, but also lose out financially by incurring expenses, loss of earning and deprivation of property. Shapland has described the victim at court as a 'nonperson' (1983) and Rossner and Wulf (1984) suggest there is a tendency to treat the testifying victim in court as an 'item of evidence' (cited in Wright 1996). Wright himself has pointed out that 'Offenders are usually passive spectators at their trial, and victims are left out of it altogether, except sometimes as witnesses' (Wright 1996).

A victim may have taken advantage of the services offered by Victim Support and they may also have received information in the form of a leaflet from either the police or a Victim Support Scheme. One leaflet is entitled *Victims of Crime*, which describes how the court can order the offender to pay compensation and how victims who are injured in a crime of violence can claim compensation from the Criminal Injuries Compensation Board (CICB). A second leaflet, *Witness in Court*, explains what is involved in being called to court and appearing to give evidence. Further policy statements and service standards emanating from the CPS can also be obtained from their publicity department. For example their *Statement of the Treatment of Victims and Witnesses by the Crown Prosecution Service* (CPS 1993). On arrival at court on the day appointed for them to give evidence, it is likely that at least some of this help, advice and information has been made available to the victim in court.

Research undertaken by Raine and Smith (1991) revealed that only 12 per cent of the victims interviewed at the Crown Court in Newcastle upon Tyne had received the Home Office's *Witness in Court* leaflet. Research at the same location a year later showed that the CPS had concerns that Victim Support volunteers might tend towards representing the witness and perhaps interfere in the judicial process (Burn and Davies 1992). Whilst at court the obligations placed upon the CPS appear to add up to little more than a suggestion for them to be courteous and polite to victims. Further, they would appear to be resisting any welcome efforts by other personnel involved in the process to help the victim at court.

Court outcomes and sentencing

Most victims of crime never get to the court stage, and for those who are called as witnesses they do not always appear in the witness box. Some offenders plead guilty in court on the day and in all of these situations the victim is unlikely to attend the final hearing of the case in court and therefore hear the verdict or the sentence. For the minority of victims who do give evidence they may be in court to hear the offender convicted or acquitted, and an even smaller number of these victims will hear in court of the sentence. Alternatively, the police may inform the victim of the outcome and/or the sentence.

There are two types of compensation for victims, one of which comes into play at this, the court stage. This type of compensation is called court compensation. If the defendant is convicted and found guilty, the court must always consider an order to pay compensation to the victim. This policy is backed up by legislation. The Criminal Justice Act 1988 requires courts to give reasons when a compensation order is not made. Moreover, compensation for the victim must come ahead of a fine if a financial penalty is being considered by the courts. The Home Office has issued magistrates with a table of injuries and typical amounts of compensation a victim might receive.

This form of compensation, compensation direct from the convicted offender to the victim, has become firmly embedded in recent government legislation. A coherent approach to this form of victim recompense appears in policy documents and is generally welcomed. Even where difficulties over payment may arise, courts have been provided with guidance as to how to best fix levels and ensure payment. However, this provision is not without its critics (Mawby and Gill 1987). Victims may be reluctant to prolong their contact with their victim, and this is likely where compensation is to be paid in small instalments over a long period of time. Some may argue this form of restitution is more beneficial to the offender in terms of a lenient punishment than to the victim as a form of recompense. Other supporters of court-based reparation strategies might argue the value is in the more civilising influence this type of process could have for all parties concerned, albeit in a coercive setting.

In the criminal justice system and in the witness box the victim's experience has been the subject of research by those who are particularly concerned about the plight of women victims of personal and sexual violence such as rape (Dowdeswell 1986) and domestic violence (Edwards 1989). Court practices have to some extent been influenced by such research and campaigning that has resulted in legislative changes (in 1988 and 1994) to eliminate the worst excesses of victims' experience in court. Such developments help prevent an overt form of secondary victimisation where women in particular have been forced to relive the nightmare of the original crime in the witness box.

Other research conducted on the CPS and pre-trial processes has uncovered severe due process problems surrounding justice for the accused (see, for example, Baldwin 1985 and McConville et al. 1991). This type of sustained critique has as yet hardly been extended to uncover the injustices sustained during the same process by victims.

Victims, Criminal Injuries Compensation and Restorative Justice

During the course of a victim's encounter with the criminal justice system a specific and traditional form of support that they might receive is help in the form of financial compensation. One type of compensation has been noted above. A second form of financial compensation is criminal injuries compensation. This was introduced in the 1960s. More recent victim-oriented innovations within the state sector have been formally introduced under the Crime and Disorder Act 1998. This Act is a clear signal of a more general movement in the late twentieth/early twenty-first century towards a more victim-conscious approach from official Home Office circles. In addition to financial compensation (for example, the Criminal Injuries Compensation Scheme and from various sentences of the court) there are signs of a move towards a less restricted form of restitution as well as a less retributive form of criminal justice. A rebirth of compensation and reparation, evident in Britain since the turn of the twentieth century (Wright 1996), has recently been given added impetus though New Labour's interest in restorative justice. This approach is holding out hope for victims being placed further to the forefront on criminal justice agendas. Both of these avenues of potential support for victims of crime are considered below.

The Criminal Injuries Compensation Scheme

As the *Victim's Charter* states: 'If you have been injured as a result of a violent crime you may be able to get compensation under the Criminal Injuries Compensation Scheme' (Home Office 1996). Victims who come into contact with the criminal justice system can expect to be offered information about criminal injuries compensation in the form of leaflets provided by the police, courts or Victim Support.

The Criminal Injuries Compensation Authority publication *Victims of Violence: A Guide to the Criminal Injuries Compensation Scheme* (CIJA 1996) describes criminal injuries compensation policy. It states that awards may be withheld when the police have not been informed and also in several circumstances where the victim engaged in violence/provocation or where the applicant has criminal convictions. Twenty-five levels of compensation exist and a corresponding 'tariff of injuries' indicates standard amounts payable for different levels of compensation which accord with different descriptions of injury. Standard amounts at the time of writing range from a lowest award of £1,000 up to a maximum of £250,000.

The scheme described above has been criticised in respect of its overall philosophy, its omissions, limitations, inadequate payments and lengthy deliberations. In sum, the scheme is limited to financial compensation for some ideal-typical victims of violent crime. Victim Support has been amongst the biggest critics of the scheme and has constantly drawn attention to the scheme's shortcomings (Victim Support 1995). These include the following;

- victims of crime are not always informed of the scheme's existence
- for those who have applied there have been long delays
- some victims are deliberately excluded
- awards have been criticised for being too low, for being reduced and for being refused
- victims dependent upon social security have had their benefit entitlements affected when a claim has been successfully made to the scheme.

Where leaflets and guidance information on criminal injuries compensation is available to victims this is often inadequate or simply states how to complain or where to send for further information. If claimants do apply for criminal injuries compensation they must do so as individuals and may often incur the expense of a solicitor to help them in this endeavour. For others who enlist the advice and help of Victim Support, the expense of this is not borne by the individual claimant.

Restorative justice

Compensation has recently taken on a rather different guise in the form of mediation and other restorative justice programmes. For victims this may mean increased chances of financial redress but also increased satisfaction with the way in which they are treated by the criminal justice system. Prior to the Crime and Disorder Act 1998 a range of mediation and reparation practices, projects and pilots had been in evidence particularly during the 1980s. New Labour's administrative arrangements for dealing with social justice, as well as the implementation of the above Act, appears to herald a more sustained commitment towards a restorative ethos in respect of dealing with crime and disorder (Home Office 2000), at least in relation to the youth justice system.

The Crime and Disorder Act has introduced a new sentencing framework. These arrangements include elements of restorative and reparative measures that were already in existence and popular use such as the compensation order, community service order and combination order. In addition a new reparation order can now be awarded in its own right or combined with other disposals such as final warnings, action plan orders and some supervision orders. In essence this order requires the young offender to make reparation to the victim where the victim wishes it or to the community at large (Nacro 1999).

Domestic changes to the legislative framework noted above were introduced in the late 1990s alongside the new Human Rights Act 1998. These convention laws will have an impact upon all our lives as well as the British justice system (Rozenberg 2000). Several of the articles are likely to have an impact upon both victims and offenders who interact with the criminal justice system. Although it is early days to gauge the impact of these new measures on victims' experiences of the criminal justice process, they clearly signal a greater potential involvement for some victims in the process should they choose to participate.

Victims and the Probation Service

The National Probation Service of England and Wales has always had some degree of involvement with victims of crime, although this has traditionally been governed by ad hoc arrangements, and the extent of their direct contact with crime victims has been very limited. In the last decade not only has the Probation Service undergone metamorphic changes per se, but this has included several changes affecting support for victims of crime. This section will provide a brief review and critical overview of some of the new roles and responsibilities that the Probation Service has in respect of victims of crime arising out of three policy guidelines: the *Victim's Charter* (Home Office 1990 and 1996), *National Standards* (Home Office, DoH and Welsh Office 1995) and *Probation Circular 61/1995* (Home Office 1995).

The *Victim's Charter* (1990) was an important spur for the Probation Service's victim contact work. The *Charter* gave probation responsibilities for providing new services to victims of serious crime. These new responsibilities and services were later extended and further work with victims was underscored by the *National Standards for the Supervision of Offenders in the Community* (Home Office DoH and Welsh Office 1995) and by *Probation Circular No. 61/1995: Probation Service Contact with Victims* (Home Office 1995) so that by the time that the second and revised version of the *Victim's Charter* (Home Office 1996) was published, the Probation Service had already revisited its roles and responsibilities towards crime victims.

In effect the 1990s saw the Probation Service develop its victim contact work in cases involving serious sexual and other violent offences. The Probation Service has also developed a more victim-oriented perspective in pre-sentence reports and in groupwork with offenders. The *National Standards* (Home Office, DoH and Welsh Office 1995) stress that Probation Officers should 'identify work to be done to make offenders aware of the impact of the crimes they have committed on their victims, themselves and their community' (Home Office, DoH and Welsh Office 1995: para. 3.14), emphasising the reparative element of probation work. The introduction of Reparation Orders for young offenders under the 1998 Crime and Disorder Act also underscores, through legislation, this growing emphasis on getting offenders to think of the impact of their behaviour upon victims. *Probation Circular 61/1995* reinforces and gives further direction on the process to be undertaken when contacting victims of life-sentence prisoners. It identifies the purpose of contact with the victim, the timescale of the process and the nature of the contact.

It is still early days to provide a full critique of the Probation Service's new roles and responsibilities towards victims of crime. However, there are some key areas that have caused debate within the Probation Service itself and most recently there has been an indication of the problematic issues from the Home Office's own Thematic Inspection Report entitled *The Victim's Perspective: Ensuring the Victim Matters* (Home Office 2000). First however, the *Victim's Charter* has attracted some critique in general (Mawby and Walklate 1994; Williams 1999), and in respect of its statements on the role of the Probation Service in particular.

The original version of the *Victims' Charter*, subtitled *A Statement of the Rights of Victims of Crime*, suggested that the Probation Service take on more direct victim contact work in the specific case of life-sentence prisoners and their victims. Although this was a significant new role for the Probation Service there was little advice, guidance or preparation for the introduction of this policy and it was left to the Probation Service to struggle to find sensitive ways of carrying out these new duties and of adopting victim-oriented rather than offender-oriented methods of operating. In the past, inquiries made of victims have on occasion been carried out insensitively (Kosh and Williams 1995). Williams (1999) has also observed there was widespread opposition to the *Victim's Charter* which put aside no new resources for the Probation Service. This led to variation in the ways in which the *Charter* was initially implemented within the Service and its members felt that unequal justice ensued.

Interestingly, by 1996 the subtitle of the *Victim's Charter* had changed to *A Statement of Service Standards for Victims of Crime* reflecting critics' views that, amongst other problems with the document, it did not provide any new or enforceable rights for victims of crime. The changes in policy adopted by the Probation Service are piecemeal and are highlighted in several 'significant milestones' (Home Office 2000: 25). In particular the 1995 *National Standards* emphasised issues relating to the protection of the public as well as the importance of considering the effect of crime on victims. In this case reparative philosophies were emphasised. However, in its thematic inspection the Home Office (2000) document illustrates how restorative justice is little developed, with only five services having a policy addressing restorative justice and only eight services running mediation/reparation projects.

The same report contains twelve specific recommendations arising out of the first inspection of the Probation Service's role in working with victims. The first recommendation is for new circular instruction guidance. Recommendations 2–6 are for the Home Office to address. Recommendation 7 is aimed at the Home Office in consultation with Probation Service's and numbers 8–12 make recommendations for Chief Probation Officers. On the whole the report is self-critical and it suggests a need to take forward its development of victim contact work with an active lead from the Home Office.

The developments noted above show several emerging themes in respect of victims and the Probation Service in the late twentieth and early twenty-first centuries. The themes have both a micro- and macro-level. At a micro-level some specific criticisms can be levelled at both the Probation Service itself and at Home Office polices and practices. In turn these impact upon inter-agency work with the police, the CPS and courts, Victim Support and other non-statutory, voluntary and feminist groups who provide support for victims of crime. Such inter-agency co-operation also affects macro-level perspectives on the crime victim. The response to the crime victim by the Probation Service as well as the police, the CPS and courts remains largely at the ideal-typical crime victim level. The response by the Probation Service to developing victim services will likely continue to struggle from the offender rehabilitation perspective (Williams 1999). There is a distinct possibility that the cultural change required within the Probation Service to properly take on board a victim-oriented perspective might not be welcomed and accepted in all parts of the service. In such circumstances role and responsibility 'confusion' could turn into overt victim-blaming (Williams 1999) A fundamentally different approach is required from probation staff to that involved in work with offenders. Like the police, whose main clients are also offenders, not victims, probation officers are likely to struggle to come to terms with meeting the requirements of their new responsibilities, in particular the requirement for them to undertake more victim contact work alongside their responsibilities to offenders.

Conclusion

This chapter has focused upon several levels of victim encounter in the criminal justice process. Two perspectives have been provided: One has been typically described as the 'top-down' approach and documents the formal road the victim may travel, as expressed in 'official' policy; the second has been described as a 'bottom-up' approach which critically reviews the same path but from a more victim-oriented perspective. It is clear that there are several inconsistencies and inadequacies in respect of the state response to the crime victim.

Contrary to the impression given, no new rights as such have been created by the most significant document to be published in respect of crime victims – the *Victim's Charter*. The *Charter's* overall philosophy on dealing with the needs of crime victims is one of individualised justice. Despite ample evidence from voluntary and feminist groups who provide a whole range of services, advice, help, practical, emotional and psychological support for different victims of crime, the Home Office largely fails to encourage this form of collective response. The debate about who is/should be responsible for meeting victims' needs and whether victims have any rights remains unresolved. The state's provisions amount to limited financial compensation and its obligations amount to the provision of service standards for the police, the CPS and the courts and the Probation Service. These standards are also devolved down to local levels, diffusing criticism away from the centre. Working practices and relationships between different parts of the criminal justice system and between parts of that system and the voluntary sector mean that responses to crime victims are often varied.

If these are the current trends in respect of crime victims and public policy, what are the future prospects? Any discussion of the victim must address the problem of definitions. Certainly it would appear that conventional definitions and common-sense understandings of crime victims have dominated the policy response. Radical and critical victimologies variously suggest the need to embrace broader visions of both the victimisers and the victims so that neglected, hidden and voiceless victims are brought within the remit of public concern and public policy. Several specific initiatives and changes to government policy are noted under their crime reduction strategy. These include provisions aimed at helping victims and witnesses in the witness box and in court, further annual funding for Victim Support and new responsibilities for the CPS in these categories too. Other experimental pilot projects are also currently being evaluated. These include One Stop Shops and Victim

Statements. Finally, research findings suggest that a guiding principle for working with victims of crime is inter-agency partnership. If an effective combination of some of these points can be achieved this will provide some limited grounds for optimism in the search for more effective public policy for crime victims in the next decade.

References

Baldwin, J. (1985) *Pre-Trial Criminal Justice*. Oxford: Blackwell.

Brake, M. and Hale, C. (1992) *Public Order and Private Lives: the Politics of Law and Order*. London: Routledge.

Burn, N. and Davies, P. (1992) *Newcastle Crown Court Victim/Witness Support Project*. Ponteland: Inspection and Development Department, Northumbria Police.

Cathcart, B. (2000) *The Case of Stephen Lawrence*. London: Penguin.

CIJA (1996) *Victims of Crimes of Violence: A Guide to the Criminal Injuries Compensation Scheme*. Glasgow: Criminal Injuries Compensation Authority.

Court Service (1995) *Charter for Court Users*. London: HMSO.

Croall, H. (1998) *Crime and Society in Britain*. London: Longman.

Crown Prosecution Service (1993) *Statement on the Treatment of Victims and Witnesses by the Crown Prosecution Service*. London: Crown Prosecution Service.

Daily Telegraph (Wednesday 26 April 2000) 'Hague: let raid victims hit back'.

Davies, P., Francis, P. and Jupp, V. (1999) *Invisible Crimes: Their Victims and their Regulation*. Basingstoke: Macmillan Press – new Palgrave.

Dowdeswell, J. (1986) *Women On Rape*. Wellingborough: Thorsons.

Edwards, S. S. M. (1984) *Women On Trial*. Manchester: Manchester University Press.

Edwards, S. S. M. (1989) *Policing Domestic Violence*. London: Sage.

Home Office (1988) *Victims of Crime*. Home Office Circular 20. London: Home Office.

Home Office (1989) *Witness in Court*. London: Home Office.

Home Office (1990) *The Victim's Charter: A Statement of the Rights of Victims of Crime*. London: HMSO.

Home Office (1995) *Probation Circular No 61/1995: Probation Service Contact with Victims*. London: HMSO.

Home Office (1996) *The Victim's Charter: A Statement of Service Standards for Victims of Crime*. London: HMSO.

Home Office (2000) *The Victim's Perspective: Ensuring the Victim Matters*. HM Inspectorate of Probation. Thematic Inspection Report. London: HMSO.

Home Office, Department of Health and the Welsh Office (1995) *National Standards for the Supervision of Offenders in the Community*. London: HMSO.

Jeffreys, S. and Radford, J. (1984) 'Contributory negligence or being a woman: the car rapist case'. In P. Scraton and P. Gordon (eds), *Causes for Concern*. Harmondsworth: Penguin.

Jones, T., Newburn, T. and Smith, D. (1994) *Democracy and Policing*. London: Policy Studies Institute.

Kinsey, R., Lea, J. and Young J. (1986) *Losing the Fight Against Crime*. Oxford: Blackwell.

Kosh, M. and Williams, B. (1995) *The Probation Service and Victims of Crime: A Pilot Study*. Keele: Keele University Press.

Lopez-Jones, N. (1999) *Some Mother's Daughter: The Hidden Movement of Prostitute Women against Violence*. London: Crossroads.

Maguire, M., in collaboration with Bennett, T. (1982) *Burglary in a Dwelling: The Offence, the Offender and the Victim*. London: Heinemann Educational.

Mawby, R. I. and Gill, M. L. (1987) *Crime Victims: Needs, Services and the Voluntary Sector*. London: Tavistock.

Mawby, R. and Walklate, S. (1994) *Critical Victimology*. London: Sage.

McConville, M., Sanders, A. and Leng, R. (1991) *The Case for the Prosecution*. London: Routledge.

Nacro Youth Crime Section (1999) *A Brief Outline of the Youth Justice System in England and Wales Incorporating the Crime and Disorder Act 1998*. Nacro Briefing London: Nacro

Newburn, T. and Merry, S. (1990) *Keeping in Touch: Police–Victim Communication in Two Areas*. Home Office Research Study No. 116. London: HMSO.

Raine, J. W. and Smith, R. E. (1991) *The Victim/Witness in Court Project: Report of the Research Programme*. London: Victim Support.

Reiner, R. (1992) *The Politics of the Police*, 2nd edn. Hemel Hempstead: Harvester Wheatsheaf.

Rozenberg, J. (2000) 'Rights Act shifts balance of power to judges'. *The Daily Telegraph*, Monday 2 October.

Shapland, J., Willmore, J. and Duff, P. (1985) *Victims in the Criminal Justice System*. Aldershot: Gower.

Southgate, P. and Ekblom, P. (1984) *Contacts Between Police and Public*. Home Office Research Study No. 77. London: HMSO.

Victim Support (1988) *The Victim in Court: Report of a Working Party*. London: Victim Support.

Victim Support (1995) *The Rights of Victims of Crime: A Policy Paper by Victim Support*. London: Victim Support.

Williams, B. (1999) *Working with Victims of Crime: Policies, Politics and Practice* London: Jessica Kingsley.

Wright, M. (1996) *Justice for Victims: A Restorative Response to Crime*, 2nd edn. Winchester: Waterside Press.

Zedner, L. (1994; 2002) 'Victims'. In M. Maguire, R. Morgan and R. Reiner (eds), *The Oxford Handbook of Criminology* (2nd edn. 1997; 3rd edn. 2002). Oxford: Clarendon Press.

7

Victims of Surveillance

Michael McCahill and Clive Norris

Introduction

In this chapter we are going to document the uses of three surveillance technologies -CCTV, drug testing, and genetic testing – in a number of different settings. Our main concern is to explore the relationship between these 'new surveillance technologies' and 'victimisation'. For many people, this relationship may seem obvious. In the context of criminal justice, for example, the common assumption is that surveillance technologies have been introduced to prevent 'victimisation', either through deterring would-be 'victimisers' or, in the longer term, by providing evidence against them so they may be punished and held accountable for their actions. The introduction of open-street CCTV systems is often justified in this way. In 1994, for example, Michael Howard said, 'I am absolutely convinced that CCTV has a major part to play in helping to detect, and reduce crimes and to convict criminals' (Home Secretary Michael Howard, 1994, in Norris and Armstrong 1998: 63). Similarly, one of the primary aims of workplace drug testing is to prevent workers from 'victimising' themselves or others by reducing 'the number of deaths, accidents, and injuries caused by workers who have been using drugs' (Newton 1999: 32). Following Gary Marx (1998), however, we wish to argue that it is also necessary to focus on the unintended consequences of the introduction of new technologies of social control. In particular, we will show how the introduction of these technologies creates a new category of victims – 'victims' of surveillance.

Asking employees to submit urine samples, or filming people in public spaces, does not automatically create a new category of 'victims', although in some jurisdictions both acts have been ruled illegal. This alerts us to the fact that there are differing opinions about whether the law contains all of the behaviour that should be prohibited. For some writers, crime (and therefore 'victimisation') is a legalistic category which should be restricted only to the activities of those convicted of offences (Tappan 1947). For other writers, criminal behaviour and its attendant 'victimisation' should include that which violates 'conduct norms' (Sellin 1938). More critical theorists, have suggested that criminalised harms be expanded to include the socially injurious activities of powerful groups against the powerless, and behaviour which violates human rights (Schwendinger and Schwendinger 1970). As Henry and Milovanovic (1996: 105) have pointed out, this notion of crime as a violation of human rights raises new victim categories such as 'abused women' or 'victims of state crimes'. To this we would add 'victims of surveillance'.

Using this broader definition of victimisation we aim to show how surveillance technologies have created three categories of 'victims'. Firstly, people are 'victims' of surveillance when they are disproportionately targeted (e.g. on the grounds of age, sex and race). Secondly, people are 'victims' of surveillance when the information gathered about them is used in a way that is inappropriate or not in accordance with stated aims and objectives. Thirdly, people are 'victims' of surveillance when they are targeted by technologies that produce 'false' information that may have negative consequences for the individual concerned. But before we turn our attention to the 'victims' of surveillance, we will document the uses of new surveillance technologies in five different locales: *public space, the workplace, the criminal justice system, civic institutions, and private space.*

Surveillance Technologies and Locations

CCTV

As Table 7.1 shows, visual surveillance systems are now commonplace in a wide range of different locales and institutional settings. The first open-street CCTV system designed to provide permanent surveillance of public space was introduced in 1985, when Bournemouth City Council installed cameras to monitor the town's promenade. Since then there has been a rapid expansion of CCTV systems in public space, largely due to Home Office backing during the 1990s. By 1996, Norris et al. (1998) reported that all major cities with a population over 500,000 had city-centre schemes, and that there were more than 500 police and local authority schemes operating in high streets and smaller towns. Other systems operating in public space include those designed to monitor residential areas, such as Newcastle upon Tyne's West End scheme

Table 7.1 Surveillance Technologies in Five Locales

	Public space	Workplace	Criminal justice	Civic institutions	Private space
CCTV	City centres, car parks, housing estates, transport (i.e. roads and railways), football stadia etc.	Manufacturing, retail sector etc.	Prisons, police cells.	Hospitals, schools, universities etc.	The home (e.g. domestic security, voyeurism).
Drug Testing	Airports, roadside testing.	Transport (train drivers, airline pilots), armed forces, police, professional sports.	Prison inmates, probationers, arrestees.	Hospitals (e.g. heart patients), school pupils, college athletes, welfare claimants.	Parental testing of children.
Genetic Testing	'Mass' DNA screening programmes.	Armed forces, police, forensic scientists.	Potentially, anyone convicted or suspected of committing an offence.	Medical/clinical DNA databases.	Paternity disputes.

where the images displayed by fifteen cameras are monitored from a dedicated police control room (Graham 1998). The use of CCTV is also becoming ubiquitous in a number of other public and semi-public spaces, including road and rail transport systems, car parks, and football stadia (see Norris and Armstrong 1998: 42–51).

The use of visual surveillance in the workplace is arguably more extensive than the use of surveillance in public spaces. For instance, despite the massive investment in city-centre CCTV systems during the 1990s, public and civil systems still only accounted for 22 per cent of the market in 1996 with annual sales of £25 million. The remaining 78 per cent of the market was dominated by the retail, commercial and industrial sectors which accounted for 33 per cent (£38 million), 30 per cent (£35 million), and 17 per cent (£17.3 million) respectively (*CCTV Today*, 1 January 1998: 20). CCTV systems in the (commercial and industrial) workplace are used to monitor both the 'external threat', posed by shoplifters, fraudsters, burglars and other 'outsiders', and the 'internal threat' posed by workplace theft.

In the context of criminal justice, CCTV systems have been installed both in prisons and police cells. A study by the Police Complaints Authority described 'how 11 forces have installed closed-circuit TV cameras in cells for the first time and that 14 more are considering the move' (*Guardian*, 14 January 2000). It is hoped that the introduction of CCTV in police cells will further reduce the number of deaths in police custody which has fallen since the publication last year of a report which condemned the restraining techniques used by some officers. Between April and December in 1999, thirty-five people died in police 'care' compared with forty-seven in the same period in 1998.

The use of CCTV systems in schools and hospitals is now commonplace. In 1996, the Conservative government 'announced a £66 million package for school security, which included provision for the installation of CCTV' (Norris and Armstrong 1998: 44). Meanwhile, in a number of hospitals doctors have decided to use covert cameras to monitor parents who they believe are displaying signs of the disorder Munchhausen Syndrome by Proxy (*Guardian*, 11 November 1999 and 19 August 1999). The extent of visual surveillance in the private sphere is difficult to gauge, although first-hand observation suggests that many private dwellings are using CCTV for domestic security purposes. There are also a number of local authority housing departments who have installed concierge-operated CCTV systems that monitor the communal areas of high-rise flats. Some of these CCTV systems are connected to the tenants' communal television aerial system on a dedicated channel. This latter feature enables the tenants themselves to visually identify callers before admitting them into their flats.

Drug testing

The 1990s saw the use of drug tests increase in a number of different institutional settings. The presence of drugs in the human body can be detected in urine, hair, blood, and other body fluids such as sweat. The most common type of drug test is urinalysis where a person is asked to urinate into a specimen bottle. The urine sample is then examined by chemical tests which are able to detect the presence of an illegal drug itself or, more commonly, the presence of chemicals produced during the breakdown of the drug in the body (Newton 1999: 17).

In the United Kingdom, workplace drug testing took off in 1991 when drug traces were found in the blood of the train driver involved in the Cannon Street rail crash (*Independent on Sunday* 1998). In the following year, British Rail introduced a strict drink- and drug-testing regime for 50,000 employees with operational or safety responsibilities. The British army introduced random drug tests in 1995, since when 323,000 male and female soldiers have been tested, with under 0.7 per cent testing positive (BBC News, 14 March 2000). Tony Jerrard, a retired army Air Corps major who co-ordinates the army's Compulsory Drug Testing (CDT) team, says that his team 'work on the Martini principle: any time, any place, anywhere' (Bound 1999). The team recently performed random drug tests on troops stationed in Belize and on mountain tops in the Falklands. The urine specimens collected by the travelling CDT teams are delivered to the laboratory of the government chemist in west London, which handled 110,000 military samples in 1998: 86,000 of these samples were from the army, while the remaining 24,000 were from the Royal Navy and the Royal Air Force (Bound 1999).

A further extension of drug testing in the workplace came in 1998 when random testing was introduced by Merseyside police chiefs 'to prevent the drugs-inspired lifestyle from spreading in the ranks' (*Independent on Sunday* 1998). The government's drug 'tsar', Keith Hellawell, believes that the fire, ambulance and motorway rescue services should also introduce drug testing immediately. The Forensic Science Service currently carries out 1 million drugs tests on employees a year, and estimates that in some companies up to 15 per cent of the workforce is taking drugs (*The Guardian*, 2 November 1998).

In the context of criminal justice, mandatory drug testing began in January 1995 when it was introduced at a number of prisons (Bristol, Holloway, Lindholme, Pentonville, Wakefield, and Wayland) and two young offender institutions (Feltham and Stoke Heath) (HM Prison Service, March 1995). The police recently gained sweeping powers to impose mandatory drugs tests on people arrested for criminal offences. Under measures disclosed by Tony Blair persistent cocaine and heroin users are to be denied bail after being arrested in an effort to prevent further drug-linked crime. There are also plans for an extension of mandatory testing to include offenders on probation (*The Guardian*, 27 September 1999).

Drug testing has also filtered into other parts of society. A London hospital, for example, wants to introduce random urine testing of patients presenting at casualty with chest pain to test for cocaine use, as the drug is well known for causing heart problems. (BBC News, 21 January 2000). Public school pupils can also be tested if a teacher thinks they are exhibiting signs of drug abuse (*Independent on Sunday* 1998). In January 1999, a report by the Headmasters' and Headmistresses' Conference on drug use in independent schools revealed that 72 per cent of private boarding schools and 28 per cent of day schools use some form of drug testing (*The Guardian*, 27 January 1999). In 1998, Eton threw out two boys, and St Paul's school in west London, expelled three teenage boys who tested positive for drugs (Russell and Rodda 1998).

While the widespread random drug testing of people in public space has yet to become a reality, several countries have provisional plans for introducing drug testing at airports and on the roads (BBC News, 26 March 2000; American Civil Liberties Union 1996). The UK's drugs tsar Keith Hellawell, for example, is considering the introduction of drug tests on airline tickets where a 'boarding pass analyser' scans the ticket to test for traces of heroin, cocaine, cannabis or ecstasy residue. This new technology is designed to target couriers, who it is believed will have had to handle the drugs they are smuggling. Meanwhile, at the two international airports in Jamaica, 'trained customs officials' are picking out 'suspicious-looking passengers' who are taken to a room and obliged to furnish urine specimens for drug testing (*Gleaner*, 17 November 1998). In the UK, in February 1998 the government announced pilot projects to try out the practicality of new roadside drug-testing equipment. One device, known as 'Drugwipe', involves taking a specimen of sweat from the forehead. If the device changes colour the use of drugs (e.g. cannabis, amphetamines, cocaine, opiates and benzodiazepines, such as valium) is claimed to have been detected (BBC News, 11 February 1998).

Genetic testing

The announcement on 26 June 2000 that researchers have recorded the entire human genome marks a turning point not only in biology and medicine, but also in the surveillance capacity of the state. DNA (Deoxy-ribonucleic Acid) is the hereditary blueprint imparted to us by our biological parents. The genetic information carried in DNA is in the form of a code or language which, when translated, determines our physical characteristics and directs all the chemical processes in the body. As Nelkin and Andrews (1999) have shown, DNA analysis was first developed in a medical context as a technique to identify the markers that indicate familial disorders, but has subsequently spread out of the medical sphere into the sphere of public surveillance.

On the 10 April 1995, a National DNA Database was set up in the UK by the Forensic Science Service (FSS) on behalf of the Association of Chief Police Officers (ACPO). Latest figures show that over one million DNA profiles from suspects have been put onto the database, plus around 73,000 profiles from evidence found at scenes of crime (*The Guardian*, 1 September 2000; Forensic Science Service 2000). The government recently announced a £109 million cash boost for the database, which is expected to see an extra 3 million samples added to the DNA database by 2004 (*The Guardian*, 1 September 2000). The database was originally established as a forensic source for helping identify those involved in serious crimes (i.e. murder and rape). However, an amendment to the Criminal Justice and Public Order Act (1994) allows samples to be taken without consent from any person convicted or suspected of a recordable offence. The trend towards more 'inclusive' databanking is also evident in those cases involving the retention of samples submitted on a voluntary basis. The police have already conducted 118 'mass screens', resulting in forty-eight hits and seven convictions. While the samples taken from those who were eliminated as possible suspects were later destroyed, a recent amendment to section 64 of the Police and Criminal Evidence Act permits the retention and use of DNA samples and data with a volunteer's written permission.

In the UK, the use of genetic testing in the workplace does not appear to be widely practised, although forensic scientists themselves are asked to submit samples to counter the problem of 'contamination' (*Police Review* 1999: 11). However, the temptation for employers to use genetic information to screen out prospective employees who are perceived as genetically abnormal and hence potentially costly is obviously a real one. In the United States, a government study based on interviews with managers found that many firms already use genetic screening (Strudler 1994: 839). The study also found that many more firms hope eventually to use these technologies to screen for a wide range of diseases and conditions, including Huntingdon's disease, sickle cell anaemia, muscular dystrophy, cystic fibrosis, schizophrenia, cancer, heart disease, Alzheimer's disease, and hamolytic anaemia. In the 'private' sphere, Nelkin and Andrews (1999) have reported that increasing numbers of men 'have brought their children to genetic clinics and had them secretly tested to determine if they were the "real" fathers or if their wives had had an affair'.

The 'Victims' of Surveillance

The idea that surveillance systems are designed primarily to reduce victimisation is a common assumption among its proponents. These assumptions are supported by the many 'success stories' that appear on a regular basis in the daily newspapers. For example, it has been reported that CCTV systems operating in public space have been used to protect victims of racial harassment. In Lancaster, for example, the racist harassment of two local shopkeepers on the Ryelands estate prompted Lancaster City Council to install three CCTV cameras which are monitored on a continuous basis in Lancaster police station (*The Guardian*, 3 April 1999). Surveillance systems also produce information that can be stored and used at some future date to provide evidence of victimisation. A number of CCTV systems operating in public space have recorded examples of police brutality (*The Guardian*, 24 August 1999; *The Hull Daily Mail*, 20 February 1998; *The Guardian*, 7 August 1999; *The Guardian*, 22 February 2000). In one court case, the prosecution produced a video recording taken from the Bournemouth CCTV system which showed a police constable bouncing a suspect's head off the back windscreen of his patrol car (*The Guardian*, 22 February 2000).

The protection of victims was also a major concern of police officers in Scotland who decided to take 'DNA samples from all racial offenders in Scotland in a covert attempt to stop attacks on ethnic minorities' (*Sunday Times* 2000). In the United States, proponents of DNA testing have argued that this new technology not only provides police with a powerful tool in the fight against crime, but that it also exonerates the innocent. Easterbrook (2000), for example, reported that DNA tests have shown sixty-eight people imprisoned by state and federal courts (including some sent to death row but not executed) were innocent. Meanwhile, proponents of workplace drug testing have argued that it 'will reduce the number of deaths, accidents, and injuries caused by workers who have been using drugs' (Newton 1999: 32).

However, we show how the introduction of surveillance technologies is creating a new category of victim – 'victims' of surveillance. As Table 7.2 shows, surveillance technologies create three types of 'victim'. Firstly,

Table 7.2 Surveillance Technologies and New Categories of Victims

	CCTV	Drug testing	Genetic testing
Fairness	Is everyone equally subject to surveillance or are some people disproportionately targeted (e.g. on the grounds of age, sex and race)?	Is everyone equally subject to drug testing or are some people disproportionately targeted?	Is everyone equally subject to genetic testing or are some people disproportionately targeted?
Misappropriation	Is photographic information used in ways that are inappropriate or not in accordance with stated aims and objectives (e.g. voyeurism)?	Are the samples collected during drug testing used in ways that are inappropriate or not in accordance with stated aims and objectives?	Are DNA profiles/samples used in ways that are inappropriate or not in accordance with stated aims and objectives (e.g. 'Third Party Access' by employers or insurers)?
False Knowledge	Do CCTV systems produce 'false' information that may have negative consequences for the 'surveilled'?	Does drug testing produce 'false' information that may have negative consequences for the 'surveilled'?	Does genetic testing produce 'false' information that may have negative consequences for the 'surveilled'?

those who are disproportionately targeted (e.g. on the grounds of age, sex or race). Secondly, those who have information gathered about them that is used in ways which are inappropriate or not in accordance with stated aims and objectives. Thirdly, those who are targeted by technologies that produce 'false' information and may have negative consequences for the individual concerned.

Fairness

CCTV

For surveillance to be 'fair' everyone should be equally subject to its regime. However, some individuals and social groups are disproportionately targeted by surveillance systems. Nowhere is this more evident than in the case of closed-circuit television (CCTV) surveillance systems.

For instance, in their study of three open-street CCTV surveillance systems, Norris and Armstrong (1998) have shown how the CCTV operators disproportionately target particular social groups. In short, the operation of these systems leads 'to the over-representation of men, particularly if they are young or black' (1998: 196). Moreover, the targeting of young, mainly working-class males was prompted 'not because of their involvement in crime or disorder, but for "no obvious reason" and on the basis of categorical suspicion alone' (1998: 197). Norris and Armstrong conclude that the disproportionate targeting of the socially and economically marginal means that open-street CCTV systems 'rather than contributing to social justice through the reduction of victimisation ... may become a tool of injustice through the amplification of differential and discriminatory policing' (1999: 201).

The disproportionate targeting of young, working-class males has also been found in the semi-public space of the shopping mall. For instance, observational research conducted in the CCTV control rooms of two shopping malls in a northern city found that almost nine out of ten (88%) of those targeted were either in their teens or twenties. Exactly one half of all targeted surveillances were of people dressed in 'subcultural attire' (i.e. tracksuits and baseball caps). The targeting of 'subcultural' youth was based on the CCTV operator's belief that this group were not shopping, and, therefore, disrupted the commercial image of the mall. As the following extract from the field-notes illustrates, these practices had negative consequences for the 'surveilled', who could find themselves excluded from the shopping mall:

> Just after 12.00 Jim does the 'Saturday Message' on the Shopping Centre Radio Link (SCRL): 'Control to all patrol guards, just a reminder that today is Saturday. If you see any groups of youths hanging around can you ask them to move along. If you have to tell them more than twice could you please ask them to leave the centre.

The formalised exclusion policy at this shopping mall was reflected in the study's figures on the social characteristics of suspects who were ejected from the mall. For instance, while no one over the age of 30 who was deployed against was ejected, around two out of ten (18%) of those in their twenties and more than four out of ten (43%) of those in their teens who were deployed against were ejected from the shopping centre. Being part of a group also compounds the influence of age. For example, McCahill found that 'when a guard was deployed to deal with groups of teenagers there was a fifty-fifty chance that someone would be ejected'.

Drug testing

For drug testing to be fair those subject to its regime should be selected on a random basis. This is recognised by HM Prison Service who have stated that 'all prisoners will be required to participate in a random testing programme, prisoners will be chosen by computer on a totally random basis' (HM Prison Service 1995). However, this document goes on to state that '*some* testing of prisoners may also be carried out on reception to prison', and that 'prison officers will have the power to require prisoners to be tested if they have *reasonable suspicion* of drug misuse by the prisoner' (HM Prison Service 1995, emphasis added). Similarly, in his announcement that the 500,000 people arrested each year will be subject to mandatory drug testing, Jack Straw indicated that the police will have the discretion to use the power to identify drug abusers (*The Guardian*, 18 November 1999). Clearly, then, prison officers and arresting officers will have wide discretionary powers when deciding whom they believe should be subject to drug testing.

In the workplace, decisions about which employees are chosen for drug testing is left entirely in the hands of employers. In the absence of any detailed empirical research, it is not yet clear how these discretionary powers are utilised. However, a review of newspaper articles suggests that workplace drug testing is being used to discriminate against certain social groups. It has been reported, for example, that some 'companies deliberately preyed on older workers with random drug tests in the hope that a positive result would release them from pension payments' (*The Observer*, 12 December 1999). Also, the National Union of Rail, Maritime and Transport Workers (RMT) has received complaints that managers of the London Underground are using drug tests 'as a disciplinary weapon, and picking on ethnic minorities' (*Independent on Sunday* 1998). Finally, it has been reported that 'a woman rail cleaner, sacked for refusing to provide a urine sample to a male manager, was unfairly and wrongfully dismissed and discriminated against on the grounds of sex by her former employers' (*The Guardian*, 4 June 1999).

In the United States, drug testing has filtered out from the workplace into other areas, including the drug testing of welfare claimants. In October 1999, the state Family Independence Agency introduced a pilot programme requiring drug testing and treatment for welfare applicants in Detroit. Any applicant who refused to submit to drug testing had their application for assistance denied, while 'those who test positive are required to participate in substance abuse assessment and comply with a required substance abuse treatment plan' (American Civil Liberties Union 2000). The disproportionate targeting of the poor can be seen as an attempt at discriminatory social engineering. The aim is 'to encourage work and personal responsibility while discouraging behaviours such as teenage pregnancy and drug and alcohol abuse' (American Civil Liberties Union 1996).

As the examples above show, drug testing can be unfair because some people are disproportionately targeted on the grounds of age, sex, race and class. However, some writers have argued that technologies such as hair testing have a built-in bias that discriminates on the grounds of race (American Civil Liberties Union 1999). As Holtorf (1998: 104) has argued, 'most drugs, including cocaine and marijuana, bind and incorporate into the hair of African-Americans [at a rate] 10 to 50 times greater than drugs are incorporated into the hair of Caucasians. Thus, with equal drug use, African-Americans are 10 to 50 times more likely than Caucasians to have a positive drug test.'

Some of these issues were raised in 1996 when a 30-year-old black police officer in the United States was sacked after failing his Police Department's new hair test for drugs. Samples of Jerome McCall's hair tested positive for cocaine, but the officer insists that he is innocent and has argued that the tests discriminate against African-Americans. In his appeal, McCall, who tested negative in urinalysis, argued that 'it is impossible to determine whether the drugs found in a person's hair come from drug abuse or other factors, such as touching a drug addict or even being in a room where someone had been smoking crack'. As a police officer, McCall was routinely exposed to drugs in this way.

Genetic testing

The emergence of genetic testing and DNA databases raises a number of important issues which to date have received very little attention from social scientists. The amendment to the Criminal Justice and Public Order Act (1994) allows samples to be taken without consent from any person convicted or suspected of a recordable offence (Home Office 1999). In some respects, the collection of DNA samples from suspects would seem to make perfect sense. The profiles of convicted offenders can be stored on the computerised database and checked against profiles obtained from scenes of crime. Any matches between suspects and scenes of crime can then be communicated to the police.

However, for the DNA databank to be most effective the majority of crimes would have to be committed by those convicted repeat offenders who have had their samples taken by the police. The greatest flaw in this policy lies in the fact that the vast majority of offenders never come into contact with the criminal justice system. Moreover, the official population of offenders is a reflection of criminal justice processing which leads to an over-representation of socially marginal groups. In this respect, it is likely to be the DNA of socially marginal groups that is stored in the database and used for investigative purposes. In relation to violent and sexual crime, for example, Canadian writers, Kubanek and Miller (1997), have argued that:

> A DNA databank could only be effective if most violent crimes were committed by convicted repeat offenders. But most sex offenders have never been convicted. Men with the most privilege in society are even less likely to have been convicted. However, we know from the experiences of women, that those men are not less likely to have offended. At present, Native men, men of colour and poor men are jailed in Canada at a rate far out of proportion with Canadian demographics. Because their DNA would dominate the DNA databank, using such a databank to identify perpetrators of crime would reinforce and even promote more inequality in our justice system.

The question of whether genetic testing is fair has also arisen in the context of employment and insurance. In the early 1970s, for example, some insurance companies in the United States 'denied coverage and charged higher rates to African Americans who were carriers of the gene for sickle cell anemia' (Colonna 1998: 4). More recent studies have documented cases of genetic discrimination against people who have a gene that predisposes them or their children to illnesses such as Huntingdon's disease. In a recent survey of people with a known genetic condition in the family, 'twenty-two percent indicated that they had been refused health insurance coverage because of their genetic status, whether they were manifesting symptoms of the genetic disease or not' (Gostin 1991). Another survey, carried out by Shriver, at a centre for public health in Massachusetts, reported 582 cases of people who were turned down for jobs or health insurance because of 'flaws' discovered in their genes. In the UK, the Council for Responsible Genetics (CRG), says 'it has documented more than 200 cases of genetic discrimination by employers' (*The Guardian*, 19 September 2000). The number of these cases could increase following the government's recent confirmation of the reliability of tests for the hereditary disease Huntingdon's. This will give insurers the go-ahead to use the results when setting premium levels for sufferers (*The Guardian*, 12 October 2000).

The Misappropriation of Personal Information

CCTV

Someone is a 'victim' of surveillance when the information gathered about them is used in ways that are inappropriate or not in accordance with stated aims and objectives. One example of the misappropriation of personal information is when a CCTV system installed for the purposes of crime control is used by the CCTV operators to monitor women for voyeuristic purposes (see Norris and Armstrong 1998: 115). In Australia, CCTV operators in Burswood Casino 'videotaped women in toilets and artists' changing rooms, zooming in on the exposed parts of their bodies and editing the video sequences on to one tape that was shown at local house parties' (Koskela 2000). Also, in the summer of 1997 'it was discovered that Swedish conscript soldiers had been "entertaining" themselves by monitoring topless women on a beach near their navy base, taping the women and printing pictures of them to hang on the barrack walls' (Koskela 2000).

While the above examples involve the misuse of CCTV systems operating in public or semi-public space, other video voyeurs are employing state-of-the-art technology (e.g. pinhole cameras and infra-red technology) to gain access into the most private places. As in the examples above, the usual victims of this form of voyeurism are women, who are covertly monitored 'as they change their clothes, perform natural functions or engage in sexual activities, (Simon 1997: 884). As the two cases described below illustrate, the use of surveillance cameras for voyeuristic purposes can result in serious psychological harm for the victim:

> A 16 year old girl was videotaped by a male classmate using a miniature colour TV camera mounted above a small hole in the ceiling tile of a high school dressing area ... One videotape was found showing her undressing and completely naked. She was quite self-conscious about her body. Almost 6ft tall, she was very thin with large breasts. Her psychological response was to withdraw from friends, dress in masculine, baggy clothes, refuse to go to school, become very depressed and lose 10 lb to try to reduce the size of her breasts. She dropped out of school for one year, received psychiatric treatment and spent much time at home with her animals. (Simon 1997: 885)

> Sexual intercourse with a co-ed was covertly videotaped by her then boyfriend using a miniature black and white TV camera mounted in a smoke detector at a fraternity house. The videotape was shown

over and over to fraternity brothers, creating a sensation on campus. The sexual encounter was surreptitiously transformed into a porno flick to the horror of the victim, when she later discovered the existence of the videotape. The victim became severely depressed and suicidal, requiring psychiatric hospitalisation. (Simon 1997: 885)

Because visual information can be stored on videotape, the anguish suffered by the victim of voyeurism does not end when the culprit has been found out. The recording can be watched over and over again. It can also be shared with others. In this respect, the experience of victimisation goes on indefinitely. One victim, for example, reported how several nights a week she 'wakes up in a cold sweat with two unanswered questions on her mind...."What has he done with those videos, and who else is he showing them to?"' (Aziz).

Drug testing

In relation to drug testing, examples of misappropriation are found mainly in the workplace. In his book, *Ur-ine Trouble*, Ken Holtorf (1998) shows that some employers in the United States are using drug tests surreptitiously to screen female candidates for pregnancy. The Washington DC police department, for example, 'has admitted that it routinely subjected urine specimens taken for drug tests from female police officers...to pregnancy testing without their knowledge or consent' (Aziz 51).

Other employers are using drug tests to learn what medication employees and applicants are using. This allows employers to target 'less desirable' candidates, including those who are likely to need sick leave or use medical benefits. One leading drug-test manufacturer, Bio Medica, has developed the 'Rapid Drug Screen' which allows employers to test for both illicit drugs and antidepressants. This information can then be used by the employer who may decide to avoid hiring applicants with a history of mental illness (Holtorf 1998: 50-1). One business owner in Holtorf's study stated:

I do have some reservations about screening for prescription medications, but I'm a businessman. I need to stay competitive. I can't afford to spend the money to train someone then have them go off on a bout of depression. I'm just protecting myself. (Holtorf 1998: 50)

Holtorf suggests that information from drug tests is also being shared via computer databases with other employers, government agencies, and insurance companies, leading to a form of 'high-tech blacklisting' (1998: 52–3).

Genetic testing

The storage of DNA profiles on computerised databases raises the issue of third-party access to genetic information. In the context of criminal justice, DNA databases consist of DNA samples obtained from both crime scene evidence and individual 'donors' (Tracy and Morgan 2000). However, rather than obtaining samples from the scene of crime or from suspects, the possibility exists for the police to obtain DNA data on a suspect from pre-existing databases. In the United States, for example, the military has admitted that it is willing to release its data to law enforcement officials, and the Human Genome Privacy Act allows 'police officers to have access to hospital diagnostic DNA collections without patient authorisation' (Nelkin and Andrews 1999: 697).

Empirical evidence of third-party access to genetic information is provided by a survey of 148 DNA diagnostic labs. This survey found that eight respondents (10%) had received requests for samples in their possession from law enforcement and other government agencies. The authors of the report go on to state that 'in five of these eight cases, the samples were in fact released' (McEwan and Reilly 1995: 1483). At present there are no proposals in the UK to use medical databases for criminal investigations, mainly because this would be prohibitively expensive. However, the authors go on to suggest that in the long term technological advances could see genetic information collected as a routine part of medical research, and this information could then be accessed by the police. At a meeting of the National Commission on the Future of DNA Evidence, Commissioner Reilly suggested that in twenty to twenty-five years' time we will 'reach universal DNA data-banking for criminal purposes through the back door of public health' (1999).

The misappropriation of genetic information has also been raised in the context of employment and insurance. In the United States, a soldier who was suspended from military training for refusing to provide a blood sample for DNA testing wrote a letter in defence of his actions:

Dear Military Superiors,

I am writing in regard to a recent notification of my indefinite suspension from cadet training of the United States Military. This suspension was a result of my unwillingness to provide a blood sample for use in a process known as 'DNA Dog-tagging' ... The military claims that they keep these samples for identification purposes only... However, my concern lies in what may happen to these samples in the future...There is no guarantee that the military will not transfer the samples to a third party, like an insurance agency or medical research agency...Physicians, insurance companies, and employers will also want DNA samples and/or the information to base decisions on...This 'future diary' not only has information on the military person, but also to his or her civilian parents, siblings and children. To release this 'future diary' of a person and his or her family to the military is an invasion of people's privacy. (Srinivasan 1996)

False Knowledge and Negative Consequences

CCTV

The idea that 'if you have done nothing wrong you have nothing to hide' has become almost a cliché among proponents of CCTV. However, as Channel 4's TV investigative documentary *Dispatches* has shown, there are already people serving prison sentences based on CCTV 'evidence' of dubious quality. In this respect, people can be regarded as 'victims' of surveillance when they are targeted by systems that produce 'false' information that may have negative consequences for the individual concerned. Norris and Armstrong (1998) provide another example in their study of open-street CCTV systems. These writers found that on some occasions when citizens intervened to quell disorder their actions were misinterpreted by the CCTV operators and became subject to criminalisation (1998: 187–8). As Norris and Armstrong point out, this may have negative consequences not only for the individuals concerned, but also for the wider society, as citizens become more reluctant to intervene and maintain the public peace.

Genetic testing

While forensic DNA technology is often presented as an infallible technique based on 'hard' scientific 'facts', other writers have raised the issue of whether this technology may also produce 'false' information (see Hoeffel 1990; McDonald 1998; Nelkin and Andrews 1999). For instance, in a paper entitled 'The Dark Side of DNA Profiling', Hoeffel has argued that one of the main problem areas 'is the contamination and degradation likely to be present in forensic samples' (1990: 479). Hoeffel points to the example of forensic samples that have been removed from carpeting or clothing previously cleaned with detergents. He goes on to argue that 'the chemicals in detergents can cause the restriction enzymes to cut the DNA at the wrong place, causing fragments to be different lengths than they would normally be'.

McDonald (1998) has argued that one of the main problems with genetic testing is the laboratory conditions under which testing takes place. For example, one DNA laboratory in Kern County, California, 'is a refurbished dog kennel with such limited space that on one occasion crucial evidence from a fatal hit-and-run case was stored in a men's lavatory'. Meanwhile, 'in the Michigan State Police Forensics Laboratory, twenty degree temperature swings every fifteen minutes caused instruments such as a $10,000 scanning electron microscope to rust and corrode' (1998: 112–13). In a 1993 study, forty-five laboratories were asked whether particular DNA samples matched. In the 223 tests performed, the study identified matches in eighteen cases where matches did not exist. As Nelkin and Andrews point out, 'if these had been real trials, innocent people would have been convicted' (1999: 701).

Drug testing

In the context of drug testing, 'false information' is produced when a urine sample (or hair sample) tests positive due to something other than illicit drugs. As Holtorf (1998: ch. 4) has shown, 'false positives' can occur in a number of ways. In the laboratory, for example, false positives can occur through 'contamination crossover'. This occurs when the 'glassware used to transfer the urine to and from the testing apparatus is contaminated by previous drug containing urine samples' (1998: 57). False positives can also occur when those tested have consumed both over-the-counter medications (e.g. decongestants, cold and allergy medications, slimming tablets, sleeping tablets, cough medicines and vitamin B2), and prescription medications (e.g. diet pills, asthma medication, migraine tablets, pain killers, and medications for insomnia, anxiety and Parkinson's disease). Finally, the metabolites of certain foods are similar to and may be mistaken for those of illicit drugs. Poppy seeds, for example, are collected from the same plant that produces morphine and codeine and can produce a false positive.

False positives can have negative consequences for those who test positive. In the workplace, for example, 'a London Underground worker was suspended after being randomly tested and found to have traces of a drug in his sample. It was subsequently found that the trace came from the poppy seeds on his lunchtime roll' (*The Independent on Sunday*, 22 November 1998). In the United States, a woman was fired when two poppy seed muffins she had eaten one morning registered a positive morphine level in a test carried out later in the afternoon (*The Guardian*,

21 February 2000). In the United States, Ford worker John Kinnie was sacked when a random drug test at his plant in Arizona showed he had been using 'speed'. While the real 'culprit' was his bronchitis medicine, Kinnie failed to prove his innocence and became long-term unemployed (*The Observer*, 12 December 1999).

As Newton (1999: 86) has pointed out, the concern among employers is that employees will use drugs that *impair* their productivity. In contrast, the concern of sports officials is that athletes may use drugs to *improve* their performance. One of the earliest examples of an athlete using performance enhancing substances took place in 668 BC when Charmis, the winner of the 200 metre sprint in the Olympic Games, prepared for the event with a special diet of dried figs (Australian Sports Commission 1999). The first drug tests on athletes were conducted at the Olympic Games in Mexico in 1968, but it was not until twenty years later that the issue became headline news when Canadian sprinter Ben Johnson was stripped of his 100 metres gold medal after testing positive for the anabolic steroid stanozolol (*The Guardian*, 20 November 1999).

Several high-profile cases have brought the issue of drug testing amongst athletes to the attention of the public. In 1999, for example, a total of 343 sportsmen or women tested positive for nandrolone, which is an easily detectable steroid (BBC News, 13 March 2000). Among those who tested positive were the Czech tennis player Peter Korda, the French footballer Christophe Dugarry, and the British sprinters Mark Richardson, Dougie Walker and Linford Christie. The amount of nandrolone found in Linford Christie's urine sample was more than 100 times the legal limit and 1,000 times more than is found in the average person (*The Guardian*, 7 August 1999: 1). However, Christie and other high-profile athletes who have failed the nandrolone test have challenged the scientific validity of the tests. For instance, the German athlete Dieter Baumann has recently instigated criminal proceedings to try to discover who injected nandrolone into his toothpaste (*The Guardian*, 8 January 2000).

Following the huge increase in the number of athletes testing positive, UK Athletics announced a joint study into the possible triggers of nandrolone. Attempts to explain the proliferation of nandrolone positives have focused upon the increased use of health supplements, the sophistication of the new detection machines, and the feeding of cattle with anabolic steroids. Following the acquittal of Dougie Walker, for example, it was argued that 'European cattle were regularly fed with nandrolone and other anabolic steroids and this was passed onto the athlete when he ate the meat'. Two years earlier, this argument was successfully used by the British bobsleigh racer Lenny Paul, who also claimed after failing a drugs test that he had eaten meat contaminated with steroids (*The Guardian*, 5 August 1999: 3).

Perhaps the most controversial case of recent years, however, took place in 1994 when Diane Modahl was sent home from defending her Commonwealth 800 metre title in Victoria, Canada. Modahl's urine sample recorded a high testosterone level and she was subsequently banned from competition for four years (*The Guardian*, 7 August 1999). However, the British runner discovered that her urine sample had not been stored properly, possibly causing its degradation and a subsequent high reading. In July 1995, the International Amateur Athletic Federation cleared Modahl after it was confirmed that her urine sample might have become contaminated because it had not been refrigerated properly. In December 2000, a High Court judge dismissed Modahl's £1 million compensation claim against the now defunct British Athletic Federation (*The Guardian*, 21 November 2000).

Discussion

The impact of surveillance

In the literature on crime victims a distinction is often made between the objective and subjective impact of crime (Walklate 1989). The objective impact refers to the immediate financial or physical effects of crime, while the subjective impact refers to the psychological and emotional effects of crime. A similar distinction can be made in relation to the 'victims' of surveillance. For instance, those who have refused to submit a DNA sample to their employer have felt the objective impact of surveillance. In January 1995, Corporal Joseph Vlacovsky and Lance Corporal John Mayfield III, two US marines, refused to supply a DNA sample. They were subsequently court-martialled for violating an order from their superior officer (Nelkin and Andrews 1999: 691). In April the following year, Sergeant Warren Sinclair a United States Air Force veteran, refused to submit samples for genetic testing and 'was convicted by court-martial on 10 May 1996 and sentenced to 14 days of hard labour and a two-grade reduction in rank' (Nelkin and Andrews 1999: 694). In the same year, 'Donald P. Power, a 1st Class Petty Officer and Navy nuclear technician, refused to give a DNA specimen because it violated his religious principles as a member of a Native American Lodge. For his refusal, Power lost a stripe, his security classification, and 40 per cent of his income' (Nelkin and Andrews 1999: 694). A similar story can be found among the many athletes whose careers have been damaged because of 'false positive' dope tests. For instance, in August 1998 a drug test found that the sample provided by top British weightlifter Paul Supple had excessive testosterone levels. The athlete was subsequently dropped from England's team for the Commonwealth Games and received a life ban from representing Britain in the Olympic Games. In 1999 all charges were dropped when Supple became the first sportsman to challenge success-fully the findings of the International Olympic Committee-accredited laboratory at King's College in London (*The Guardian*, 24 March 1999).

However, as the Diane Modahl case illustrates, it is the subjective impact of 'victimisation' that has the greatest impact on the lives of 'victims' of surveillance. As we saw earlier, in 1994 Diane Modahl recorded a high testosterone level and was banned from competition for four years. In an attempt to clear her name Modahl sold the family home to help meet legal and medical fees of £480,000. Following a recent High Court ruling which dismissed her claim for compensation, Vicente Modahl (Diane's husband) said that the couple 'were now on the point of bank-ruptcy and that they faced a bill of £1 million for contesting the case' (*Times* 2000b: 1). However, the financial cost incurred by Modahl was nothing compared to the psychological and emotional impact of the case. As Modahl herself put it, the case cost her 'hundreds of thousands of pounds in emotional turmoil' (ITV News, 14 December 2000). The psy-chological impact on Modahl was so great that during the case 'she tried to commit suicide on more than one occasion' (*The Guardian*, 21 November 2000).

The subjective impact of surveillance is likely to vary depending on the type of 'victimisation'. For instance, the disproportionate targeting of young, working-class people by CCTV operators is likely to induce anger and resentment in those who feel they are being unfairly targeted. As Norris and Armstrong have shown, on most occasions this social group has done nothing to attract the attention of CCTV operators. Yet they 'are being treated as ... unwanted outsiders ... This technologically mediated and distanced social interaction is, then, loaded with meaning and for literally thousands of black and working-class youth, however law-abiding, it transmits a wholly negative message about their position in society' (1998: 151).

The experience of victimisation for those asked to submit urine samples, on the other hand, may be one of shame or humiliation. During the Georgia Power drug-testing programme in the United States, for example:

Suitable drug testing meant being forced by a nurse to drop her pants to her ankles, bend over at the waist with her knees slightly bent, hold her right arm in the air, and with her left hand angle a specimen bottle between her legs. She sobbed and shook, wet herself, and vomited. She was fired for insubordination: refusal to take another test. (Newton 1999: 64–5)

A similar story was found in a study of US college athletes of whom 36.8 per cent experienced drug testing as humiliating and 26.5 per cent as upsetting (Coombs 1991). One young athlete tested at a national event said:

They grabbed me and locked me into a room for three hours with a bunch of other athletes, gave me a gallon of water to drink, and said that I couldn't leave the room until I completed the drug testing. I was dehydrated, had stomach cramps and was very upset. I never got a chance to cool down and was very upset that I had to urinate in front of somebody I didn't even know . . . I was very embarrassed and upset. (Coombs 1991: 209)

The tape recording of a person's nude body or intimate acts also produces intense feelings of shame, humiliation, and embarrassment. For 'victims' of voyeurism the impact of surveillance can have serious social and psychological consequences. From his experience of consultation with a number of covert videotaping victims, Simon (1997) suggests that there are four major overlapping areas of psychological damage. These include 'the development of psychological symptoms and disorders, distrust in relationships, fear for personal safety, and shame and humiliation (narcissistic injury)' (Simon 1997: 886). Simon also found evidence of the 'differential impact' of victimisation, with some victims of voyeurism being more severely affected than others. Thus, adolescent girls, solitary individuals, and those with pre-existing psychological problems or disorders were all particularly vulnerable to psychological injury from covert videotaping.

Repeat victimisation

Surveillance systems produce information that can be stored and used at some future, as yet unspecified, time and place. This raises the issue of 'repeat victimisation'. Holtorf (1998: 52), for example, suggests that in the United States when an employee fails a drug test 'the government and insurance companies are notified to deny all possible benefits to those who test positive'. Thus a person who tested positive in one institution may find that this information is stored and used at a later date to deny employment in another institution. Visual surveillance systems also produce information (i.e. images) that can be stored and used at a later date. We have already noted how CCTV operators disproportionately target young, working-class males. In one case study, it was reported how this social group can often find themselves excluded from the semi-public space of the shopping mall. With the aid of the hard-copy print-out machine, photographs of the 'excluded' can also be stored in 'rogue's galleries' for future reference. This allows those responsible for such systems to share (mainly photographic) information with other CCTV operators, the police, and security officers based in other shops and supermarkets. This raises the possibility that those who receive intensive monitoring and possible exclusion from one site may be targeted and excluded from other sites regardless of whether they are shopping or shoplifting.

The 'victim' of voyeurism is also subject to 'repeat victimisation'. Firstly, 'the video voyeur can view his desired objects in the comfort of his home and play back the videotape as many times as he pleases' (Simon 1997: 884). Secondly, the video voyeur usually brags 'to others that they have an intimate videotape of the victim or actually show the tape to a group of friends or acquaintances' (1997: 884). Thirdly, even after the culprit has been caught the 'victim' can never be sure that all the tapes have been recovered. As Simon point out, the 'victim' of voyeurism rarely discovers the surveillance cameras that have been used to spy on her most intimate moments. Instead the victim usually finds out about the existence of the taping from others who have viewed it. In this respect, 'the fact of multiple viewing is well established' (1997: 886). This is important because, as Simon points out, the more times the tape has been played and the more people who have watched it, the greater the psychological trauma to the victim. Victims of voyeurism also fear being stalked, raped or killed by someone who has viewed the videotapes. As for the duration of victimisation, Simon notes that the 'fear of commercial distribution of the videotape may stay with victims over a lifetime' (1997: 886).

The fear of surveillance

In a study which examined the drug testing of American college athletes, it was found that nearly half (47.4%) of the athletes worried about being inaccurately identified as a drug user. As one athlete explained, 'It scares me because I realise that, although the drug tests are basically very efficient, there may be a five percent chance of error. If I'm one of the five percent, it could ruin my reputation and my athletic opportunities'

(Coombs 1991: 208). However, the most common fear amongst 'victims' of surveillance is the 'fear of misappropriation' – that the information gathered about them will be used in a way that is inappropriate or not in accordance with stated aims and objectives.

One question that is often posed in the 'victimology' literature is whether certain people limit their activities because of the 'fear of crime' (Mawby and Gill 1987: 13). Similarly, in the context of genetic testing it has been suggested 'that worries about obtaining insurance were deterring those at risk of a treatable disorder from taking genetic tests and receiving early treatment' (Cook 1999). These fears are reinforced by a study in Washington which 'found that fear of discrimination has led one in 10 people at risk deciding against testing for genetic traits linked to cystic fibrosis, Huntingdon's disease, colon cancer and other conditions with a hereditary link' (*The Guardian*, 19 September 2000). Meanwhile, 'people who are aware that their prescription medication will be revealed to their employer...are abstaining from using necessary medications' (Holtorf 1998: 53). In light of the above examples it could be argued that 'the fear of future discrimination can be as damaging as discrimination itself, as people forgo screening for potentially treatable conditions for fear the information will be used against them in the future, (*The Guardian*, 19 September 2000).

Victims' needs

Finally, the surveillance 'revolution' shows no signs of slowing down. One issue of Index on Censorship states that Britain spends more on CCTV surveillance than any other European country (*The Observer*, 18 June 2000). Meanwhile, Jack Straw has announced plans for mandatory drug testing of the 500,000 people arrested each year (*The Guardian*, 18 November 1999). Also, the government recently announced a £109 million cash boost for the database, which is expected to see an extra 3 million samples added to the DNA database by 2004 (*The Guardian*, 1 September, 2000). As we have shown in this chapter, one of the unintended consequences of these developments is the creation of a new category of victims – 'victims of surveillance'. One key question for the future, therefore, is how should we address the 'needs' of these 'victims'?

At present, the prospect that a legal 'remedy' can deal with this issue would appear to be remote. As a number of writers have pointed out, the Data Protection Act does not appear to be an adequate mechanism to deal with modern surveillance technologies. Moreover, when a state agency breaches the law in the name of crime control its actions become subsequently legitimised by changes in the law. In a recent case, for example, a 'ruling by the law lords paved the way for judges to admit compelling DNA evidence in future cases, even where it had been unlawfully held' by the police (*The Times*, 15 December 2000: 1). In light of this we don't feel particularly confident that a standard legal approach can address these issues. However, the implementation of the European Convention on Human Rights is likely to have an impact on some of the issues raised during this discussion. For instance, in relation to genetic testing, to what extent does the taking of body samples infringe upon the Human Rights Act (Article 8)? Also, does the disproportionate targeting of certain individuals and social groups infringe upon Article 14, which states that no one should be discriminated against on the grounds of sex, race, colour, language, religion etc.? It is around these issues perhaps that we may see the emergence of a 'Victims' Movement' that will address the needs of 'victims of surveillance'.

References

Adams, D. (1999) 'Prints among thieves'. *Police Review*, 16 April, 26–7.

American Civil Liberties Union (1996) 'FL county plans drug tests for welfare clients', 24 September.

American Civil Liberties Union (1999) 'Hair tests: unreliable and discriminatory', 27 June.

American Civil Liberties Union (1999) 'Hair testing by schools intensifies drug debate', 14 June.

American Civil Liberties Union (2000) 'Court rejects Michigan's attempt to end ACLU challenge to urine testing of welfare recipients', 18 April.

Aziz, C. 'Who's watching you? The men who spy on your most intimate moments'.

Bound, G. (1999) '"Any time, any place, anywhere" is drug-busters' Martini motto'. *Soldier: Magazine of the British Army*, December.

Brignon, E., Bastien, C. and Pfitzinger, H. (1999) 'Forensic DNA typing of single hair samples: mitochondrial DNA sequencing of hypervariable region HV1/HV2'. Paper given at the First International Conference on Forensic Human Identification in the Millennium.

Colonna, T. E. (1998) 'Protection of privacy in personal genetic information'. *West Virginia Journal of Law and Technology*, 2, 2.

Cook, E. D. (1999) 'Genetics and the British insurance industry'. *Journal of Medical Ethics*, 25, 157–62.

Coombs, R. H. (1991) 'Drug Testing as Experienced by Mandatory Participants'. In R. H. Coombs and L. J. West (eds), *Drug Testing: Issues and Options*. Oxford: Oxford University Press.

Daily Express, 'Worried police refuse to give DNA samples', 2 July 2000.

Easterbrook, G. (2000) 'The myth of fingerprints'. *The New Republic*, 31 July 2000.

Forensic Science Service (1999), 'Employee drug screening'.

Forensic Science Service (2000) 'DNA profiles on national database top one million', 13 November.

Gostin, L. (1991) 'Genetic discrimination: the use of genetically based diagnostic and prognostic tests by employers and insurers'. *American Journal of Law and Medicine*, 17, 109–44.

Graham, S. (1998) 'Towards the Fifth Utility? On the extension and normalisation of public CCTV'. In C. Norris, J. Moran, and G. Armstrong (eds), *Surveillance, Closed Circuit Television and Social Control*. Aldershot: Ashgate.

Hammond, H. A. and Caskey, C. T. (1997) 'Automated DNA typing: method of the future?'. *National Institute of Justice Research Preview*, February 1997.

Henry, S. and Milovanovic, D. (1996), *Constitutive Criminology: Beyond Postmodernism*. London: Sage.

Hoeffel, J. C. (1990) 'The dark side of DNA profiling: unreliable scientific evidence meets the criminal defendant'. *Stanford Law Review*, 42 (January), 2, 465–538.

Holtorf, K. (1998), *Ur-ine Trouble*. Arizona: Vandalay Press.

Hull Daily Mail (1998) 'PC is caught on camera', 20 February.

HM Prison Service (1995) 'Mandatory drug testing: questions and answers'.

Independent (1998) 'Police to be tested for use of drugs', 12 October.

Independent on Sunday (1998) 'Random testing puts drug users' jobs on the line', 22 November.

Koskela, H. (2000) ' "The gaze without eyes": video-surveillance and the changing nature of urban space'. *Progress in Human Geography*, 24, 2, 243–65.

Kubanek, J. and Miller, F. (1997) *DNA Evidence and a National DNA Databank: Not in Our Name*. Vancouver: Rape Relief and Women's Shelter.

Marx, G. (1998) *Undercover Police Surveillance in America*. Berkeley: University of California Press.

Mawby, R. I. and Gill, M. L. (1987) *Crime Victims: Needs, Services and the Voluntary Sector*. London: Tavistock.

McDonald, R. (1998), 'Juries and crime labs: correcting the weak link in the DNA chain'. *American Journal of Law and Medicine*, 24, 2/3.

McEwan, J. E. and Reilly, P. R. (1995) 'A survey of DNA diagnostic laboratories regarding DNA banking'. *American Journal of Human Genetics*, 56, 1477–86.

Mulloy, P. J. (1991) 'Winning the war on drugs in the military'. In R. H. Coombs and L. J. West (eds), *Drug Testing: Issues and Options*. Oxford: Oxford University Press.

National Commission on the Future of DNA Evidence Meeting VII, 27 September 1999.

Nelkin, D. and Andrews, L. (1999) 'DNA identification and surveillance creep'. *Sociology of Health and Illness*, 21, 5, 689–706.

Newton, D. E. (1999) *Drug Testing: An Issue for School, Sports, and Work*. Aldershot: Enslow.

Norris, C. and Armstrong, G. (1998) *The Maximum Surveillance Society: The Rise of CCTV*. Oxford: Berg.

Police Review (1999) London: Police Review, 11.

Russell, B. & Rodda, M. (1998) MarijuanNews.Com, 'State schools using random drug tests', 29 March.

Schwendiger, H. and Schwendinger, J. (1970) 'Defenders of order or guardians of human rights?', *Issues in Criminology*, 51, 123–57.

Sellin, T. (1938) 'Culture, Conflict and Crime New York'. Selected in M. Wolfgang et al. (eds), *The Sociology of Crime and Delinquency*. New York: New York Press 1962: 22–69.

Simon, R. I. (1997) 'Video voyeurs and the covert videotaping of unsuspecting victims: psychological and legal consequences'. *Journal of Forensic Science*, 42, 5, 884–9.

Srinivasan, J. (1996) 'Mandatory DNA fingerprinting in the military: an unjust system'. http:/ /www-pgss.mcs.cmu.edu/1996/people.

Steadman, G. W. (2000) 'Survey of DNA crime laboratories, 1998'. *Bureau of Justice Statistics*, February, 1–8.

Strudler, A. (1994) 'The social construction of genetic abnormality: ethical implications for managerial decisions in the workplace'. *Journal of Business Ethics*, 13, 839–48.

Sunday Times (2000) 'Police use DNA to beat racists', 2 April.

Sunshine, I. (1993) 'Mandatory drug-testing in the United States', *Forensic Science International*, 63, 1–3, 1–7.

Tappan, P. (1947) 'Who is the criminal?', *American Sociological Review*, 12, February, 96–102.

Times (2000a) 'Modahl vows to win in long run', 15 December, 40.

Times (2000b) 'Judges back wider use of DNA evidence', 15 December, 1.

Tracy, P. E. and Morgan, V. (2000) 'Big brother and his science kit: DNA databases for 21st century crime control?'. *The Journal of Criminal Law and Criminology*, 90, 2, 635–90.

Van Oorschot, R. A. H. et al. (1999) 'Retrieval of genetic profiles from touched objects'. Paper given at the First International Conference on Forensic Human Identification in the Millennium.

Walklate, S. (1989) *Victimology: The Victim and the Criminal Process*. London: Unwin Hyman.

Zedner, L. (1994) 'Victims'. In M. Maguire, R. Morgan and R. Reiner (eds), *The Oxford Handbook of Criminology*. Oxford: Clarendon Press.

Websites

http:/ /www.aclu.org/news
http:/ /www.ausport.gov.au/drug
http:/ /www.guardianunlimited.co.uk
http:/ /www.hightimes.com
http:/ /news.bbc.co.uk

8

The Provision of Victim Support and Assistance Programmes: A Cross-National Perspective

Rob Mawby

Introduction

As statistics on recorded crime and victim survey data indicate (Mawby and Walklate 1994; Mayhew and van Dijk 1997), while crime is a significant factor in all modern societies the extent of crime, and the most common offence types, vary between different societies. Nevertheless, victims' responses are broadly similar (Mawby and Walklate 1994). They are affected both by the crime itself and, in many cases, by the response of different agents within the criminal justice system. They commonly experience anger (Ditton et al. 1999); in many cases they register fear and anxiety (Maguire and Kynch 2000; Mawby et al. 1999; Norris et al. 1997). While violent crimes appear to have the greatest impact, many property crimes, including burglary, also affect victims. In cases of property crime, victims may suffer financial losses, or anguish at having lost items of sentimental value. They may also express concern that their private space has been 'invaded' and register fear. They often admit to crying or experience difficulties with sleeping (Mawby et al. 1999).

It is against these concerns that the victims' movement has emerged in the last forty years. But here lies the crux of the issue. The so-called 'victims' movement' is not one movement at all. The victims' lobby emerged independently in Britain and the USA, and while other countries, such as the Netherlands and Australia, introduced services that were to some extent based on those tried and tested elsewhere, variations in emphasis are considerable.

The response of victims will vary depending upon the structure and ethos of the criminal justice system and its varying agencies, as well as other agencies involved with victims. For example, whilst police services in many countries have become more appreciative of victims' needs in recent years, in others, including many post-communist societies, changes have been slower (Mawby 1998; Zvekic 1998). And while in England and Wales most victims of property crime will find that the bulk of their financial losses are met through insurance, the same does not apply in post-communist countries (Mawby et al. 1999).

At least three different forms of support that victims might receive can be identified. First, there is help at, or shortly after, the offence, which may be given by the police (Mawby 1998, 1999; Mawby and Kirchhoff 1996), a generalist victim assistance programme (such as Victim Support in England), or a specialist agency (like a rape crisis agency) (Hanmer et al. 1989; Joyner 1999). Second, there is help at the court stage. Finally, there is help in the form of financial or other forms of compensation, through compensation orders, criminal injuries compensation, or – more recently – mediation or restorative justice programmes. The following sections focus upon victim assistance programmes. First, the overall situation is described. Then, a range of countries are considered. As del Frate (1998: 75) illustrates, services are most common in western Europe and the New World. The following four sections thus focus on England and Wales, the Netherlands, the United States, and Germany. Recent developments are, however, evident in some post-communist societies, or 'countries in transition', so two of these, Hungary and the Czech Republic, are discussed.[1]

Victim Assistance Programmes: An Overview

There are considerable variations in emphasis between victim assistance programmes, both within and between nations. Mawby and Walklate (1994) identified four broad areas within which to describe the key features of such services. First is the organisational structure of the agency; second is its relationships with other agencies; third is the nature of the service provided; fourth is the nature of the victim population targeted, or prioritised, by the organisation.

Taking the organisational structure of the agency, one might first distinguish between public services and voluntary or private services (NGOs). The established image is that England and Wales are distinctive in having a strong voluntary sector involvement. In contrast, state involvement is evident in some countries, such as Spain (Vidosa 1989), Belgium (Peters and Meyvis 1989) and Germany (Schädler 1989). However, these are the exceptions: most victim assistance programmes appear to be provided by non-state agencies, and although the profit-making private sector is sometimes involved, at least at the specialist end of the market, most services are based in the voluntary, or non-profit-making, private sector. This itself raises a number of questions about the running and financing of such services (Gill and Mawby 1990; Mawby and Gill 1987). Generally speaking, services are heavily dependent upon government funding. In the Netherlands, for example, services receive financial support from three central government departments (van Dijk 1989a; Penders 1989). In other countries, such as Germany (Doering-Striening 1989), specific taxes or fines may go directly to fund victim services. Nevertheless, government financial support is rarely on a scale that allows for a service based on professional paid staff, and in almost all countries where support services are provided there is a heavy dependence on volunteers. In Canada, McClenahan (1987) reported that in Vancouver, services funded by the Solicitor-General were based on the assumption that 140 volunteers could be recruited. This often means that services are patchy and available where volunteers are easy to recruit rather than where they are most needed (Mawby and Gill 1987). Equally important, the dependence on volunteers means that services may be competing with rival agencies to recruit from a far from bottomless pit (Gill and Mawby 1990).

Similar problems arise *vis-à-vis* a dependence on the voluntary sector. In most cases funding is on a short-term basis and may be withdrawn with a change of political climate, or it may be provided for a limited period on the expectation that the agency will become self-financing in the long term. Voluntary bodies may therefore spend considerable amounts of time fund-raising rather than providing services!

Partly because of the dangers of fragmentation, many countries have created national co-ordinating bodies that provide national standards, advice, examples of best practice, direct routes to central government, and links with similar agencies abroad such as through the European Forum. In England and Wales, the National Association of Victim Support Schemes (now Victim Support) was formed in 1979. In France, the National Institute for Assistance for Victims (INAVEM) was created in 1986 as a co-ordinating body for the (at that time) sixty local associations (Piffaut 1989); in the Netherlands the equivalent body is the National Organisation for Victim Support (NOVS) (van Dijk 1989a).

The United States does not have an equivalent national organisation. However, the National Organisation for Victim Assistance (NOVA), as a national umbrella organisation, provides a similar role for a much wider range of victim services, including specialist ones concerned with rape and domestic violence, services provided specifically for victims at later stages in the criminal justice process, and services provided by state agencies.

Perhaps the most notable aspect of the relationship between victim assistance programmes and external agencies, is their link with the police. In North America, some services are actually run as parts of the police departments; in many others victim support is a distinct agency physically located within the police station (Dussich 1976; Waller 1982). The key advantage of this is that co-ordination of services, and particularly co-operation between police and victim service, is enhanced, although at the other extreme some victims may be reluctant to contact an agency which appears to be part of the police organisation. Elsewhere, some victim services, like the Hanau Victim Assistance Centre in Germany (Schädler 1989) and WCS in Prague, operate as a 'shop front', depending on publicity for their clientele. Some other countries report difficulties with ensuring that the police refer appropriately to victim assistance programmes; in Scotland, for example, the police have traditionally been reluctant to contact victim support without the victim's explicit permission (Moody 1989). In England and Wales, Victim Support has built up good relations with individual police forces such that most of the initial police suspicion has been eliminated and referral levels are high, apparently producing the best of both worlds (Mawby and Gill 1987).

What then of the types of service provided by Victim Support? Whilst in Britain the emphasis has traditionally been placed on a combination of sympathetic support and advice, in the USA 'support' has tended to include a greater emphasis on crisis counselling, with professional therapists seen as a common resource (Young and Stein 1983). In contrast, in much of western Europe emphasis has been on the provision of legal advice and financial assistance rather than *emotional* support (Maguire and Shapland 1997). This is certainly the case in France (Piffaut 1989) and in Spain the main service offered concerns advice on legal rights (Vidosa 1989).

Finally, the nature of the victim population targeted or prioritised can be compared for different countries. There are some variations according to the social characteristics of the victims. In the US many programmes are geared exclusively to the elderly, for example, whilst Ireland has a separate organisation catering for tourist victims (Tourist Victim Support Service 2000). Another contrast is by offence type. In some countries (such as England and Wales) the needs of property victims have been prioritised, in others (like the USA) those of victims of violent crimes. Variations, even between Western industrialised societies, are well illustrated from responses to the international crime victims survey (ICVS)

(Mayhew and van Dijk 1997: 44–6). In Sweden, 21 per cent of victims of assaults and threats said they received help from a specialised agency; in neighbouring Finland only 6 per cent did. On the other hand, only 1 per cent of burglary victims from Sweden received help, compared with 21 per cent of victims from England and Wales.

It is also pertinent to note the extent to which victim assistance programmes have been willing to provide help to non-crime victims, a debate with its roots in the formative years of victimology itself. In England, many of the rural, less pressurised schemes have tended to cover non-crime victims and, while this has been a contentious issue nationally, in times of national disaster such as Hillsborough in 1988 – when many football fans were killed or injured when barriers gave way – Victim Support has been to the forefront in providing support services. Similarly in France INAVEM has made contingency plans to deal with any disasters (Piffaut 1989) and in the US Crisis Response teams have been organised by NOVA (Davis and Henley 1990: 164).

There are, then, marked variations between victim assistance programmes in different countries. To provide further illustration of such differences, and a more detailed picture, the following sections concentrate on countries within which victim schemes are perhaps most fully developed, as well as some post-communist societies in which services have been more recently established.

Victim Support in England and Wales

In England and Wales, the first victim support scheme was launched in Bristol in 1973/4 as an independent agency relying on the co-operation of statutory agencies such as the police, probation service and magistracy. In 1979 the national association was formed and by 1980 there were 256 schemes and an annual rate of referral of 125,000 (Mawby and Gill 1987: 87–8). Not surprisingly, this phenomenal rate of increase could not be maintained, and the growth in the number of schemes decelerated. Nevertheless, by 1999 there were 374 schemes, including one on Jersey, one on Guernsey, twelve in Northern Ireland, and thirty-five in Wales (Victim Support 1999).[2] Scotland has its own, separate organisation. During the year 1998/9 1,141,198 cases were referred to Victim Support.

Victim Support operates as a co-ordinating and validating body. Over the 1970s and 1980s it developed a close relationship with the Home Office, whilst maintaining its independence (Rock 1990). It employs some fifty-three staff, is paid for by the Home Office and is based in London. At the other extreme lie individual schemes that are affiliated with Victim Support and linked to the centre via a county structure and a number of national committees. There is a Code of Practice, which includes requirements covering service provision, training and management structure, and individual schemes that do not conform to the code will be excluded from the organisation, and, effectively, from receiving police support. The national organisation is also responsible for allocating central government funding to individual schemes, which gives it an additional level of control. At local level, each scheme has a management committee, at least one co-ordinator, and a number of visitors who make direct contact with crime victims.

Throughout the UK, victim support schemes are voluntary organisations and registered charities, the latter allowing them to claim tax relief. Financial support was originally gained from a number of private sponsors and from the government (Russell 1990). The most significant development came in 1986 when the government announced a £9 million grant to Victim Support over the period 1987–90. In the year ending March 1999, Victim Support (1999) reported an income of over £13 million, of which £12,725,000 came from the Home Office.

These developments herald both a significant shift in government commitment to Victim Support and a major change in the nature of the organisation (Rock 1990; Russell 1990). Nevertheless, the bulk of the work of individual schemes depends on volunteers. Although a *majority* of schemes have paid co-ordinators, the total of 964 paid staff is dwarfed by 14,670 volunteers, of whom 9,477 visited victims, 3456 were volunteer office staff, 25 supportline volunteers and 3,700 members of management committees (Victim Support 1999: 13).[3]

What of the *location* of Victim Support *vis-à-vis* other agencies? Two of the key features of Victim Support, evident from the first Bristol scheme, were the fusion of independence and co-operation. While some schemes, especially in the early years, were located in probation offices, schemes were independent of both police and probation. At the same time, they built up good relationships with these and other agencies within the criminal justice system, and the close co-operation between the police and Victim Support has been a notable feature, contributing much to the successful establishment of the organisation (Mawby and Gill 1987; Rock 1990).

The importance of the police to Victim Support is centred on the role of the police as referrers of clients. Unlike many other European countries, almost all victims assisted by Victim Support are referred to schemes by the police (Maguire and Kynch 2000).[4] Originally the police were reluctant to relinquish control of referrals, and passed on to schemes victims whom officers felt to be in need of help, a practice that resulted in a disproportionate number of elderly, and clearly fragile, victims being seen by Victim Support (Maguire and Corbett 1987; Mawby and Gill 1987). In Scotland there is still a reluctance to refer victims without their explicit consent (Moody 1989). However, in the rest of the UK it is now common practice for scheme co-ordinators to liaise directly with the police and record all known victims of predetermined crime types as referrals, a system known as the 'direct referral system'. Schemes will then decide for themselves which victims will be contacted or, more commonly, what sort of contact will be made. Whilst clearly preferable to the original practice, this does raise some difficulties. First, given that referrals have increased at a faster rate than volunteers (Russell 1990), schemes are increasingly having to make decisions about who gets visited, or what means of contact is preferable. Secondly, whilst the police no longer act as gatekeepers, co-ordinators in the schemes are themselves increasingly deciding, on the basis of very little information, which victims are 'in need' of personal contact within a day or two of the offence being reported (Maguire and Wilkinson 1992). Despite these problems, however, it is arguable that the English system has achieved a successful balance and remains a distinctly separate organisation while receiving full co-operation, by way of referrals, from the police.

In contrast, relationships with other agencies working with victims, largely from the voluntary sector, are patchy, partly because agencies may be competing for the same clients (Russell 1990), and correspondingly for what limited funding is available, partly because of marked variations in the philosophies of the different organisations. Thus whilst Victim Support has engaged in discussions with a range of other agencies, and has drawn representatives of such agencies into its formal structure through annual conferences, specialist working parties, and so on, relationships with Rape Crisis and the Refuge Movement especially are tenuous and most fragile where Victim Support has moved in to accept victims of those crimes referred from the police (see below). On an organisational level, though, there is no equivalent agency to NOVA in the US that provides an umbrella for the various agencies and services in the victims' movements.

In relation to the nature of the services provided, Victim Support in Britain is also distinct from its North American equivalent in emphasising the service nature of its work, rather than educational or political goals (Mawby and Gill 1987). This does not mean that Victim Support is apolitical. On the contrary, as Rock (1990) pointed out, it has quietly and uncontroversially built itself an impressive power base within the political establishment. It is consulted by the Home Office over impending changes to the law, and has on various occasions campaigned publicly or instigated working parties to push for changes that would improve the lot of the crime victim. But any such political role is tightly circumscribed. The national Code of Practice bars members from expressing party political viewpoints when representing Victim Support and from commenting on sentencing policy, other than where it is of direct relevance to victims.

For Victim Support then, the most important focus is on the service provided by volunteers for victims. Co-ordinators receive details of victims from the police, or directly from police files, within a day or so of the crime being reported, and decide whether or not contact is to be made and if so whether in person or by letter or phone (Maguire and Kynch 2000). If a victim is considered in need of a visit, the co-ordinator arranges for a volunteer to pay the victim a visit, which will normally take place within the following twenty-four hours. Only in exceptional circumstances will a victim be visited when the crime is 'live'. Where contact is made, most victims will be seen only once (Maguire and Corbett 1987), although in areas with less crime return visits are more normal (Mawby and Gill 1987), and more serious crimes, where victims are more severely affected, are allocated markedly more time (Victim Support 1999). Russell (1990) also suggested that those in inner city areas, where victimisation is only one of a number of problems faced, may be visited more frequently. In most cases, however, the emphasis is on four or five levels of support: personal support, reassurance and the demonstration that 'someone cares'; immediate practical help where the victim needs to repair windows, fit secure locks or take other crime prevention measures; the provision of information and advice on what resources or services might be available, for example on compensation; as a link between victim and police to feed back details of case progress to victims; and, a more recent development, specific security advice (Maguire and Kynch 2000; Mawby and Walklate 1994).

The original scheme, in Bristol, prioritised burglary victims, partly because of the need to restrict services to a manageable proportion, partly to match needs to what help could realistically be offered. It was 'accepted' that victims of certain types of crime, such as vehicle-based offences, were little affected and would not require assistance, whereas at the other extreme sex and violence offences were considered too difficult for volunteers to deal with (Gay et al. 1975; Maguire and Corbett 1987). As a result, as Victim Support expanded into a national service, burglaries came to dominate its case files. In 1985, for example, some 80 per cent of referrals were of victims of burglary. At the same time, only 8 per cent of victims were victims of violent crime, 11 per cent of other property crime and 1 per cent non-crime victims, the latter being more common in rural, low-crime areas (Mawby and Gill 1987).

Since then, the most dramatic change has been in the increase in help for victims of more serious crimes, including violence. Partly in recognition of the unmet needs of such victims, partly in an attempt to expand services and extend credibility, and partly in response to Home Office and police willingness to turn to Victim Support for help rather than rely on more militant feminist alternatives, Victim Support has shifted its emphasis to include domestic violence, rape, homicide and so on. Special courses have been provided to train dedicated volunteers for this more intensive and demanding work; working parties have been used to set agendas, improve credibility and effect liaison with other agencies; and special projects have focused on needs and service provision. Partly reflecting these shifts, in 1998/99 only 38 per cent of Victim Support's referrals were burglary victims and Victim Support dealt with 4,184 rape cases and 671 homicides (Victim Support 1999: 10). Nevertheless, burglary victims are more likely than most to receive a personal visit (Maguire and Kynch 2000; Mawby et al. 1999).

Victim assistance in the Netherlands

Victim Support services emerged in the Netherlands in the 1970s with the first experimental projects created in 1975. The probation service was heavily involved and, partly as a result, these early schemes included a commitment to mediation (van Dijk 1989b). In 1979 Humanitas, a voluntary agency, set out a model for future initiatives, which in many respects paralleled developments in England. Schemes were to focus on the material and emotional problems of crime victims, and be independent organisations run by one paid co-ordinator and dependent upon volunteers. Police stations were seen as the ideal location for schemes. The Ministry of Justice agreed to finance three pilot projects based on this model, but these, and later schemes, evidenced a degree of variation not experienced in Britain (van Dijk 1989b). The picture in the Netherlands is thus one of considerable diversity.

This is confirmed by the stance taken by the national co-ordinating body. The National Platform for Victim Assistance (LOS), now renamed the National organisation of Victim Support, was formed in 1983–4 by the individual schemes with the active encouragement of the Ministry of Justice. In 1985 a national office was established to promote local developments. Even then, however, it was made explicit that LOS would not attempt to impose a uniform structure upon local schemes. The Ministry of Justice funded four staff posts in the national office, and in 1985 provided a grant for the establishment of local schemes; in 1987–9 some £1.2 million was provided and in 1990 this was increased to £1.2 million per annum, to pay for the staff at the national office and one co-ordinator each for local schemes, with the assumption that local councils would pay the administrative costs of each scheme.

By 1999 funding for victim assistance programmes, or *Slachtofferhulp*, had become more firmly established, with about two-thirds of funding derived from the Ministry of Justice and 19 per cent from local municipalities.[5]

By 1999 victim assistance was co-ordinated through a national office and twenty-five regional offices (coinciding with police force boundaries) that employed about 250 professional staff who themselves supported seventy-five local *Slachtofferhulp*. Most of the direct contact with victims was provided by some 1,500 volunteers who, as in England and Wales, tended to be white, middle-class, older people. About two thirds were female.

In 1985 there were twenty-three schemes in the Netherlands, a figure that had risen to seventy-five by 1989. In the same period, referrals had increased from 1,800 to 17,000 (Groenhuijsen 1990). By the end of the 1980s, about a third of schemes were independent, with most of the remainder based in either welfare or police departments. Almost all schemes utilised volunteers and use of volunteers had been encouraged by the government. Funding was available only for scheme co-ordinators, and only where the scheme deployed volunteer workers. The number of volunteers, correspondingly, increased from 295 in 1987 to 579 in 1989. In comparison, there were then some sixty paid workers in victim assistance programmes (Groenhuijsen 1990).

In the Netherlands many social services are provided through local, relatively small voluntary organisations which are heavily subsidised by central government (Brenton 1982), and victim assistance programmes appear to fit in with this model for provision. Partly for this reason, partly because many schemes were originally based in welfare departments, and partly because schemes initially covered a wide range of property *and* interpersonal crimes, relationships with other welfare and voluntary agencies appear to be relatively close.

Relationships with the police seem to be mixed. Some schemes are run completely independent of the police and rely on self-referrals for their clientele, and where the police are involved official policy seems to be that victims will not be referred unless they *explicitly* give their permission (Steinmetz 1989). The main advantage of police-based services is, allegedly, the fact that police – victim support co-operation is enhanced. The fact that the police were not routinely referring victims to programmes, however, caused concern even in those schemes operated by the police. Hauber and Zandbergen (1991) reported on the situation in the Hague, where the scheme was police-based but located centrally rather than in local stations, resulting in low rates of referral and poor knowledge of the programme among police officers. Relocation of victim assistance in local police stations apparently resulted in improvements in police relationships and in police 'victim-mindedness'. By 1999 most referrals came from the police.

The importance of improving police service to victims was recognised by two committees: the Beaufort Committee of 1981, which addressed sex offences, and the wider-ranging Vaillant Committee of 1983 (Wemmers and Zeilstra 1991). As a result a series of guidelines for police and prosecutors, what Penders (1989) calls 'pseudo-laws', was issued. The guidelines required the police to treat victims sympathetically, provide all the relevant information and, where necessary, refer them to other agencies, and victims have a right to cite the guidelines should they subsequently take legal action against the police. In this sense then, these circulars provide victims with legal rights that the British government's Victims' Charter does not. Nevertheless, in a meticulous evaluation of the subsequent operation of the police Wemmers and Zeilstra (1991) argued that improvements were limited, on the one hand because victims were unaware of their rights, on the other hand because the vagueness of the guidelines allowed the police considerable discretion in their interpretation. It thus seems that even in a system like the Dutch, where considerable emphasis has been placed on victim services, changing *police* practices is not always easy.

With regard to the nature of the service provided, there is a greater level of accord. Descriptions of services include an emphasis on information and advice and emotional support, a 'listening and caring ear'. Assistance with practical problems, such as the installation of locks or the preparation of insurance claims, has been stressed (van Dijk 1989b; Groenhuijsen 1990), as has legal assistance.[6] There are, however, perhaps three key differences. First, rather more emphasis is placed on the limitations in the skills of volunteers and the consequent need to refer victims with serious problems to professional agencies. Second, mediation is often seen as a key feature of victim assistance programmes (van Dijk 1989b). In each of these examples, one might speculate that the closer link between schemes and probation or other welfare agencies may have contributed to the difference. Third, and partly related to the types of cases covered (see below), the amount of time spent on each referral is considerable and follow-up appointments are the norm.[7]

Finally, the cases dealt with by victim assistance programmes can be considered. Unlike in England and Wales, early schemes were involved with victims of violent crime and different schemes appeared to cater for markedly different client profiles. As a result, in the Netherlands the proportion of clients who are the victims of property crime is much lower than in Britain, with only about 15 per cent of referrals in 1999 being for burglary, compared with 36 per cent for sex/violence. Indeed, the third sweep of the ICVS suggested that only 6 per cent of burglary victims received specialist support, compared with 7 per cent of robbery victims and 13 per cent of victims of assaults and threats (Mayhew and van Dijk 1997: appendix 4). Another feature of the Dutch situation is the inclusion of victims of road traffic accidents: these victims accounted for about 11 per cent of all referrals by the late 1980s (Groenhuijsen 1990), a figure that had grown to 30 per cent by 1999.

Clearly in many respects victim assistance programmes in the Netherlands have developed in similar ways to those in England and Wales. In other ways, however, there are differences, and in some instances there are similarities with provisions in the United States.

Victim assistance programmes in the United States

Policies aimed at helping the victims of crime emerged in North America in the 1960s and early 1970s, with a number of progammes geared towards helping specific groups of victims – such as rape victims, battered spouses or abused children – or rectifying faults in the criminal justice system (Davis and Henley 1990; Dussich 1981; Roberts 1990; Young 1990). Combined with victim-initiated services for parents of murdered children and relatives of those killed in drink-driving incidents, the range of victim initiatives has been considerable.

Given the diversity of the US criminal justice system, it is not surprising that there is no established operational model for these programmes. The approaches differ from one another in relation to the target audience, the types of services provided, programme organisation, the purposes of the programme, and the underlying rationale for the services being provided (Schneider and Schneider 1981: 365; Ziegenhagen and Benyi 1981: 377).

This variety is to some extent exaggerated by the fact that NOVA incorporates a range of service areas outside the scope of Victim Support

in England and Wales. Nonetheless, it seems that, as in the Netherlands, there is considerably less uniformity than in England and Wales,
a point to be borne in mind as the US situation is considered in more
detail.

It was a government funding programme, the LEAA, that stimulated
service development in the mid-1970s, when almost $50 million was
provided for schemes that aimed to promote greater public co-operation
with the criminal justice system (Schneider and Schneider 1981). Then,
when the LEAA initiative shifted its priorities, and victim funding began
to be phased out, the 1984 Victims of Crime Act (VOCA) and the 1984
Justice Assistance Act provided new central government sources of funding, with a variety of local taxes and court fines being used by individual
states or counties (Roberts 1990: 87–8; Young 1990). In Pima County,
for example, services were originally developed with the aid of an LEAA
grant of some $150,000 in 1975, and when LEAA sponsorship ended in
1978 local government took over financial responsibility (Lowenberg
1981). For 1985, Roberts (1990: 86) found that almost two-thirds of
programmes had an annual budget over $50,000, with 15 per cent
receiving at least $250,000. While the extent of funding, and the corres-
pondingly high numbers of paid professional project staff, make such
examples stand out from the situation in England and Wales, there is
an equal degree of uncertainty attached to the funding, and NOVA has
regularly had to 'fight its corner' when government restrictions have
threatened to savage victim services monies.

Yet while the volunteer element is more often stressed in Britain than
in the US, many services do depend on volunteer support. True, Roberts
(1990: 122–7) described the victim assistance unit within the police
department of Rochester, New York, which was at that time staffed by
paid workers with only one volunteer in support, and Davis and Henley
(1990) also noted the key role of professional workers within agencies,
but elsewhere volunteers appear to play a key role. For example, the
crime victim centres of Minneapolis and St Paul, Minnesota, incorporated eleven full- or part-time workers, thirty volunteers and three
student interns (Roberts 1990: 129) and in Pima County the original
service was based around eight paid workers and thirty volunteers
(Bolin 1980; Lowenberg 1981). Indeed, by making eligibility for federal
funds dependent upon the use of volunteers within applying agencies,
VOCA demonstrated a government commitment to the volunteer
principle.

Roberts' (1990) survey also revealed that most services were based in
government agencies (see also Dussich 1981). A majority, many of which

were court-based services for victims or witnesses, were based in prosecutors' offices or with the state attorney, 7 per cent were in police
departments and 4 per cent in probation departments, with only 13 per
cent in independent agencies, these tending to be grassroots organisations more reliant on volunteers and private donations. Whilst many of
the programmes that are physically located in public service agencies *are*
independent, and have a separate management committee, this nonetheless illustrates a marked difference between the US and most of
Europe. For example, the Pima County programme was the result of
a joint initiative from the police and the Attorney's Office (Bolin 1980;
Lowenberg 1981), and in Minnesota the programme was also heavily
dependent upon police initiatives (Chesney and Schneider 1981).

As already noted, this may have the advantage of ensuring close
co-operation with the police and enhancing a high level of referrals. But
this is not necessarily the case, and in Minnesota Chesney and Schneider
(1981: 401) report that a *lack* of referrals led the scheme to shift towards
personal checking of police files. There is also evidence of schemes having
their priorities defined for them by the police. In Minnesota the police
insisted that the scheme should be 'on call' at all hours (Chesney and
Schneider 1981: 403) and in Pima County the police appeared to define
the victim assistance programme as one whose role was to take any clients
with whom the police did not want to deal (Bolin 1980).

Basing a service in a criminal justice or health service agency, with its own
predefined priorities, may also of course affect the relationship that the
service can develop with victims or other agencies. In general, studies
from the US suggest a fair degree of co-operation between different
agencies, and the fact that NOVA incorporates such a disparate range of
services means that it provides a forum for the interchange of ideas. In
some areas agencies may be structured so as to prioritise inter-agency
co-operation. In Pima County inter-agency relations were defined as a
key part of the service, and individual staff were assigned responsibilities
vis-à-vis certain named agencies with which the victim assistance programme was expected to interact (Lowenberg 1981). Chesney and
Schneider (1981) also noted that relations with welfare agencies were good
in the Minnesota scheme, although they pointed out that where the police
saw the scheme as most appropriate for sexual assault victims, this inevitably raised conflict with specialist grassroots organisations in the area.

What of the range of services provided? A variety of response options
appear to have been followed from the beginning (Mawby and Gill
1987). Services range from routine letters or phone calls with only a few
personal contacts (and those generally requiring the victims to attend

the victim assistance office), to provisions for counsellors to visit the victim immediately the crime is reported (Roberts 1990: 64). To some extent this latter option was included because of the focus on victims of more serious offences, such as rape or other physical violence, and has been used with discretion. Nevertheless, the use of counsellors (volunteers or professionals) 'on call', in rapid-response cars, has been a feature of a number of programmes, for example in Minnesota (Roberts 1990: 127–30) and Pima County (Bolin 1980).

Another feature of the US situation, promulgated by the early emphasis on court-based services, is the fact that many agencies either provide a co-ordinated service from time of offence to sentence and beyond, or operate within a network that provides such comprehensive coverage (Young 1990). Focusing on the most immediate victim assistance end of the spectrum, however, the services offered seems to follow a broadly similar pattern to those in the UK and the Netherlands: 'The services provided include such things as transportation from the scene of the crime, counselling to relieve fears and emotional trauma, emergency facilities, referrals to other community agencies that can provide short-term or longer term social welfare services' (Schneider and Schneider 1981: 368).

The emphasis upon immediate support and crisis counselling, very much a feature of US initiatives, follows from the early focus on violent crime and often produces a mismatch between needs and services. In fact, in reviewing much of the material, Davis and Henley (1990) suggested that the predominance of a mental health lobby within the victims' movement may have meant that more commonly requested basic services, are not always available. Roberts (1990: 47) reported that 54 per cent of his sample provided crisis intervention, but that only 25 per cent provided emergency money and 12 per cent lock repairs. More recent research by Davis et al. (1999) reiterates this point. Thus in their survey victims wanted help *vis-à-vis* practical assistance and crime prevention advice, whereas victim assistance programmes were more likely to offer counselling.

These issues and concerns are also reflected in the types of incident dealt with by different schemes. Initially, many services focused on interpersonal crimes – violence- or sex-related – and even now services for more general crime victims may prioritise more vulnerable groups. Roberts (1990) described a number of services specialising in helping older victims, while in Pima County a specialist service for the older people was provided by separate additional funding (Bolin 1980). The emphasis upon special groups or offences is indeed a core issue in discussions in the US, where VOCA enshrined the 'first among equals' principle whereby in allocating funding services for victims of sexual offences, domestic violence or child abuse received priority (Young 1990). But although many services specialise in such cases, even among more general victim services the range of offences covered is fairly broad. For example, Chesney and Schneider (1981: 401) reported that in 1977 in the two Minnesota victim crisis centres the most common offences dealt with were burglary (45%) and assaults (21%), while in Pima County Bolin (1980) noted that 30 per cent of incidents were domestic violence. However, the ICVS found that none of the burglary victims interviewed had received specialist help, compared to 27 per cent of robbery victims and 14 per cent of victims of assaults and threats (Mayhew and van Dijk 1997: appendix 4).

In Pima County, largely due to 'requests' from the police, victim assistance seemed to cover a whole range of non-crime victims, termed PINAS, or 'persons in need of assistance' – such as the poor, elderly, the suicidal, or families of accident victims. As in England and Wales, whilst organised response to major disasters is seen as a legitimate role for victim support, *routine* services for non-crime victims are a matter of some controversy (Young 1990).

Victim Assistance in Germany

In Germany two different victim assistance agencies coexist. In the state of Hanau, county-based services are provided that are financed by local government, although volunteers are crucial to the scheme's success (Schädler 1989). For the whole country, the Weisser ring was founded in 1976 as a voluntary sector agency providing victim services (Doering-Striening 1989). Unlike the Hanau scheme, the Weisser ring does not receive government funds directly, although it does receive financial support via court fines. It too is reliant upon volunteers and affiliated members, who pay an annual membership fee. The Münchengladbach chapter of the Weisser ring, described by Mawby and Kirchhoff (1996), did not employ any paid staff. It received its funding primarily from the courts and from the fees paid by its 170 local members. However, at the time of their survey only five of these members were actively involved in providing direct services to victims.

Whilst the Hanau scheme has operated independently of the police and received mainly direct referrals, the police have been the closest statutory agency to the Weisser ring. Indeed in Münchengladbach the chapter's president was a senior police officer deployed as press officer for the local police chief. However, with much more restrictive confidentiality laws, the Weisser ring in Germany has not been able to access police records in the same way as Victim Support in England and Wales. Thus while it is argued that the police link is a means of overcoming the difficulty of gaining access to official records, in practice this still provides a formidable barrier.

There are other differences between the services provided by Victim Support and the Weisser ring. While in England and Wales Victim Support has traditionally restricted its lobbying to that which is directly related to victims' interests, in Germany the Weisser ring sees crime-prevention work and political lobbying as major features of its work. Thus most of its resources are spent on crime prevention initiatives, the production of brochures and lobbying work. Where it does provide support for victims, moreover, this is commonly legal advice or emergency financial advice. In Münchengladbach, for example, the chapter had the discretion to provide victims with up to 500 Marks to pay for emergencies such as repairs, and higher amounts could be paid if cleared with head office.

As a result, the Weisser ring's small number of volunteers made few personal contacts with crime victims. In 1991 only twenty-five victims were dealt with in Münchengladbach. Most of these involved rape, sexual abuse of children and robbery. None related to burglaries, and it was clear that burglary victims were not recognised as experiencing problems. As the president of the local chapter put it, 'Burglaries are so everyday an offence that people do not get upset by them' (quoted in Mawby and Kirchhoff 1996). While the Hanau scheme provided more by way of counselling services, it too seemed to focus on victims of violent crime (Schädler 1989).

Mawby and Kirchhoff (1996) asked respondents if they knew of 'any organisations other than the police that assist victims of crime'. Those who did not mention victim assistance programmes were subsequently asked if they had heard of any such schemes. In answer to the first question, 49 per cent of burglary victims in Münchengladbach spontaneously named the Weisser ring. Combining answers to the two questions, the numbers saying they had heard of victim support rose to 65 per cent. Clearly then, the Weisser ring had a relatively high profile in Germany.

However, contact with the Weisser ring was almost non-existent. Given a prompt card with a list of agencies that might have offered help, only one German victim said that they had had some form of contact with the Weisser ring (Mawby and Kirchhoff 1996). Victims of crime in general, and victims of burglary in particular, were unlikely to receive direct support from the Weisser ring. Yet it was equally clear that where no specialist services were available, respondents were unlikely to identify any other agencies from which they had received help. For example in Münchengladbach no more than 4 per cent mentioned help from any other official source (in this case medical services). Other than family and friends, then, victims were reliant upon the police and specialist victim assistance programmes, where available, for any help they received after the offence.

In western Europe, Victim Support and the Weisser ring are often seen as two of the leading national agencies in providing help for crime victims. Certainly in both countries the majority of victims appear aware of their existence. However, while Victim Support attempts contact with most burglary victims, in Münchengladbach the strict Germany confidentiality laws, emphasis of the Weisser ring upon campaigning work rather than service delivery, and apparent lack of appreciation of the needs of burglary victims, resulted in negligible support.

Victim assistance in eastern Europe

Victim assistance programmes are highly dependent upon governmental support. They also tend to be lodged in the voluntary sector and depend on volunteers. For these reasons, at least, they have been slow to emerge in post-communist societies. The new democracies have had little by way of extra funding to spend on victim services, and public association of volunteering with the old party elite combined with the need to take second jobs have suppressed the emergence of significant numbers of volunteers. Not surprisingly, then, del Frate (1998: 75) reported that few victims interviewed as part of the third NCVS said they had received any specialist support. Help was most common for victims of assaults and threats, but even here only 4 per cent received any specialist assistance; 2.5 per cent of burglary victims were helped. Nevertheless, two countries where victim assistance programmes have been initiated are Hungary and the Czech Republic, and these will be considered briefly here.

The German Weisser ring was instrumental in encouraging the formation of the Weisser ring in Hungary in 1991. That said, it has developed rather differently from its progenitor. It appears to have adopted a much more proactive approach and to provide support for victims of burglary and other property offences as well as violence. In discussions with Mawby et al. (1999), the president of the Weisser ring estimated that of 4,200 clients seen over a three-year period approximately three-quarters were victims of property crime and 30–40 per cent were victims of burglary. Clients received psychological help and legal advice, as well as support with making insurance claims and, in exceptional circumstances, financial compensation.

The Hungarian Weisser ring is a voluntary body receiving some government funding but heavily dependent upon corporate and individual membership fees and upon the work of volunteers. Lack of funding also means that the agency is geographically restricted. At the time of Mawby et al.'s (1999) research, the largest branch operated in Budapest and there were smaller branches in four other cities.

Clearly the Weisser ring has yet to achieve a national profile in the minds of victims of crime. When Mawby et al. (1999) asked respondents in one Hungarian city if they knew of any organisations other than the police that assisted victims of crime none spontaneously mentioned the Weisser ring, although when they were subsequently asked directly if they had heard of victim assistance programmes 13 per cent answered in the affirmative.

In the Czech Republic the White Circle of Safety (WCS) was founded in 1991. The WCS, which is a non-governmental organisation (NGO), is based in Prague, although it has recently opened branches in a few other cities. In Prague it has some twenty-five volunteers who take it in turns to manage the central office on one evening each week. However, there are no arrangements whereby the WCS can receive referrals directly from the police and its dependence on self-referrals inevitably restricts the number of victims using its services. In 1993 only about 200 victims sought help from the WCS. Moreover, many of these were victims of violent crime, and staff estimated that only about 5 per cent of its clientele were victims of burglaries (Mawby et al. 2000). This was confirmed by findings from the ICVS. In the Czech Republic, few victims received any such support. Victims of sex offences were most likely to say that they received help from a specialist agency, but this only accounted for 7 per cent of all sex offence victims (Valkova 1998: 193–4).

Interviews with burglary victims indicated that even in Prague the WCS has a relatively low profile. Asked to name any organisations that provided help for victims, 14 per cent mentioned it. A further forty-two said they had heard of the WCS when asked directly, so that overall 35 per cent could be said to have had some awareness of the organisation. However, only one victim out of 200 interviewed said they had either asked for or been offered help from the WCS (Mawby et al. 2000).

Summary

Victim assistance programmes have emerged in a number of Western societies over the past twenty-five years. However, just as the victims' movement is multifaceted, and varies in its emphasis in different countries, so programmes aimed at helping victims at the time of the offence vary markedly between different countries. Building on Mawby and Walklate's (1994) identification of four broad areas within which to describe the key features of such services, this chapter has compared service provision in England and Wales, the Netherlands, the USA, Germany and post-communist societies.

Taking first the organisational structure of the agency, it seems that in most countries they are located in the voluntary sector and depend on volunteers, although this can cause difficulties in countries where voluntarism is poorly established or is discredited. Second, we can consider the relationships between victim assistance programmes and other agencies. Here it seems that relationships with the police are a key feature of victim assistance. While in general such programmes rely on a good relationship, this provides no guarantee that victims will be readily referred, as the German example illustrates. Third, programmes vary according to the nature of the service provided: in the USA more emphasis has been placed on counselling, although many victims would have appreciated more practical help; in contrast, in countries like Germany, services may be restricted to legal and financial support. Finally, the nature of the victim population targeted, or prioritised, by the organisation may differ. While in England and Wales the initial emphasis was on burglary victims, the range of victims contacted has expanded. None the less, cross-national comparisons reveal England and Wales as still distinctive in this respect.

Cross-national analysis of victim assistance programmes provides ample illustration of the benefits of comparative work. From a theoretical perspective, the ways in which victim services have developed can be linked to the key players at the forefront of developments and the agendas that were set out. In Germany, for example, the involvement of the police might be linked to the emphasis on crime prevention rather than individual need; in the US the prioritisation of court-based services and the severity of impact might stem from the centrality of the law and order lobby and mental health services, respectively, in early developments (Mawby and Gill 1987). The type of service provided continues to depend as much on cultural perceptions of need and on the agendas surrounding victim assistance as it does on the actual experiences of crime victims. Equally, it may be that socio-cultural conditions may hinder the transference of services from one society to another: variations in police culture, legalistic perceptions of privacy, and the place of voluntarism in society are examples that have been touched on here.

Despite this, it is possible to identify examples of best practice that might be attempted elsewhere. Co-operation between Victim Support and police in England and Wales is a case in point, as is the emphasis on victims' practical needs. In the Netherlands, the involvement of probation is a notable feature, whilst in the USA co-operation between different victim agencies appears well established. Conversely, evidence from the Netherlands and Czech Republic illustrates the difficulties of relying exclusively on self-referrals.

However, there is relatively little information available on what services are available for victims in many countries, and the ICVS provides only rudimentary data. There is, consequently, a need for further in-depth research that systematically allows comparison between different countries. Such research will need to include some wider appreciation of the societies concerned.

Thus, while the global village may allow different counties to become better informed about practices elsewhere, distinctions remain. Although victim services emerged in a number of countries at a similar point in time, the differences between them are as marked as are the similarities. Attempting to understand the reasons for these differences, and evaluating the success of different programmes, offer distinctive and equally important challenges to future researchers.

Notes

1. The following four sections are an abbrieviated and updated version of Mawby and Walklate (1994: 107–26).
2. Data taken from the annual report (Victim Support 1999) sometimes include figures for the Victim/Witness Services as well as victim assistance.
3. The remaining 1,112 were Witness Service Volunteers.
4. Some 18,000 were self-referrals in 1998/99. A Victim Supportline was established in 1998 to allow victims to telephone Victim Support direct, and received 11,500 calls in 1998/99 (Victim Support 1999, 11).
5. This and later data from 1999 are taken from presentation by A. van Beckhoven at the tenth International Symposium on Victimology, Montreal, August 2000.
6. See n. 5.
7. See n. 5.

References

Bolin, D. C. (1980) 'The Pima County victim witness program: analysing its success'. *Evaluating Change*, special issue, 120–6.
Brenton, M. (1982) 'Changing relationships in Dutch social services'. *Journal of Social Policy*, 11, 1, 59–80.

Chesney, S. and Schneider, C. S. (1981) 'Crime victim crisis centres: the Minnesota experience' in B. Galaway, and J. Hudson (eds), *Perspectives on Crime Victims.* St Louis: C. V. Mosby, pp. 399–404.

Davis, R. C. and Henley, M. (1990) 'Victim service programs'. In R. C. Davis, A. J. Lurigio, and W. G. Skogan (eds), *Victims of Crime: Problems, Policies, and Progress.* Newbury Park, CA: Sage, pp. 157–71.

Davis, R. C., Lurigio, A. J. and Skogan, W. G. (1999) 'Services for victims: a market research study'. *International Review of Victimology*, 6, 101–15.

Dijk, J. J. M. van (1989a) 'Recent developments in the criminal policy on victims in the Netherlands'. In *Changing Victim Policy: The United Nations Declaration and Recent Developments in Europe.* Helsinki: HEUNI, pp. 68–82.

Dijk, J. J. M. van (1989b) 'The challenge of quality control: victim support in the Netherlands', unpublished paper.

Ditton, J. et al. (1999) 'Reactions to victimisation: why has anger been ignored?' *Crime Prevention and Community Safety: An International Journal*, 1, 3, 37–54.

Doening-Striening, G. (1989) 'The advantages of Weisser ring's approach to victim support compared with state policy'. In First European Conference of Victim Support Workers, *Guidelines for Victim Support in Europe.* Utrecht: VLOS, pp. 48–51.

Dussich, J. P. (1976) 'Victim service models and their efficacy'. In E. Viano (ed.), *Victims and Society.* Washington, DC: Visage Press, pp. 472–83.

Dussich, J. P. (1981) 'Evolving services for crime victims'. In B. Galaway and J. Hudson (eds), *Perspectives on Crime Victims.* St Louis: C. V. Mosby, pp. 27–32.

Frate, A. A. del (1998) *Victims of Crime in the Developing World.* Rome: UNICRI.

Gay, M. J., Holton, C. and Thomas, M. S. (1975) 'Helping the victims'. *International Journal of Offender Therapy and Comparative Criminology*, 19, 263–9.

Gill, M. L. and Mawby, R. I. (1990) *Volunteers in the Criminal Justice System.* Milton Keynes: Open University Press.

Groenhuijsen, M. (1990) 'Victim support for road traffic accident victims'. Paper presented to National Association of Victim Support Schemes, annual conference, Warwick.

Hanmer, J., Radford, J. and Stanko, E. A. (1989) *Women, Policing and Male Violence.* London: Routledge.

Hauber, A. R. and Zandbergen, A. (1991) 'Victim assistance in police stations on the move: An experiment of victim assistance in police stations'. *International Review of Victimology*, 2, 1–13.

Joyner, M. (1999) 'Surfing the crime net: domestic violence'. *Crime Prevention and Community Safety: An International Journal*, 1, 2, 51–8.

Lowenberg, D. A. (1981) 'An integrated victim service model'. In B. Galaway and J. Hudson (eds), *Perspectives on Crime Victims.* St Louis: C. V. Mosby, pp. 404–11.

McClenahan, C. A. (1987) 'Victim/witness services: Vancouver, British Columbia, Canada'. Paper presented to American Criminological Association annual conference, Montreal.

Maguire, M. and Corbett, C. (1987) *The Effects of Crime and the Work of Victim Support Schemes.* Aldershot: Gower.

Maguire, M. and Kynch, J. (2000) *Public Perceptions and Victims' Experiences of Victim Support: Findings from the 1998 British Crime Survey.* London: Home Office.

Maguire, M. and Shapland, J. (1997) 'Provision for victims in an international context'. In Davis et al. (eds), *Victims of Crime.* London: Sage, pp. 211–28.

Maguire, M. and Wilkinson, C. (1992) *Contacting Victims: Victim Support and the Relative Merits of Letters, Telephone Calls, and 'Cold' Visits*. Report to Home Office. London: Home Office.

Mawby, R. I. (1998). 'Victims' perceptions of police "services" in east and west Europe'. In V. Ruggiero, N. South and I. Taylor (eds), *European Criminology: Crime and Social Order in Europe*. London: Routledge, pp. 180–200.

Mawby, R. I. (1999) 'Police services for crime victims'. In R. I. Mawby (ed.) *Policing Across the World: Issues for the Twenty-First Century*. London: UCL Press, pp. 187–203.

Mawby, R. I. and Gill, M. (1987) *Crime Victims: Needs, Services and the Voluntary Sector*. London: Tavistock.

Mawby, R. I., Gorgenyi, I., Ostrihanska, Z., Walklate, S. and Wojcik, D. (1999) 'Victims' needs and the availability of services: a comparison of burglary victims in Poland, Hungary and England'. *International Criminal Justice Review*, 9, 18–38.

Mawby, R. I. and Kirchoff, G. (1996). 'Coping with crime: a comparison of victims' experiences in England and Germany'. In P. Francis, P. Davies and V. Jupp (eds), *Understanding Victimisation: Themes and Perspectives*. Newcastle: University of Northumbria, pp. 55–70.

Mawby, R. I., Koubova, E. and Brabcova, I. (2000) 'Victims' needs and support for victims in Prague', *International Journal of the Sociology of Law*.

Mawby, R. I. and Walklate, S. (1994) *Critical Victimology: International Perspectives*. London: Sage.

Mayhew, P. and Dijk, J. J. M. van (1997) *Criminal Victimisation in Eleven Industrialised Countries*. Amstelveen, Netherlands: WODC.

Moody, S. (1989) 'Referral methods in victim support: implications for practice and philosophy'. In First European Conference of Victim Support Workers Proceedings, pp. 87–96.

Norris, F. H., Kaniasty, K. and Thompson, M. P. (1997) 'The psychological consequences of crime'. In R. C. Davis, A. J. Lurigio and W. G. Skogan (eds), *Victims of Crime*. London: Sage, pp. 146–66.

Penders, L. (1989) 'Guidelines for police and prosecutors: an interest of victims; a matter of justice'. In First European Conference of Victim Support Workers Proceedings, pp. 75–86.

Peters, T. and Meyvis, W. (1989) 'Recent projects of victim support and assistance in Belgium'. In First European Conference of Victim Support Workers Proceedings, pp. 52–9.

Piffaut, G. (1989) 'Concrete achievements toward the implementation of the fundamental principles of justice for victims'. In *Changing Victim Policy: The United Nations Declaration and Recent Developments in Europe*. Helsinki: HEUNI, pp. 113–39.

Roberts, A. R. (1990) *Helping Victims of Crime*. London: Sage.

Rock, P. (1990) *Helping Victims of Crime*. Oxford: Clarendon Press.

Russell, J. (1990) *Home Office Funding of Victim Support Schemes: Money Well Spent?* Home Office, Research and Planning Unit paper 58. London: HMSO.

Schädler, W. (1989) 'Experiences from the victim and witness assistance centre in Hanau'. In First European Conference of Victim Support Workers Proceedings, pp. 60–3.

Schneider, A. L. and Schneider, P. R. (1981) 'Victim assistance programs'. In B. Galaway and J. Hudson (eds), *Perspectives on Crime Victims*. St Louis: C. V. Mosby, pp. 364–73.

Steinmetz, C. (1989) 'The effects of victim support'. In First European Conference of Victim Support Workers Proceedings, pp. 120–8.

Tourist Victim Support (2000) *Annual Report 1999*. Dublin: TVS.

Valkova, J. (1998) 'The international crime victim survey in the Czech Republic 1996'. In O. Hatalak, A. A. del Frate, and U. Zvekic (eds), *The International Crime Victim Survey in Countries in Transition: National Reports*. Rome: UNICRI, pp. 179–95.

Victim Support (1999) *Annual Report 1991*. London: Victim Support.

Vidosa, F. G. (1989) 'Improving the position of the victim of crime in Spain'. In *Changing Victim Policy: The United Nations Declaration and Recent Developments in Europe*. Helsinki: HEUNI, pp. 209–18.

Waller, I. (1982) 'Declaration on victims of crime'. *WSV Newsletter*, 2, 2, 88–100.

Wemmers, J. M. and Zeilstra, M. I. (1991) 'Victims services in the Netherlands'. *Dutch Penal Law and Policy*, 3. The Hague: Ministry of Justice.

Young, M. A. (1990) 'Victim assistance in the United States: the end of the beginning'. *International Review of Victimology*, 1, 181–99.

Young, M. A. and Stein, J. H. (1983) *The Victim Service System: A Guide to Action*. Washington, DC: NOVA.

Ziegenhagen, E. A. and Benyi, J. (1981) 'Victim interests, victim services and social control'. In B. Galaway and J. Hudson (eds), *Perspectives on Crime Victims*. St Louis: C. V. Mosby, pp. 373–83.

Zvekic, U. (1998) *Criminal Victimisation in Countries in Transition*. Rome: UNICRI.

9
Preventing Harm, Promoting Harmony

Martin Wright

Introduction

Until quite recently the study of crime focused almost exclusively on the perpetrator. Offenders were, and are, researched, treated, punished, and sometimes helped to recover from the punishment. Attempts are made to classify them and to find patterns, but there are no characteristics which are shared by all of them and not shared by those who are not (or not known to be) offenders. Later the families and social backgrounds were scrutinised (only of those who were detected, of course, apart from some self-report studies). But people who committed certain types of crime, such as 'white-collar crime', received much less attention, and many harmful acts are not defined as crimes. Either they remain outside the criminal law, to be dealt with if at all by tribunals or the self-regulatory bodies of the major professions, or in some cases the criminal law is used at one remove: instead of 'You have broken the law and must be prosecuted and punished', the accused are told 'You have broken the law and unless you put matters right you will be prosecuted.' This is a very different approach; originally it was chiefly used where the 'victim' was the state, in cases such as tax fraud, but it is beginning to be used for the benefit of individual and corporate victims.

In the mid-twentieth century victimology came on the scene, as Sandra Walklate outlines in her chapter. Here patterns are at least as hard to find: anyone can be a victim, rich or poor, powerful or vulnerable, young or old, male or female. Of the traumas which people suffer in their lives, a very small proportion are defined as criminal, as the Dutch criminologist Louk Hulsman (1986) has pointed out. They attract particular attention because they are seen as involving one person who deliberately, or recklessly, satisfies his or her own wants or interests (or attempts to do so) in a way that harms another individual, and this is presumably why they are defined as criminal. However, some behaviour that is not criminal can cause at least as much financial loss and physical and psychological harm, and some of it is no less selfish or reckless. Thus the study and treatment of crime victims parallels that of offenders; it is commonly limited to those who have suffered certain types of harm.

Victimology, like the study of most social questions, tends to fall into two main parts. As regards victimisation, we ask what are the facts, and as regards the response, what can be done about them? This book has not attempted to give a comprehensive survey of the whole field; rather it has selected aspects which throw light on the subject from particular angles. The picture might be summarised by saying, firstly, that the people we think of as victims of crime are not the only ones who suffer at the hands of their fellow citizens, nor even necessarily the most seriously harmed. Similarly, the acts we label as crimes are often less damaging than some of those which are not treated in that way. Thirdly, when people harm each other, the criminal justice system may not be the only, or the best, way of helping victims, and it can even make things worse. Turning to the search for a victim-oriented response, two particular forms of assistance are appreciated by many victims: support from the community and, when the offender is known, the opportunity to take part in resolving the matter. Finally, this dialogue between victims, offenders and other members of the community gives an opportunity to learn from the crimes that occur, and use the information to develop crime-reduction policies, but also to create a much broader strategy to encourage people, from childhood up, to respect each other, to handle competing interests by negotiation, and to resolve conflicts non-violently, as a contribution to the creation of a safe and harmonious society.

Victimisation

If we first ask what are the facts, this question in turn has two aspects: who are the victims, and what are they victims of?

Who are the victims?

Stereotypes of victims were often used without being recognised as such until victimology was established, and contributors to this book have shown that they are still common. The number of types of victims is almost as great as the number of types of human beings; this book has considered four categories: young people, women, older people, and communities. In the case of young people, especially males, John Muncie points out that the stereotype usually points to them as offenders; in the popular press they are often labelled with derogatory terms such as 'thugs'. In fact, however, they are especially likely to be victims (as the Gulbenkian report *Children and Violence* (1995) has shown in greater detail). In their first year of life children are at the greatest risk of murder. In adolescence, young people are often bullied because they are from minority ethnic groups or 'different' in some other way. Their parents may use physical violence on them in the name of discipline, which would be classed as an assault, or worse, if done to an adult, and increases the likelihood that they in turn will be violent. If they do become violent, they may be placed in institutions where violence is endemic, and where conditions have in some cases been found to contravene the United Nations Convention on the Rights of the Child. These are of course further examples of harm which is not classified (or at least not treated) as criminal victimisation.

The women's movement has focused on violence against women and female children, but young males are most at risk, as Walklate has pointed out, citing the work of Betsy Stanko and Kathy Hobdell, an academic and a Victim Support worker respectively. Women and girls are of course also at risk, and much of their victimisation is invisible, although as Walklate says the women's movement has now made it in some ways more visible than men's. So once again there is some doubt about 'what constitutes the real', and she reminds us that it includes offenders as well as victims: both are trying to deal with difficult circumstances, and the key to understanding is to treat both with respect.

Another stereotype is that old people are more likely to be victims of young violent criminals and to suffer disproportionately. It is true that they are sometimes harassed by children – a process which seems to have much in common with bullying – and obviously some elderly people are vulnerable. The fact is, however, that they can be physically and mentally tough, and less fearful than younger victims; Victim Support workers have numerous anecdotes about how elderly victims have thought up stratagems to frighten off intruders. They can also be sustained by being thoughtful, like one seriously injured elderly woman, who was concerned less about herself, since she had not much time left anyway, than about her young attacker, who was only just starting his life and she didn't want him to waste it. Some of the worst victimisation of elderly people is by their supposed carers, through physical or mental cruelty or embezzlement of their assets, and Rachel Pain has raised once again the question of how best to intervene: is it more helpful to prosecute it as a crime, or to regard it as a problem for social services? Braithwaite (1998) quotes evidence that nursing homes checked by inspectors with a reintegrative shaming philosophy had improved two years later, while those dealt with by inspectors whose approach was either stigmatising or tolerant and understanding got worse. In some cases ill-treatment results from frustration over apparently small matters, and to pre-empt this Age Concern (England) has recently appointed a Manager of Alternative Dispute Resolution Services whose remit includes, for example, disputes in sheltered housing.

It is usual to think of victims as individuals, or institutions such as shops and schools; but Karen Evans and Penny Fraser have provided another perspective by looking at some communities in high-crime areas as victims. It has been observed for some years that crime is spatially patterned (see, for example, Brantingham and Brantingham 1975). Individuals (or groups) commit crime, but the conditions in which it is prevalent can be created by 'the community' in the form of its elected representatives and paid officials, through architectural design, housing allocation, and general neglect. Evans and Fraser refer to the 'broken windows' theory; this had been foreshadowed already in the 1970s, in the Cunningham Road Project in Widnes, in northern England, which showed that outside help can act as a catalyst to bring together groups within a run-down community, enabling it to pick itself up and tackle the incivilities which have demoralised it; these included a mixture of criminal and non-criminal problems (Nacro 1978; Wright 1982: 220–1). There have been many other similar projects, for example in Hartford, Connecticut (Fowler et al. 1979), and in Kirkholt, Lancashire (Forrester 1990); this suggests the possibility that an important part of a cost-effective crime reduction strategy should be, rather than sporadic short-term one-off pilot schemes, a regular programme introducing such projects wherever they are needed – and reintroducing them if they run out of steam.[1] Needless to say they should be evaluated and, if effective, adequately funded.

Victimology has also dispelled the assumption that 'lightning doesn't strike twice': Genn (1988) painted a bleak picture of a housing estate where victimisation, being an everyday occurrence, was hardly thought of as such; Farrell and Pease (1991) looked behind the statistics to show that becoming a victim actually increases the chances of being targeted again, and suggested how the community could help to counter this, for example by concentrating assistance on those who have just been victims, to try to prevent a repetition.

What are they victims of?

The effect of various crimes on victims has become well-trodden ground since Maguire's (1982) pioneering work on burglars and their victims. Less is heard about victimisation by acts which have not been defined as criminal, and by the very efforts to deal with crime. One example of the former, among many, is provided by the food industry. Not only are people exposed to salmonella poisoning through battery chickens, among which the infection is rife, but farming practices are the likely cause of the hugely costly BSE (bovine spongiform encephalopathy). Large figures are often quoted for the cost of crimes such as retail theft and criminal damage (£2,100 million in 1992/3 : Home Office 1995: 74), but it has been estimated that present-day farming practices cost the public £2,343 million in 1996. The costs, according to Professor Jules Pretty of the Centre for Environment and Society at the University of Essex, included £191 million for the removal of pesticides, nitrates and phosphates, £1,113 million from emissions of gases likely to con- tribute to climate change, £169 million from food poisoning, and £607 million from BSE. While shoplifting may add a few pence to the price of retail goods, Pretty argues that consumers pay for their food three times: over the counter, through farming subsidies of some £3 billion a year, and through cleaning up the mess (Pretty 2001; McCarthy 2001). The methods proposed for dealing with this form of victimisation are, of course, economic rather than through the criminal law.

In world trade, drugs are an addictive, damaging and ultimately lethal product, yet thousands of poor people and a smaller number of very rich ones make their living by producing and selling them. Each of those statements is also true of tobacco, and it is hard to see the moral difference, except that one has widely been declared criminal and the other has not. At a micro-level, there is a thin line between crime and various perfectly legal rip-offs. One man uses a trick to get into your house and steal; another tells you that your roof needs repair, and charges you a ridiculous, but lawful, amount. I am one of those who has been victimised by a drain-clearing company, and it was all legal: the operative asked me to agree to each new operation which turned out to cost several times what I had expected. I felt like the man invited on to the stage, where the conjurer asked for his permission to take his gold watch and pound it into small pieces with a pestle and mortar. End of trick – all done with permission. The drainage firm was so law-abiding that it charged me VAT as well; and I also experienced the shame of the victim: to this day I cannot admit how much I was charged.

It is perhaps even worse when we are victimised not by criminals or unscrupulous traders but by those who are supposed to protect us. Michael McCahill and Clive Norris have shown how closed-circuit television (CCTV) has been used to target particular social and racial groups, who may then be ejected from a public place where they had every right to be, and the cameras can be misused in other ways as well.[2] Similarly with identity cards: since the attack on the World Trade Centre and the Pentagon, the British media have been full of debate about how ID cards, ostensibly a safeguard, could put innocent civilians at risk. Respectable-looking citizens would seldom be stopped; if they were, and had left their ID cards at home, they could probably talk their way out of it; while those of foreign appearance, or wearing 'subcultural attire' (such as the tracksuits and baseball caps which get them excluded from shopping malls) could be harassed and criminalised, possibly by private security guards against whom there is less redress than against police officers (see national newspapers, late September and early October 2001, *passim*).

Genetic testing, and drugs testing for athletes, can also victimise people, as McCahill and Norris have shown; once again the victimisation is outside the scope of the criminal law, although it can be seriously unjust: since, for example, a badly conducted drugs test can ruin an athlete's career, and the insurance industry is contravening the whole insurance philosophy of shared risk if it uses tests to exclude people with certain genetic features.

Re-victimisation by the criminal justice system

In a system still largely focused on offenders, the first milestone towards the development of awareness of victims, in Britain, was the creation of Victim Support in 1974. Within a decade it had grown across the country, and provided a focal point where those who had hitherto suffered in isolation could tell their stories of how they had been treated, or more often ignored, by 'the system'. Joanna Shapland's innovative research showed how casually victims were treated by the police, whether a suspect was apprehended or not (Shapland et al. 1985). This was complemented by Roger Graef's television documentary in 1982 about police attitudes to rape victims. As Pamela Davies has suggested in her chapter, victims seem to come third in police priorities, after convicting offenders and preventing crime; moreover, their work is often biased by stereotypes of victims as deserving, innocent, negligent, provocative and so on.

The number of victims who have dealings with the courts is much smaller, but the impact can be much more traumatic, ranging from not even being told that the trial is taking place to being publicly humiliated by a defending barrister. Victim Support drew attention to this, as Davies has mentioned, in the report of a working party led by a former chairman of the Magistrates' Association, Lady Ralphs (Victim Support 1988), and followed it up with an action research project which showed how trained volunteers can help victims (and other witnesses) through the process (Raine and Smith 1991). This is now happening in all Crown Court centres, and being extended to magistrates' courts. The Royal Commission on Criminal Justice (1993), after being nudged by Victim Support, included some recommendations for improvement; the General Council of the Bar, for example, modified its Code to allow prosecutors to speak to victims before the trial (Bar Council 1997).

In their fieldwork in 1990–2, Cretney and Davies (1995: 149–54) still found many of the familiar complaints – delays, lack of information, hostile cross-examination – and rape victims studied in 1993–5 by Temkin (2000) were still exposed to barristers who tried to discredit them and to ask about their previous sexual histories. Although judges' permission has to be asked before raising previous histories, and prosecutors should, according to the *Victim's Charter*, challenge untrue statements in pleas for mitigation of sentence (Home Office 1990, 1996), these safeguards have not been entirely effective. Child witnesses in cases involving sex, violence or cruelty, can give their evidence by a closed-circuit television link (Home Office 1990, 1996); this protection has not, however, been extended to other vulnerable witnesses. I have argued elsewhere that victims are always likely to have a rougher ride in a system that is adversarial and based on the punishment of the offender: the more severe the threatened punishment, the more he will do to try to avoid it, sometimes by intimidating witnesses (Wright 1999).

Towards a Restorative Response

Support from the community

What should be the response? We need to begin by reminding ourselves that many victims can take crimes, especially the less serious ones, in their stride. But there are two forms of assistance which many of them welcome: support from the community and, when the offender is known, the opportunity to take part in the process of resolving the matter. Much of what is needed is implicit in the foregoing critique. Rob Mawby has described how a range of countries have offered assistance to victims. Thought also needs to be given to the best structure for the provision of victim assistance; Mawby's survey provides various examples. Obviously this depends on local cultures and circumstances. In some countries it is done by statutory agencies; but there are attractions in the idea of members of the community spontaneously forming a voluntary organisation (NGO) in which volunteers express neighbourly concern and show solidarity, and refer them to professional help such as counselling or financial advice where needed. Financial support from central or local government can relieve such groups of the struggle of fund-raising. Among the advantages are that this is a way of involving the local community, volunteers are available outside office hours, and they cost less – though they need salaried staff to train, support, and supervise them. However, in high-crime areas there may be too few volunteers to contact all victims personally; in some countries the data protection laws mean that the police must obtain the victim's permission before passing on their name; and in countries where working hours are very long, it may be difficult to recruit enough volunteers.

It is also difficult to *guarantee* a service provided by volunteers, but statutory services are not always available either, unless there is some enforcement system. A country which wants to do the best it can for victims would ensure that victim assistance services are adequately funded, and (as some do) provide financial assistance to victims who want to engage a lawyer to claim their entitlement. As Mawby has shown, there may be different organisations for various types of victims (the elderly, tourists), and for victims of different traumas, especially domestic violence and abuse of children; in England there is one for victims of road traffic crashes and another for medical negligence, for example, and in Italy there is no 'umbrella organisation' for assistance to victims but there are associations for victims of terrorists, the Mafia, railway crashes and so on, usually created by survivors and relatives.

For many victims, a practical form of help is compensation. The basis for this is not entirely consistent. Society's response can vary on the basis of quite extraneous factors; for example, compensation for an iatrogenic injury may depend not on the victim's needs but on whether the doctor is proved to have been negligent, and compensation for a criminal injury (in the United Kingdom) on whether the victim has a previous criminal record, as Davies has mentioned in her chapter.

For crimes against property, individuals and organisations are supposed to cover themselves through insurance, if they choose to, and to rely on social security if the crime has left them destitute. For crimes of violence, in countries such as the United Kingdom most medical costs are borne by the National Health Service, and the Criminal Injuries Compensation Authority pays an additional sum related to the seriousness of the injury, mostly thought of as compensation for pain and suffering. In some countries the state compensation is swallowed up by the medical costs. In a welfare state, it is not obvious why a person who is disabled by an injury should be treated differently according to whether the injury was caused through, say, an accident at work, a sporting accident, medical negligence, or crime. In New Zealand the Accident Compensation Commission provides only for 'work and non-work' injuries, with no separate criminal category except for sensitive cases such as sexual abuse; it is funded through premiums, and can help with medical and surgical bills, rehabilitation, support in the home, and up to 80 per cent of lost earnings (subject to a maximum), with allowances for serious long-term effects (New Zealand 2001). The needs of people with a particular injury are similar, whatever the cause. The source of the compensation might vary, however: if an individual or organisation was responsible or negligent, they might be required to pay, with the state making up the difference if they were unable to, as is often the case with individual offenders. Perhaps there should be a clearer distinction between the *cost* of treatment, loss of earnings, and so on, and *compensation* for intangibles such as the particular fear, anger and other emotions which victims of crime of violence are likely to experience (for further discussion see Victim Support 1993; Wright 1998).

Several countries tackle the problem of the offender who cannot pay by establishing a 'resocialisation fund'. The fund is created by the state, or from fines, or private donations, or a combination. An offender can apply to it for the sum he needs for compensation (and often other debts), and if he appears to be a good risk the fund pays.[3] Thus the victim receives the amount at once, not in small irregular instalments, and the offender pays it back either in cash, when he finds work, or by doing community service for which a notional hourly rate is paid (Wright 1988).

If the court is to order the offender to pay compensation (whether by a compensation order as in the United Kingdom – 'restitution order' in the United States – or in a linked civil action as in some continental countries) the victim needs to indicate the loss or harm suffered. There are arrangements for this, but a common criticism of the criminal justice process has been that it focuses only on the financial aspect, while the victim's voice remains unheard. The apparent solution is to let them be heard. Unfortunately it is not so easy. In much of North America and Australasia victims can make victim impact statements before sentence is passed, but in Britain it has been felt that that could be burdensome to victims and lead to unfairness to offenders. A modified scheme was therefore introduced, in October 2001, in which victims are invited to make a 'personal statement' at the beginning of the process. In this way, the statements are distanced from sentencing and can be used for other purposes such as providing prosecutors with information so that they can challenge inaccurate pleas in mitigation. However, the researchers of the pilot projects have pointed out that there are two contradictory aims. The first they call cathartic, enabling victims to describe what they have suffered and their feelings, but not affecting sentence; the second is instrumental, providing information which may influence decisions. They recommend that the scheme should decide which its aim will be, but it appears to be trying to combine both. The leaflet for victims, in line with the *Victim's Charter*, says that the courts may use the statement when deciding if a defendant should be given bail; that the CPS will 'consider the consequences for the victim and will take account of the views of the victim or the victim's family' in deciding whether to prosecute; and the court will 'take account of' how the offence has affected them; the victim's views on sentence will not however be considered (Home Office 2001). Despite this, it appears that many victims expect the sentence to be affected, and are disillusioned when it is not. This helps to explain why, in the pilot projects, few victims chose to make a statement,[4] only a third felt better as a result, and nearly a fifth felt worse (Hoyle et al. 1998; Morgan and Sanders 1999). Moreover, the statement becomes part of the case papers and may be seen by the defence; this could inhibit victims from expressing their feelings fully, because offenders, being potentially seriously affected, could cross-examine them about the statement, or even intimidate them.

An opportunity for dialogue

Sanders et al. (2001: 450), who researched the pilots of victim personal statements in England, have pointed out that what is missing in this system is *dialogue* between the victim and the criminal justice agencies (or, they might have added, with the offender). They would expect victims participating in restorative justice to be more satisfied than victims in conventional common or civil law systems (Sanders et al. 2001: 456): 'The more participative the process, the more satisfied the victim' (Sanders et al. 2001: 457), and research appears to support this (Liebmann 1998). This, I would suggest, is the benefit for victims offered by processes such as victim/offender mediation and conferencing, specifically because they take place away from the courtroom and the prospect of punishment. Victims want different things: some simply want compensation; others want to show the offender that his action was hurtful, and why.

Some want to enable him/her to put it right and do better in future. In some cases the expression of feelings is the only outcome, in others there is an element of reparation, but not of punishment (defined as a measure whose primary purpose is to inflict pain: see Christie 1982). It is true that this only comes into operation when the offender does not deny the act of which he is accused, but that is the great majority of cases, and the reduced prospect of punishment is likely to reduce the number of denials. The less punitive the response, the greater the likelihood of finding the truth,[5] and hence the greater the prospect that some good will come from the harm – a common wish amongst victims. Victims are enabled to ask questions and discuss reparation; offenders are enabled to speak for themselves, apologise, and show that there is also some good in them.[6] As Sanders and colleagues conclude, 'Only a genuinely participative system can treat victims with the respect they deserve without giving them the power to influence decisions that are not appropriately theirs' Sanders et al. 2001: 458).

A learning experience for the community

Offenders, it is said, should learn their lesson. But it should be the right lesson. As Sir Louis Blom-Cooper, former Chair of the Howard League for Penal Reform, has written:

> The message of punishment, in effect, is: 'Behave well, because otherwise you will be made to suffer (if you are caught).' Is it not more appropriate to admonish the offender and everyone else: 'Behave well, because otherwise you will hurt *other people*, whether you are caught or not; and if you are caught, you will be required to pay back'? (Blom-Cooper 1988: 55, italics in original)

It is not only the offender, however, who has to learn a lesson; in a restorative process other people learn from what took place. An advantage of the wide-ranging dialogue which victim/offender mediation and conferencing make possible is that, unlike the courtroom process, it is not focused on the narrow question of what sanction should be imposed on the offender, but it can help to explain how the crime came about. It holds the offender accountable for what he has done; but it can also throw light on the circumstances. Where the mediators are volunteers, this spreads understanding of crime through the community; at a more formal level, the information can be passed to those responsible for crime-reduction strategies.

These are commonly divided into 'situational' ones, based on the principle that virtue is lack of opportunity, and 'social' approaches, recognising that society as well as the offender shares responsibility for anti-social behaviour. Mediation and conferencing can contribute to both of these; and I will propose a third.

On situational influences, we may learn from mediations and conferences that, for example, windows were left open or cars unlocked. There may have been failures of supervision: too few shop assistants or railway station staff, or peripatetic concierges and park keepers instead of permanent ones. The implications for crime reduction are clear.

Social crime prevention is focused on the pressures towards crime (a more accurate term than 'causes'): society as well as the individual shares responsibility. A mediation service may find that a number of young people come from a local school which has a high truancy rate, or has been dealing with problems by excluding its troublesome pupils, putting them and the community at risk. It may find that many of them have been in care, in which case we need to ask what needs to be done to improve the care of vulnerable young people. It might find problems with housing allocation (e.g. too many children in one housing estate), unemployment, youth clubs or sports facilities closed or starved of funds, or lack of adult involvement.

The dialogue may also show that attempts to control misbehaviour can be counterproductive: Muncie points to some practices conducive to crime, such as locking children in institutions; this should not be done except when it is unavoidable for the protection of themselves or the public from serious harm, and the regime should be based primarily on respect for their humanity and their needs. Physical punishment should be avoided altogether. (A fuller survey is provided by the Gulbenkian Foundation: Gulbenkian 1995). These examples are not new; they are well known to be potential influences on crime rates. The point is that a mediation service is well placed to observe which factors are present in its area, and pass the information to those responsible for crime-reduction policy.

The third strategy might be called 'individual': the converse of the previous point is that the individual as well as society shares responsibility, and this third pillar of a crime-reduction policy is based on encouraging people, especially young people, to want to refrain from committing crime. The primary method is to promote their self-respect by treating them with respect; this also encourages them to respect other people, and indeed other living creatures and the environment. Methods in schools, such as circle time, peer mediation, and the 'shared concern' approach to bullying, can show children how to resolve conflicts by listening to each other without either using violence or giving in (Alderson 1997; Mediation UK 1998; Curtis 2001). Contributors to this volume have given further examples. Rachel Pain has described how, if there is little contact between young and old in a community, older people may be afraid of local teenagers, sometimes with good reason, sometimes without; when such a situation is identified, a project like 'Lifelink' can bring different age groups together. As Evans and Fraser put it, in more general terms, crimes are committed when certain factors are present: motivated offenders, vulnerable victims and opportunity. The process of responding should include establishing which of these factors contributed, in what way, and how they can be removed or reduced.

Initiatives like these should form the basis of general social policies which are right not merely because they reduce crime and victimisation but because they enable people and communities to develop their full potential. They are beginning in schools, as has been mentioned, but the use of mediation and related conflict-resolving techniques can be extended to adults and to other spheres of society: the workplace, the family, commerce, professionals and their clients, the environment, and between communities and indeed countries. Crime and conflict can never be eliminated – and perhaps the world would be dull if they were – but they can be used constructively to enable individuals and communities to 'have life, and have it abundantly'.

Notes

1. Projects of this kind may be generated by local initiatives (for example Waterville Projects (1997) in north-east England), local projects stimulated by national NGOs such as Nacro and Crime Concern (Warburton et al. 2000; Findlay et al. 1990, and numerous other publications of these organisations); or by local action encouraged by governments (King 1988; Crime Prevention Council 1994).
2. CCTV can also protect citizens, for example by recording police who assaulted a young black man in Brixton, south London, and attacked a white couple who tried to intervene (*Evening Standard*, 2 October 2001, 12).
3. Sometimes the fund negotiates a discount from large creditors such as hire purchase and electricity companies, on the analogy of bankruptcy proceedings.
4. It should be remembered that, although the rhetoric speaks of helping victims to recover from harm, in practice there is often more inconvenience than trauma; another reason why the labour-intensive process of arranging mediations or conferences should be reserved for cases where the victim has been much affected.

5. One example of this is that when the CPS does not prosecute because it does not consider that it can satisfy the criminal standard of proof, some victims or their relatives take civil action in order to bring the offender to book: since the potential outcome is compensation rather than punishment, the standard of proof is less demanding.
6. There are various issues about the use of restorative justice, especially when linked to the criminal justice process, for example the degree of voluntariness of the offender's participation, but they cannot be explored here; suffice it to say that they seem no more problematic than those raised by the conventional system.

References

Alderson, Priscilla, ed. (1997) *Changing our School: Promoting Positive Behaviour.* Plymouth: Loxley Enterprises.

Bar Council (1997) Code of Professional Conduct (as amended). General Council of the Bar, 3 Bedford Row, London WS1R 4DB.

Blom-Cooper, Louis (1988) *The Penalty of Imprisonment.* (The Tanner Lectures 1987.) London: Howard League for Penal Reform and Prison Reform Trust.

Braithwaite, John (1998) *Restorative Justice: Assessing an Immodest Theory and a Pessimistic Theory.* Canberra: Australian National University webmaster@aic. gov.au.

Brantingham, Paul J., and Brantingham, Patricia L. (1975) 'The spatial patterning of burglary'. *Howard Journal*, 14, 2, 11–23.

Cretney, Antonia, and Davies, Gwynn (1995) *Punishing Violence.* London: Routledge.

Crime Prevention Council (1994) *Co-operation for Prevention in Local Areas.* Det kriminalpræventive Råd, 5 Odensegade, DK-2100 Copenhagen Ø. Denmark.

Curtis, Barbara (2001) *Conflict Resolution, Peer Mediation in Schools: A Directory of Services and Training.* Bristol: Mediation UK.

Farrell, Graham, and Pease, Ken (1991) *Once Bitten, Twice Bitten: Repeat Victimisation and its Implications for Crime Prevention.* Home Office Crime Prevention Unit Papers 46. London: Home Office Police Research Group.

Findlay, Jim, Bright, Jon and Gill, Kevin (1990) *Youth Crime Prevention: A Handbook of Good Practice.* Swindon: Crime Concern.

Forrester, David, et al. (1990) *The Kirkholt Burglary Prevention Project: Phase II.* Home Office Crime Prevention Unit, 23. London: Home Office.

Fowler, Floyd, et al. (1979) *Reducing Residential Crime and Fear: The Hartford Neighborhood Crime Prevention Program.* Washington: US GPO.

Genn, Hazel (1988) 'Multiple victimisation'. In Mike Maguire and John Pointing (eds), *Victims of Crime: A New Deal?* Milton Keynes: Open University Press.

Gulbenkian (1995) *Children and Violence.* London: Gulbenkian Society.

Home Office (1990, 1996) *The Victim's Charter: A Statement of Service Standards for Victims of Crime* (1st and 2nd edns). London: Home Office.

Home Office (2001) *Making a Victim's Personal Statement.* London: Home Office Communications Directorate.

Home Office Research and Statistics Department (1995) *Digest: Information on the Criminal Justice System in England and Wales.* Croydon: HO RSD.

Hoyle, Carolyn, Cape, Ed, Morgan, Rod and Sanders, Andrew (1998) *Evaluation of the 'One-Stop Shop' and Victim Statement Pilot Projects*. London: Home Office Research, Development and Statistics Directorate.

Hulsman, L. (1986) *Critical Criminology and the Concept of Crime Contemporary Crises*, 10, 1, 63–80.

King, Michael (1988) *How to Make Social Crime Prevention Work: The French Experience*. London: Nacro.

Liebmann, Marian (1998) *Restorative Justice: Does it Work?* Bristol: Mediation UK.

McCarthy, Michael (2001) 'The way we eat'. *The Independent, Review*, 5 September, 1, 8.

Maguire, Mike (1982) *Burglary in a Dwelling: The Offence, the Offender and the Victim*. London: Heinemann.

Mediation UK (1998) *Mediation Works! Conflict Resolution and Peer Mediation Manual for Secondary Schools and Colleges*. Bristol: Mediation UK.

Morgan, Rod, and Sanders, Andrew (1999) *The Uses of Victim Statements*. London: Home Office Research, Development and Statistics Directorate.

Nacro (1978) *Vandalism: A Pilot Project*. London: Nacro.

New Zealand (2001) Accident Compensation Commission. website *http://www.acc.org.nz/*

Pretty, Jules (2001) *New Farming for Britain*. London: Fabian Society. *www.fabian-society.org.uk.*

Raine, J. W., and R. E. Smith (1991) *The Victim/Witness in Court Project: Report of the Research Programme*. London: Victim Support.

Royal Commission on Criminal Justice (1993) *Report*. Cm 2263. London: HMSO.

Sanders, Andrew, Hoyle, Carolyn, Morgan, Rod and Cape, Ed (2001) 'Victim impact statements: don't work, can't work'. *Criminal Law Review*, 447–58.

Shapland, Joanna, Willmore, Jon and Duff, Peter (1985) *Victims in the Criminal Justice System*. Aldershot: Gower.

Temkin, Jennifer (1987) *Rape and the Legal Process*. London: Sweet & Maxwell.

Temkin, Jennifer (2000) 'Prosecuting and defending rape: perspectives from the bar'. *Journal of Law and Society*, 27, 2, 219–48.

Victim Support (1988) *The Victim in Court: Report of a Working Party*. (Chair: Lady Ralphs.) London: Victim Support.

Victim Support (1993) *Compensating the Victim of Crime: Report of an Independent Working Party*. (Chair: David Faulkner.) London: Victim Support.

Warburton, Frank, Boys, Andy and Fox, Chris (2000). *Putting the Community into Community Safety: A Practitioners' Guide*. London: Nacro.

Waterville Projects (1997) *Projects for Children and Young People*. St John's Terrace, Percy Main, North Shields, Tyne and Wear NE29 6HL

Wright, Martin (1982) *Making Good: Prisons, Punishment and Beyond*. London: Burnett Books.

Wright, Martin (1988) 'Out of the morass: a rational approach to debt'. *Probation Journal*, 35, 4, 148.

Wright, Martin (1998) 'Why should victims of crime be compensated?' In Ezzat Fattah and Tony Peters (eds), *Support for Victims of Crime in a Comparative Perspective*. Leuven: Leuven University Press.

Wright, Martin (1999) *Restoring Respect for Justice*. Winchester: Waterside Press.

Glossary of Terms

ACPO	Association of Chief Police Officers
BCS	British Crime Survey
BSE	Bovine Spongiform Enccephalopathy
CAPE	Community and Police Enforcement
CAPI	Computer Assisted Personal Interviewing
CDT	Compulsory Drug Testing
CICA	Criminal Injuries Compensation Authority
CPS	Crown Prosecution Service
DNA	Deoxyribonucleic Acid
FSS	Forensic Science Service
HO	Home Office
ICS	International Crime Survey
ICVS	International Crime Victims Survey
INAVEM	National Institute for Victims Support
LGA	Local Government Association
NGO	Non-governmental Organisation
NOVA	National Organisation for Victim Support
NOVS	National Institute for Victim Support
PINAS	Persons in need of assistance
RMT	Rail Maritime and Transport Workers
VOCA	Victims of Crime Act
WCS	White Circle of Safety

Index